WEAK PLANET

Weak Planet

LITERATURE AND ASSISTED SURVIVAL

Wai Chee Dimock

The University of Chicago Press   CHICAGO AND LONDON

The University of Chicago Press, Chicago 60637
The University of Chicago Press, Ltd., London
© 2020 by The University of Chicago
All rights reserved. No part of this book may be used or
reproduced in any manner whatsoever without written permission,
except in the case of brief quotations in critical articles and reviews.
For more information, contact the University of Chicago Press,
1427 East 60th Street, Chicago, IL 60637.
Published 2020
Printed in the United States of America

29 28 27 26 25 24 23 22 21 20   1 2 3 4 5

ISBN-13: 978-0-226-47707-7 (cloth)
ISBN-13: 978-0-226-47710-7 (paper)
ISBN-13: 978-0-226-47724-4 (e-book)
DOI: https://doi.org/10.7208/chicago/9780226477244.001.0001

This book is published with the assistance of the Frederick W. Hilles
Publication Fund of Yale University.

The University of Chicago Press gratefully acknowledges
the generous support of the Modern Language Association
toward the publication of this book.

Library of Congress Cataloging-in-Publication Data

Names: Dimock, Wai-chee, 1953– author.
Title: Weak planet : literature and assisted survival /
Wai Chee Dimock.
Description: Chicago ; London : University of Chicago Press, 2020. |
Includes bibliographical references and index.
Identifiers: LCCN 2020006489 | ISBN 9780226477077 (cloth) |
ISBN 9780226477107 (paperback) | ISBN 9780226477244 (ebook)
Subjects: LCSH: Literature, Modern—20th century—History and
criticism. | Literature, Modern—21st century—History and criticism. |
American literature—History and criticism. | English literature—
History and criticism.
Classification: LCC PN771 .D57 2020 | DDC 809/.93353—dc23
LC record available at https://lccn.loc.gov/2020006489

♾ This paper meets the requirements of ANSI/NISO Z39.48-1992
(Permanence of Paper).

FOR GD AND BEATRICE, AS ALWAYS

Find Your Strength

—Spaulding Rehab

Contents

II

Figures

Introduction

ENDANGERED

One moment the street was quiet and drizzly, so familiar that I barely gave it a thought. The next moment the headlights were on me, direct, blinding, a flood of illumination so incandescent and unexpected that what paralyzed me wasn't fear but stupefaction. Then I was on the ground, screaming with a rage that took even me by surprise: "No, I'm not OK! I'm not OK! I'm not OK!"

A lot happened during the four weeks I spent at Spaulding Rehab.[1] The Red Sox won the World Series. A record number of women and minorities were elected to Congress. Participating in these bonds of anticipation, suspense, and elation didn't make me forget that I was wedded to my wheelchair, another kind of bond, never before contemplated and in many ways more interesting than the others. This unsightly contraption, a marvel of metallic flexibility, was never apart from me or out of my mind: not the new normal but simply part of life, taken for granted and integral to my sense of myself. Not being able to live without it defined me, an identity I got used to with surprising ease.

The motto of Spaulding is Find Your Strength. It's also the motto of this book, one long in the making. Evolving from a more general engagement with "weak theory"[2]—shaky paradigms with incomplete resolution—to one occasioned directly by the shaky future of the planet Earth, it's an attempt to write literary history as part of the collective run-up to our climate crisis. I argue that the large-scale harms now opening up on so many fronts have a long past, that ecological disruptions have been part of human life for centuries. Mass casualties from European colonialism—a death toll of 56 million across the Americas—changed the earth's climate,[3] making adaptation and experimentation key to indigenous survival.[4] Works of literature have much to tell us about this arc of vulnerability and resilience, and the attempts by endangered populations to "find their strength," to avoid paralysis, to stay in the fray against all odds.[5]

While the broad argument of the book seemed clear enough, I couldn't initially think of a good way to connect the macro narratives about ecosystems to what must remain micro narratives about the literary form: the ebb and flow of genre; the idiosyncratic use of verb tense, pronouns, and punctuation; the countless ways authors animate and accentuate the works bearing their signatures; and the countless ways these signatures instruct and delight. The planetary narrative and the literary narrative seem to pull in opposite directions. How could accounts of catastrophic change square with the sense of persistence that we get from individual literary works, works that (if only because they continue to be read) must attest to the staying power of their authors? Is the longevity of these works a tribute to their strength, or is that a fantasy, an optical illusion?

The question takes a different turn when the weakness of my own body makes itself felt so matter-of-factly, an odd kind of mechanical generalizability. It's a reality check, a necessary amendment to the stories we tell about ourselves and our objects of study. For those of us living with the unpredictable course of the injured body, strength is not a given, not a fact in the present tense. Not securely lodged, it is rather an aspired-to outcome, the promise of a yet-to-be-realized future.[6] One must work for it, try to find it. What one finds varies greatly from one person to another. There's always the chance that the search would be in vain, that this aspired-to outcome would always remain aspired-to, beckoning from a place just beyond our reach.

That uncertain future brings to mind the taunt popularized by disability advocates: "temporarily abled-bodied."[7] Most of us think of injury as short term, coming to an end when we recover fully and return to normal life. These advocates remind us that this might not happen, that full recovery might elude us, and that the assumption about able-bodiedness as the condition of normalcy is misguided to begin with. Robert McRuer calls it "compulsory able-bodiedness."[8] Compulsory it might be, but this bodily norm also turns out to be sadly unenforceable over the course of a life, for a simple reason: time does not always cooperate. The trajectory that posits able-bodiedness as the end point is more honored in the breach, for time tends to go in the opposite direction, offering an entropic spiral, sending all of us to some form of disability as the baseline, a state of maximum likelihood.

Seen in this light, disability studies is not a minority discourse, of interest only to a small segment of the population. It speaks to all living things, calling out the vulnerability inscribed in our physical embodiment, an inscription dictated by time itself. Humans join other species on this common ground, the broadest and most egalitarian, uniting us where we least want to be, amid the age-induced weakness and general susceptibility to harm more likely than not to come our way. But disability studies is also broad and egalitarian in another sense. Accepting susceptibility to harm as our common lot, it turns that shared weakness into an injunction for shared labor, a planetwide imperative to provide access and accommodation, to redistribute agency in such a way as to correspond to the widest spectrum of abilities.[9] Experiments in nonparalysis rather than terminal handicaps give rise to disability studies. Action rather than identity propels it. Resilience is its limit-accepting goal, its clear-eyed and nondespairing claim to the future.

What opens up here is what Donna Haraway calls a "tentacular" bond, linking different life-forms across the planet, allowing us to "make kin" among ecological devastations and to "stay with the trouble" we have collectively brought on ourselves.[10] For 3.6 billion years the planet has nurtured life, meeting the needs and providing a robust reproductive environment for the myriad species making their homes here. That nurturing has been eroding since the Industrial Revolution, and with speed and ferocity in recent decades. The now-familiar term *Anthropocene* names human behavior as the cause for this catastrophic speed-up, a transformation so abrupt and so massively disruptive as to constitute a new geological epoch. No longer a reliable home, the planet has become overnight a disabling environment. Record cold alternating with record heat, devastating floods with devastating wildfires, this environment poses an ever-growing threat to all those dependent on it. A "sixth extinction" seems well under way: the elimination of a "significant proportion of the world's biota in a geologically insignificant amount of time."[11] The 2019 UN report on biodiversity warned that 1 million species might disappear within the next decades, making a weak claim to existence as much the rule as the exception.[12]

Can this weak claim lead to something like the "species thinking" envisioned by Dipesh Chakrabarty? Will humankind, a newly constituted endangered species, rally under this elemental threat, a "form of life" taking its place among other endangered life-forms on the planet?[13] If so, will its primacy, long taken for granted, give way to non-species-based "regions of existence," as Elizabeth Povinelli argues?[14] At once perpetrator and victim, will this culpable species replace the innocently laboring "species-being" of Marx, yielding a politics enmeshed in and taking responsibility for the Anthropocene, as urged by Jedidiah Purdy?[15] And can literary history bear witness to this no longer sovereign life-form, offering glimpses into its large-scale hazards, its inherited and ongoing harms, but also its attempts to rebuild, repair, and resuscitate?[16]

While literature has often been depicted as a sovereign domain—the home of masterly authors, hegemonic institutions, and dominant ideologies—turning that narrative on its head and beginning instead with vulnerability can take us outside this muscular preserve, human-centered and coming always in maximum strength. Friedrich Kittler famously says that writing is inscription "burned into silicon by means of electron beam lithography."[17] We don't have to go that far to see that authorship is no longer the work of a sovereign species; it bears the imprint of the nonhuman as well as the human, speaking to the coevolution and codependence of these two.[18] Agency here is laterally distributed rather than vertically integrated. Emerging at different locales, on different levels of a "stack" that can be continually reshuffled, it speaks to the limited power but also relative autonomy of each, as Benjamin Bratton reminds us.[19] Input will come from many: from the peripheries, from lower elevations, requiring no mastery from the contributors, only the happenstance of being there and happening to pitch in.

What results are ad hoc networks with low membership threshold. Like Gilles Deleuze and Felix Guattari's rhizomes, these networks multiply across species boundaries and along horizontal planes, not through linear ordering or vertical chains of command.[20] Bruno Latour calls attention to the variety of actors in such networks. In *Reassembling the Social* (2005), he urges us to be "less wooden, less rigid, less stiff" in imagining "what sort of agencies populate the world."[21] He distinguishes between two in particular, practiced by *intermediaries* and *mediators*—the former, rubber stamps that transmit information without change; the latter, catalysts that alter the relation between any aggregate form and its low-level participants,[22] creating a new dynamics out of several newly connected and now jointly contributing localities. Mediation, on this view, is what keeps a network input-rich, providing links where none previously existed and new forms of action born of this new connectivity. Through such mediation, even a weak network can weigh in where it would otherwise have no say, paralyzed neither by dominant institutions nor powerful single individuals.[23]

The nonparalysis of "multiple weak ties" forged "with strangers" was noted by Manuel Castells in *The Rise of the Network Society* (1996), his pioneering study of the internet. Castells was struck by the ability of weak networks to make structural inequalities less determinative, "less influential in framing, or even blocking, communication."[24] More recently, Lee Rainie and Barry Wellman analyze such networked agency in terms of online "partial membership": intermittent engagement in more than one group, freely entered into rather than institutionally prescribed, and more likely to result in faster, nimbler, and more imaginative responses in an emergency.[25]

Sociologist Mark Granovetter captures this paradox in a memorable oxymoron: "the strength of weak ties." Granovetter coined this phrase back in 1973, inspired by the crucial role of "informal interaction in systems that are formally rationalized."[26] Focusing on the personal networking that facilitates job mobility, he argues that having a large pool of casual acquaintances, each with his or her own information network, is a decided plus here, a weak connectivity providing far more venues for action than a small, tight-knit circle with information overlap. Indeed, weak ties of this sort are the most reliable links to out-groups, allowing for the broadest dissemination of information across different social localities and serving as a "macro-micro bridge"[27] between large-scale statistics and small-scale outcomes.

How might literary history honor such low-bar networks, not powerful but also not trivial, alternating between the macro and micro, and between weakness and strength? One outcome could be a field multiplane and continually crowdsourced, often below the line for public record, though not for meaningful action. Improvised from the ground up, with emerging vectors at every turn and input bearers always on hand, a field like this will never have enough finality to effect closure, even its own. It is involuntarily ongoing. Cause and effect could trade places here; foreground could become background; what's momentarily in focus could become blurry, depending on the location and the mediating plane we happen to be on.

Among the dwellers of this unprepossessing field, none is more energized and less conclusive than literary genre, involuntarily ongoing in just this way. Far from being a done deal, a complete catalog of what exists and what is to come, genre is a mixed attempt at cataloging, doomed to come up short because there will always be more specimens coming its way, inconvenient specimens, unforeseen and unrecognizable on its terms. Genre cannot ban such evidence or deny its empirical force.[28] It's a taxonomy that never quite taxonomizes. Its labels never keep everything straight. Ontologized out of habit but in practice without an ontology, it's "weak" in the sense Gianni Vattimo would use that term.[29] Forever vulnerable to what has not yet materialized, genre is inadequate and interminable in the same breath, less a finished product than a virtual infrastructure, plagued by shortfalls, always only a fraction of what it could be.[30]

As a virtual infrastructure, genre is a key player in the global mediascape that Arjun Appadurai associates with modernity.[31] Lisa Parks and Nicole Starosielski highlight the plurality of scales and venues in such a mediascape.[32] This is a very different world from the print-unified one analyzed by Benedict Anderson.[33] In this platform-rich universe, it's helpful to think of literature as also platform-rich, only weakly standardized by print. Proliferating visually and sonically, as Marshall McLuhan predicted back in 1962, it's a heterogeneous field, with no single medium achieving absolute domination.[34] Fan fiction, singled out by Henry Jenkins as a vibrant participatory culture, also speaks more generally to the bottom-up energies of contemporary media.[35] Weakly integrated and weakly policed, it flourishes through its scalar variety and platform plenitude, surprised by unscheduled appearances among its ranks and able to respond to crisis thanks to these.

These unscheduled appearances enable literature to weigh in on those situations where neither the solution nor even the nature of the problem is self-evident, and where unexpected input from unexpected quarters could make a significant difference. Faced with the impending catastrophes of the twenty-first century, literature offers many options, including the counterintuitive one of going forward by reaching back, giving the present a prehistory, an archive notable for its granularity and depth. Amid our fears about what's to come, these past records of similar fears—

but also of tenacity and inventiveness—have a special meaning. If nothing else, they show that susceptibility to harm could have reparative spinoffs; that diversification and collaboration often follow; and that humans as a species have a track record of bouncing back, turning the endgames of finite individuals into linked chapters in our ongoing life.

Resilience rather than strength is what humans can reasonably hope for in the twenty-first century. Starting out with susceptibility to harm as a baseline condition, resilience is a wager with time, a bet that we would be able to come out at the other end. It's a long-term undertaking, a collateral effect, demonstrable only over the long haul and only through the steadfast presence of a mediating network. Survival here is *assisted* survival. Hanging on perilously and not by its effort alone, it needs an infrastructure, a support team on permanent standby, making up for imperfect outcomes with incessant labor.

Literary history has yet to be seen as a mediating network of this sort: imperfect and incessant.[36] Seen that way, as a nonsovereign field weakly durable because continually crowdsourced, it offers one of the best examples of redress as an incremental process, never finished because never without new input.[37] Mindful that the world isn't what it should be and rarely able to effect a definitive cure, it always has room for one more try. The persistence of literature stems from that very incompleteness, a sequel-producing deficit giving it an extended relation to time. Especially striking in Native American literature and African American literature, this persistence is also generally true of any trial-and-error experiments by the historically handicapped, bent on repairing the past and reclaiming the future, learning from long practice not to be paralyzed by flawed attempts.

Not paralyzed, and coming up short as a matter of course, literary history finds its closest kin in pragmatism, the experimental method of William James and John Dewey, often found wanting yet not devastated by it. Public-facing and field-tested, such a method marks a crossover point from hermeneutics to politics, from the leisureliness of textual analysis to the urgency of repairing and reviving. It faces a unique challenge in that capacity. To repair and revive in the twenty-first century, it must be a *climate* pragmatism, speaking to the exigencies of the Anthropocene, owning up to all the ways we have imperiled our home and not looking away from the possibility that redress might not happen soon enough, might not be able to reverse the accelerating chain of events to give us a future. What does it mean to be finite as a species? How to keep going, when time seems to have run out, giving us no guarantee that the world inhabited today would be world inherited tomorrow?

The future is both a threat and a rallying cry for climate pragmatism. The starting point here is evidence of harm, empirically observable in humans and nonhumans, calling for a damage-responsive method. Such a method, venturing into uncharted waters, is necessarily improvised, drawn from many fields: environmental humanities, disability studies, Native American studies, and African American studies, as well as the radical empiricism of James and Dewey. Experimental and therefore inconclusive, it offers no confident forecasts. It has no ability to enforce conduct, to carve policy in stone. Its practical advocacies can appear "onerous" and dismissible, which, Dewey says, is usually the case with "practical doing and making," the more so here "because of the uncertainty which attends it." Such a weak method, subject to miscue, misdiagnosis, mismatch between means and ends, "can never attain more than a precarious probability," Dewey concedes.[38] And yet, weak as it is, nothing but "skin and bone," it tries nonetheless to "mould" itself "upon the particular shape of this particular world's carcass," James says,[39] stretching its capabilities as best it can, as if some kind of future were still a live option, still up to it to decide.

Climate pragmatism is, in this sense, shorthand for a more general form of open-eyed quixotism. We can think of it as a crisis-necessitated form of the subjunctive mood, a verb form persevering against the seeming negation of "as if," against the strong likelihood of things being otherwise. Chastened but not deterred by the "noise of facts,"[40] it gives us a counterfactual agency, a wager with time and against time to save a world probably beyond saving at this point. Not fully justified in its procedures yet pitching in all the same, climate pragmatism is fact-based but not outcome-obsessed. Merely trying can pass for an acceptable effort when the indicative is loosened by the subjunctive. Modest but stubborn, this verb form enables those who don't have much time left to spend it without reservation and without panic, as if an infinite future were still at their disposal. Such weak daring summarizes both the contents of the book and my own experimental method.

Six chapters—organized under two broad headings, "Revamped Genres" and "Rebuilt Networks"—chronicle these precarious and persistent experiments. Featuring authors far apart in space and time, some celebrated and some not, this literary history pays special attention to low-grade, low-visibility phenomena that, not always developed to their fullest or most forceful extent, have often been overlooked. Bringing these weak phenomena into relief and making them the occasion for further effort, such a history speaks to the crisis of the moment by offering literature as a crisis-responsive art form, long in its emergence and provisional in its expression, bearing the input of many, and surviving as an ad hoc archive, a preliminary report, though also a cautiously hopeful vote on behalf of the future.

Chapter 1, "Still Hungry," features Mary Rowlandson, Louise Erdrich, and Sherman Alexie in just this light. These three authors, the last two unknown and most likely unwelcome to the first, make up a mediating network ongoing by necessity and not to be resolved anytime soon. The three in fact have more in common than one might think. Rowlandson, a "wolfish" reader by her own account, made so by her raging and unappeasable hunger, perpetuates that eating disorder as a reading disorder, devouring the gastronomic language of the Bible as addictive substance. Hunger here is energizing rather than disabling. Extending from Rowlandson to Erdrich and Alexie, it turns the captivity narrative into a long-running and user-amended genre, linking the hungry Puritan to two Native readers with hungers of their own and writing counterfactual histories out of that deficit. These histories won't please everyone or work to the benefit of all. Still, they turn the most inhospitable of genres into the most intimate, aligning it with indigenous agency and reclaiming the past as a yet-to-be-realized future, an experiment with time apparently built into the captivity narrative.

Chapter 2, "Almost Extinct," chronicles the hazards and resilience of the planet through two other genres, elegy and pastoral, each bearing witness to prospects of nonsurvival faced by humans and nonhumans—by frogs and toads, wolves, loons, and Native Americans. Taking these genres through an emerging field, sound studies, I trace a history of near extinction as a sonic history, running from the works of Thoreau to Maya Lin's *What Is Missing*, a sound installation and "last memorial" to all endangered and vanished species. This history, though dire, is not without a counterpoint, a double helix with harm and tenacity entwined. In the climate activism of Native Americans against the Dakota Access and Keystone XL pipelines, coupled with the resurgence of indigenous languages and the eloquence of recently elected Native legislators, we hear an audible alternative to the silence of extinction. A call to action rather than an act of mourning, these newly arisen sounds are those of a crisis-honed "new pastoral," reaching beyond elegy to propose an experimental genre for the twenty-first century. Dedicated to life while mindful of death, this is a "green print" improvised out of devastation, responsive to both past and future, and honoring ancestors and descendants both.

Chapter 3, "Less Than Tragic," begins with the reported demise of yet another genre, tragedy. If true, what does this extinction say about the current state of the world? And if not, what might this not-quite-dead genre tell us about ways of surviving and not surviving? I argue that tragedy is still flourishing in modernity but in a weaker form, less invested in catastrophe as a necessary end and becoming user-friendly and user-amended as a result. Turning to *Moby-Dick* as a case of tragedy at maximum strength, I trace some comically diluted sequels emerging at a tangent to Melville's novel, linking C. L. R. James, Frank Stella, and Amitav Ghosh in an ongoing search for less-than-tragic forms. Especially important to these three is the experiment of genre switching, a reversal of background and foreground that allows James to alternate between his hands-on dedication to cricket and his archive-researched faith in the black Jacobins; Stella, between the high-concept abstraction of his painting and the artisan routine of his printmaking; and Ghosh, between the devastations of the opium trade and the vibrant pidgin tongues spoken by the migrant labor of the Indian Ocean. These authors and artists keep alive the idea of catastrophe but also keep it at bay by taking a second look. Finding a flip side far more habitable, they bring to light a dimension of the world not paralyzed by tragedy and only sometimes under its jurisdiction.

Chapter 4, "Contagiously Irish," explores a weak Irishness as another less-than-tragic form, derived not from one's nationality but from contact with others, an induced effect. Drawing from recent scientific work on viral infection as variant-producing as much as life-threatening, I propose a way to think about global ecologies through communicable diseases, highlighting side effects, both good and bad, that go hand in hand with our susceptibility to harm. With an eye to climate-related pandemics, literature is imagined here as a contagious site, a risk ecology necessitating adaptive hybridization. Beginning with Henry

James's risky sojourn in Colm Tóibín's *The Master*, I trace a hazard-filled arc extending across the Atlantic and from the nineteenth century to the twenty-first. Putting James in the company of Oscar Wilde and W. B. Yeats as well as Gish Jen, it also brings into play the Abbey Theatre, World War I, and Hanna Sheehy-Skeffington, the Irish suffragette and antiwar activist whose book, *British Militarism as I Have Known It*, was banned in Britain for the duration of the war. In such unsafe company, Henry James's less-than-complete naturalization as a British citizen emerges as a weak Irishness, a contagious effect, but far more dynamic than his actual Irish descent. As with the HIV in Tóibín's *Blackwater Lightship*, carriers of diseases here generate a future-building network, weaving assisted life into threats of infection.

Chapter 5, "Vaguely Islamic," turns to weak forms of a strong faith, asking what they might have to offer. The abstract, atmospheric, and out-of-focus versions of Islam in the works of Henri Matisse, James Joyce, Ezra Pound, and Langston Hughes often seem to have a significance that belies their marginality, especially against the contrasting examples of Paul Bowles, Mark Twain, and Edith Wharton. I argue that a "Calypso effect" is in play in all four, enlisting Islam less as a religion on its own terms than as a low-resolution spectrum underwriting some of the boldest experiments in twentieth-century art, fiction, poetry, and politics. Embedded in the visual syntax of Matisse's Moroccan paintings, Islam allows for a play of colors—an intense, opaque black against a pervasive blue green—inspiring Matisse's observation that black is the "color of light" rather than the "color of darkness."[41] Dissolved into a sensory blur in *Ulysses* and scrambled as portmanteaus in *Finnegans Wake*, a barely legible Islam allows Joyce to write as a nose-thumbing hybrid—a "Mohammadhawn," at once a Mohammedan and a *homadhaun*, Irish for "a lout." An equally scrambled but largely idealized Islam, traced back to the splendors of medieval Granada, holds out for Pound the hope and solace of intellectual labor, a refuge from his life in a cage at the American Disciplinary Center at Pisa, awaiting trial for treason. But a vague Islam can also have troubling consequences, as we see in Langston Hughes's off-key vignettes when he traveled to Soviet Central Asia and Civil War Spain in the 1930s. State-sponsored religious persecutions in the former and deep-rooted anti-Islamic prejudices in the latter are both out-of-focus in Hughes's utopian accounts of these countries. His fraught encounter with a black Muslim soldier in a Madrid prison hospital—one of "General Franco's Moors"—makes it clear that a weak Islam serving a political experiment often does so at a cost.

Chapter 6, "Remotely Japanese," takes up the question of reparation. How can we begin to make amends, and how to ensure that such efforts are not fantasies? I look at the long-distance atonement of Faulkner as he reaches out in apology to Japan after World War II, hoping in the same gesture to reach out in apology to displaced indigenous populations in Mississippi. This attempt at reparation, largely wishful, becomes less so when it's crowdsourced by chance, distributed to Native and immigrant authors far from Faulkner's orbit, whose weak connectivity makes them resourceful mediators. Gerald Vizenor, Jim Barnes, and Lucien Stryk are names almost never seen in the company of Faulkner. Unbeknownst to him, they have built a resilient set of ties giving substance and context to his hoped-for atonement. Taking many forms over the years, from teaching appointments in regional universities, to dedicated translation of haiku, to the sending and receiving of postcards, this trans-Pacific network, low-key and steadfast, links the catastrophe of New World genocide to the catastrophe of the atomic bombs without being fixated on either—a dynamic, nonlinear mediation, speaking for Faulkner on his behalf and perhaps in his despite.

In the afterword, "Not Paralyzed," I come back to these mediating networks one more time, making an explicit case now for a form of nonlinear agency I call collateral resilience. Left-field developments rather than targeted hits, collateral resilience inversely matches collateral damage and, like the latter, speaks to the importance of cascading side effects, multi-cause and peripherally propagated, emerging where one might not expect them to. The nonlinear sequels to Sitting Bull's late-life frailties are a case in point. The nineteenth-century Lakota warrior, celebrated for his military prowess in his youth, was assigned by the US government to the Standing Rock Reservation in his last decades. I look at the present-day climate activism of the Standing Rock Sioux Tribe and the Lakota language classes at Sitting Bull College as oblique responses to these past defeats, a reparative network bearing the input of many. Persevering against all odds and granting assisted life to finite beings, these precarious mediations release us from paralysis, sustaining hope in a future still unforeclosed, weakly but meaningfully open to our efforts.

Part One
Revamped Genres

1 · Still Hungry

LOUISE ERDRICH AND SHERMAN ALEXIE
EDIT MARY ROWLANDSON

On the face of it, there's no genre more triumphant than the captivity narrative. Its basic features—involuntary sojourn among non-Europeans, ensuing trials and tribulations, and eventual deliverance—are unified across the genre and self-evident to all. Equally self-evident is its staying power, its ability to project cognate forms into the future and dominate imaginative life for centuries.

Even by conservative estimates, captives taken by Indians numbered in the tens of thousands, beginning with the first European settlements in the sixteenth and seventeenth centuries and extending well into the nineteenth century with the westward expansion.[1] Captivity was a recurring trauma, touching the entire community and woven into the fabric of everyday life. It brought home the dangers of the frontier and the treacheries of racially marked neighbors. The genre seems to be an epitome of settler colonialism, a stark binary—*us* versus *them*—making violence both necessary and legitimate.[2] At the same time, the many economic vectors at play, from the sizable ransom money to the market value of this print commodity on both sides of the Atlantic, also made it an epitome of early capitalism. The captivity narrative stood at the intersection of several force fields, occupying a central place in the national pantheon, "one of America's oldest genres and its most unique,"[3] inaugurated in 1682 by Mary Rowlandson and still going strong, still overshadowing subsequent writings.

AT SEA

This powerful genre becomes less so, however, when viewed across the fluid expanse of oceans. Linda Colley in particular has argued that "like much American exceptionalism," a land-based, nation-centric, and single-track approach is misleading when it comes to these "persistent, tricksy writings."[4] For one thing, the genre was not invented in the New World but transported across the Atlantic by English emigrants, themselves hailing from a culture permeated by the "abundant literature and sermonizing that surrounded men and women captured at sea by Barbary corsairs and enslaved in North Africa" (201).[5] These seaborne narratives didn't originate from any one nation or any one language "any more than they were exclusively Protestant," for the ancient topoi of sin, enslavement, and redemption had long been a staple across the Mediterranean, "standard reference points for all societies exposed to the Old Testament" (202). With the "proliferation of autobiographical and biographical writings that occurred throughout Western Europe around 1400," the captivity narrative was disseminated as a "Europe-wide genre," speaking to Catholics as well as Protestants and written in "Portuguese, French, German, and Russian" as well as English (202).

An ocean-based archive shifts the center of gravity away from a few seventeenth-century texts headed by *The Sovereignty and Goodness of God* (1682). This small and tight-knit canon now becomes looser, less univocal. No longer bound by a common language or a common purpose, it reemerges as emotionally as well as physically at sea, pulled hither and thither by contrary currents. Colley sees it as "protean, profusely distributed across time and place," and "downright plebeian" (202) in its lack of insulation from material necessity, and lack of expertise navigating a world stretched beyond its comprehension. The captivity narrative is "low literature" in at least three senses: improvised "wholly or in part by amateurs"; torn by cultural prejudices running "perplexedly deep"; and driven at its core by "some form of desperation," a neediness "often wrenched from the guts" (200).

"FROM THE GUTS"

"Guts" for Colley is a manner of speaking—she has in mind not so much the digestive tract as visceral responses to trying circumstances. And

Mary Rowlandson would probably not be her candidate for such implacable promptings. In what follows, I'd like to be more literal-minded, taking "guts" at face value as a form of physical embodiment central to the captivity narrative, dramatized through a peremptory need for food. Saturating the narrative voice and yoking it to a clamorous body, this elemental force produces obsessive readings no less than frequent breaches of decorum. It puts Rowlandson, however briefly, in a "low" continuum, exposed to want and exhibiting all its ignoble traits, an abjection as unbecoming to her Christian piety as to her social station.

Born in Somerset, England, in 1637 to a "middling" couple, John and Joan White, Rowlandson arrived with her family in Massachusetts Bay in 1639, settling first in Salem, then in Wenham, which her father helped found, and eventually in Lancaster, a frontier town whose closest neighbors were the Nipmuc. In 1656 she married Joseph Rowlandson, minister of Lancaster, a man whose prosperity and prominence entitled her, alone among all the other "goodwives," to be addressed henceforth as Mistress Mary Rowlandson. Captured in 1676 during Metacom's (or King Philip's) War, Rowlandson was ransomed with twenty pounds, a testament to her family's social and financial wherewithal. Hunger wouldn't have been her lot, wouldn't even have been a worry, except for those three months spent among the Nipmuc, Narragansett, and Wampanoag.

During those three months, it did reign as the principal obsession, a raging torment not to be reasoned with or conjured away. Its traces are everywhere, evident in the way she interacts with her Indian captors, the way she reads her Bible, and of course the way she tells her story in *The Sovereignty and Goodness of God*. In a typical moment in the Seventeenth Remove, Rowlandson writes:

I laid down my load, and went into the Wigwam, and there sat an Indian boyling of Horses feet (they being wont to eat the flesh first, and when the feet were old and dried, and they had nothing else, they would cut off the feet and use them). I asked him to give me a little of his Broth, or water they were boiling in; he took a dish, and gave me one spoonful of Samp, and bid me take as much of the Broth as I would. Then I put some of the hot water to the Samp, and drank it up, and my spirit came again. He gave me also a piece of the Ruff or Ridding of the small Guts, and I broiled it on the coals; and now I say with Jonathan, *See, I pray you,*

how mine eyes have been enlightened, because I tasted a little of this honey,
1 Sam, 14: 29.[6]

In one sense, not much has happened here: no atrocity branding the Indian as heathen, nothing that would help sell the book. The narration is flat, slow-paced. And yet the micro details—from the cataloging of anatomical parts of the animal not ordinarily mentioned, to the litany-like repetition of certain food items, to the peculiar spin put on 1 Samuel 14:29—all make it clear that what transpired here was a significant occurrence.

What makes it one? And what sort of narrator would tell the story this particular way? Someone food-crazed, for whom anything edible counts as a blessing. Horses' feet, the ruff or ridding of the small guts—all are choice morsels for her. This lack of nicety is not an individual failing but rather a behavioral norm common to all those facing starvation. Fastidiousness is a luxury no one could afford. Material necessity here exerts a downward pressure on both what's consumed and who partakes of it. Plagued by hunger, the captivity narrative here cuts across entrenched divisions, putting the famished of all races on the same footing, sharing the same gut-level knowledge. Rowlandson's parenthetical remark, explaining that horses' feet are eaten by Indians only when everything else is gone, is one example of this new, admittedly situational but nonetheless nontrivial gut tutelage. The plain-spoken reporting and tonal neutrality of the empirical data suggest that the captivity narrative is as much field report as jeremiad, an eyewitness account steeped in firsthand knowledge of hunger. The racial binary of *us* versus *them* remains in effect but no longer with uniform strength. The bond of deprivation here offers an alternative protocol, setting *us* and *them* adrift, making it possible for these pronouns to fluctuate, to stray from their default membership.

FLUCTUATING PRONOUNS

Hannah Swarton, whose captivity narrative was published twice by Cotton Mather—first in his *Humiliation Followed with Deliverances* (1697) and then in *Magnalia Christi Americana* (1702)—plays fast and loose with pronouns in just this way. No longer reserved for whites alone, her hunger-chastened *we* fluctuates from sentence to sentence:

The Indians wanted themselves and we more, so that then I was pined with want. We had no corn or bread but sometimes ate Groundnuts, Acorns, Purslain, Hogweed, Weeds, Roots, and sometimes Dogs Flesh but not sufficient to satisfy hunger with these, having but little at a time. We had no success at hunting save that one bear was killed, which I had part of, and a very small part of a turtle I had another time. And once an Indian gave me a piece of moose's liver, which was a sweet morsel to me.[7]

This fluctuating *we*, sometimes including Indians and sometimes not, and alternating with periodic returns of a racially differentiated *I*, makes for an unusually volatile pronominal field. Interestingly, when the first-person singular does reappear, it is often in the form of a grammatical object—on the receiving end syntactically as well as experientially, as is the case here. This twice-repeated *me* is the grateful recipient of a piece of moose's liver, given to her by an Indian apparently without any begging on her part, making the "sweet morsel" all the sweeter.

Still, such usages were rare—indeed, they were the exceptions that proved the rule. For Hannah Swarton had scant reason to make common cause with her captors, let alone modify her grammatical habits to honor that new bond. Despite the "Deliverance" promised by Cotton Mather, her captivity was prolonged, deeply traumatizing, and by all counts uncompensated for. She was held captive for five and a half years; her husband and one of her children were killed; two others were never redeemed. These devastating outcomes were clearly stated in the opening sentences of the narrative:

I was taken by the Indians when Casco Fort was taken (May 1690), my husband being slain and four children being taken with me. The eldest of my sons they killed about two months after I was taken, and the rest scattered. I was now left a widow and as bereaved of my children though I had them alive, yet was very seldom that I could see them, and I had not liberty to discourse with them without danger either of my own life or theirs; for our consoling each other's condition and showing natural affection was so displeasing to our Indian rulers unto whose shares we fell, that they would threaten to kill us if we cried each to other or discoursed much together.[8]

The *we* here, self-evidently unified around a racialized family and pitted against "our Indian rulers"—without question a *them*—would seem to rule out any alternative form of the first-person plural. And yet the fact remains that such an alternative does exist. Weak but not dismissible, this unfamiliar *we* does materialize, in the same paragraph no less, nor can it be said to be altogether an aberration. Born of need, it can be counted on to recur, as indeed it does, prompted by the same threat of starvation and taking an even more striking form when it appears a second time:

> One time my Indian mistress and I were left alone while the rest went to look for eels and they left us no food from Sabbath-day morning till the next Saturday, save that we had a bladder (of moose I think) which was well filled with maggots; and we boiled it and drank the broth, but the bladder was so tough we could not eat it. On the Saturday I was sent by my mistress to that part of the island most likely to see some canoe and there to make fire and smoke to invite some Indians, if I could spy any, to come to relieve us, and I espied a canoe and by signs invited them to come to shore. It proved to be some squaws who, understanding our wants, one of them gave me a roasted eel which I ate and it seemed unto me the most savory food I ever tasted before.[9]

As before, the *we* here is ephemeral, situational, coalescing briefly around a dire need. Still, its membership is clearly interracial, as is the need for food. Simple arithmetic meant that the two women would have to help each other out, resulting in this case in a limited partnership, with one of them venturing out and doing the begging for both. Swarton's freedom of movement, evidenced by the food she was able to secure, underscores just how elastic "captivity" could be. This enterprising captive had plenty of opportunity to show off her talents. Swarton was in fact better equipped to survive than her captor, even on the latter's home turf. Her resourcefulness, however, also brought the situational *we* to a quick end—the interracial pronoun was dropped the moment "our wants" had served its purpose. There wasn't much guilt on Swarton's part as she reverted to the first-person singular, eating the eel alone rather than sharing it with her mistress, making it clear that the ravages of hunger would always trump any budding cross-racial friendship.

ALTERNATE UNIVERSE

Swarton's lack of guilt points to something like an alternate universe, observing a separate code of conduct and allowing for dubious behavior of all sorts. Rowlandson, interestingly, had a roughly similar episode, a lapse from customary norms recounted with some sheepishness but followed immediately by self-justification:

> I went into another Wigwam, where they were boyling Corn and Beans, which was a lovely sight to see, but I could not get a taste thereof. Then I went to another Wigwam, where there were two of the English children; the Squaw was boyling Horses feet, then she cut me off a little piece, and gave one of the English children a piece also. Being very hungry I had quickly eat up mine, but the Child could not bite it, it was so tough and sinewy, but lay sucking, gnawing, chewing and slobbering of it in the mouth and hand, then I took it of the Child, and ate it myself, and savoury it was to my taste. Then I may say as *Job* Chap. 6.7. *The things that my soul refused to touch, are as my sorrowful meat.* Thus the Lord made pleasant refreshing, which another time would have been an abomination.[10]

Not a form of behavior Rowlandson is proud of, but, like Swarton, she also feels no particular need to apologize. For both, implacable hunger allows for behavior inadmissible in civilized society. What would have been an "abomination" anywhere else is not only acceptable here but confessed to with some pride.[11]

EATING AND READING

The "abomination" in this case is horses' feet, inedible to the starving child but "savoury" to Rowlandson herself. But the conversion of what "my soul refused to touch" into "sorrowful meat" also seems to be a general axiom, true of other situations. As in her previous reference to 1 Samuel 14:29 ("See, I pray you, how mine eyes have been enlightened, because I tasted a little of this honey"), Rowlandson here literalizes the Bible's gastronomic language, taking "meat" and "honey" as if they were actual food. This is arguably a greater impiety than snatching a tough morsel from a child's mouth, but in this hunger-driven world, readers have the license to read differently as well as act differently. Rowlandson isn't holding up her literal-mindedness as a bad example; on the contrary, it's more than warranted—the Bible, as she sees it, is a kind of instructional manual both hermeneutic and gastronomic. That's certainly the case with Job 6:7—it teaches us that anything edible that comes our way is to be gulped down, a lesson equally applicable to eating and reading.

Rowlandson does wonder what it means to be such a reader, fearful of its long-term consequences. In a rare moment reflecting on hunger as a life-changing event rather than a passing affliction, she frets about being permanently stuck in this alternate universe, as contrary to common sense as to prevailing decorum:

> I cannot but think what a Wolfish appetite persons have in a starving condition; for many times when they gave me that which was hot, I was so greedy, that I shou'd burn my mouth, that it would trouble me hours after, and yet I should quickly do the same again. And after I was thoroughly hungry, I was never again satisfied. For though sometimes it fell out, that I got enough, and did eat till I could eat no more, yet I was as unsatisfied as I was when I began. And now could I see that Scripture verified (there being many Scriptures which we do not take notice of, or understand till we are afflicted), *Mic.* 6.14. *Thou shalt eat and not be satisfied.*[12]

Hunger has instilled a wolfishness in this otherwise decorous woman. Now that she's safely redeemed, this wolfishness ought to go away; but it seems only to have gone underground, breaking out periodically as a chronic obsession, rooted in an eating disorder also chronic, an inability to feel full no matter how much food she puts into her belly. Hunger is a now a lifelong condition. Caught in its insatiable urges, Rowlandson reads everything through such compulsions. To such a reader, obscure verses from obscure books of the Old Testament were suddenly divine vindication of her singular needs, such as this one from Micah 6:14, "Thou shalt eat and not be satisfied." This verse and many other ones make the Bible a treasure trove, feeding Rowlandson's obsessions and giving the lie to her supposed return to civilized life.

WOLFISH FOR LIFE

Wolfish Rowlandson is reunited with her neighbors only in name. Her captivity in fact has no terminal date, an eating disorder doubling as a reading disorder, turning the most sacred of books into addictive substance. To the extent that the Bible is an indispensable spiritual guide for the captivity narrative, the genre would seem fraught at its core, with pathology built into the very practice of reading. All Rowlandson's future is eaten up in this way, alienating her forever from her neighbors and indeed from her former self: "I can remember the time when I used to sleep quietly without workings in my thoughts, whole nights together, but now it is other ways with me. When all are fast about me, and no eye open, but his who ever waketh, my thoughts are upon things past, upon the awful dispensation of the Lord towards us." And, turning once again to the Bible, she now seizes on this line from Psalms 6:6, "I watered my couch with my tears," to justify her savage refusal to be redeemed: "Oh! The wonderfull power of God that mine eyes have seen, affording matter enough for my thoughts to run in, that when others are sleeping mine are weeping."[13]

This lifelong wolfishness to some extent resembles the "bare life" described by Giorgio Agamben, stuck in a permanent "state of exception." In "The Ban and the Wolf," a chapter in *Homo Sacer* (1995), Agamben links the bare life of "the *wargus*, the wolf-man," to the compulsions of "the *Friedlos*, the man without peace."[14] Both are latter-day incarnations of *zoe*, a term the ancient Greeks used to designate life brutishly lived, as opposed to *bios*, higher forms of organized life proper to an individual or a group. For Aristotle, *zoe* and *bios* were antithetical. Agamben insists, however, that this is no longer the case. According to him, *zoe* and *bios* are now the seamlessly matching halves of the modern biopolitical regime: bare life is at once excluded and coopted by this regime, subject to state power even while being cast out, "constitut[ing], in its very separateness, the hidden foundation on which the entire political system rested."[15]

Wolfish Rowlandson seems both anterior and external to what Agamben posits. A reading disorder such as hers is largely beyond the biopolitical power of the Massachusetts Bay Colony, effective, in this case, neither in its policing of savage appetites nor in its control over biblical exegesis. *Zoe* and *bios*, rather than being seamlessly contained and co-opted, are here endlessly at odds, spilling out into the future on the most elemental level, the guts, a hunger-driven hermeneutics fed by an endless supply of addictive material.

COMPULSIVE EDITING

That hunger-driven hermeneutics is reproductive above all. It has many offspring—readers feeling similarly deprived and feeding on the captivity narrative itself as the first step toward amelioration. The genre extends for hundreds of years for that reason, a cross-time lineage generating ever more determined feedback and resulting in an ever more divergent spectrum of variants.

Not surprisingly, some of the most spirited feedback has come from Native American authors. Faced with this too-durable genre and not finding much to like, these authors take things into their own hands, devouring the few texts they find nourishing and editing the rest to restore some balance to the literary diet. In what follows, I explore the work of two such compulsive editors, Louise Erdrich and Sherman Alexie, the former presiding over a Penguin edition, and the latter improvising on his own. Struck immediately by the food obsession saturating this genre, they made a point of reclaiming it, realigning it with the sufferings of Native populations. Reclaimed in this way, the captivity narrative becomes an indigenous genre, hungry to begin with and still hungry after all these years, eager for sustenance and determined to summon it into being, even if it would have to be served up in ways not palatable to all.

In her introduction to *The Falcon: A Narrative of the Captivity and Adventures of John Tanner*, originally published in 1830 and reissued as a Penguin paperback in 1994, Louise Erdrich lists the well-thumbed volumes standing on a bookshelf in her grandparents' house on the Turtle Mountain Reservation. Tanner's narrative stood "alongside the *New Testament*, the Book of Mormon, and Bishop Baraga's Ojibway Dictionary." It's a "family touchstone," read "until the binding broke and the pages had to be gathered in a heap, secured with rubber bands."[16]

John Tanner (1780–1846) was kidnapped in Kentucky in 1789 when he was nine, brought north, sold, and adopted, spending thirty years of his life among the Ojibwa (1790–1820), fathering three mixed-blood children. Given this degree of integration into Ojibwa society and his less-than-edifying return to white settlements, Erdrich urges us to put his narrative in a separate category, outside the captivity genre altogether. Tanner's account "is more rightly classified as an autobiography than as a captivity narrative—one of those cautionary and often inflammatory tales of abduction and redemption" (xii).

Even though Tanner did in fact leave the Ojibwa and, for the last twenty-six years of his life, worked first as an employee of the Hudson's Bay Company and then as an interpreter for the Indian agents George Boyd and Henry Rowe Schoolcraft, Erdrich doesn't dwell on these facts; nor does she mention his stated desire to take his daughters with him. For her, Tanner had gone Native and would always remain Native: "he was culturally an Ojibwa" (xi). His eventual return to his white relatives was done more "out of curiosity than longing," she insists, and in the end "sicken[ed] him almost to death" (xii–xiv). No redemption graces this narrative, a "desanctified" story of unmitigated suffering (xii). "No odor of piety" tempers the brute fact of "starvation haunt[ing] Ojibwa winters," brought on by the market pressures of "large fur companies" demanding "huge numbers of fur-bearing animals" (xii–xiii). Tanner's Indian family was "forced to boil and eat their own moccasins" (xiii) at one point, she tells us, and concludes that "the driving force of this story is *food*—how to get it, how to hunt it, where to sell the skins to buy it" (xiii). Next to this "all-absorbing task" of bare "survival" (xiii), everything else pales in significance.

In putting hunger front and center, Erdrich puts *The Falcon* firmly on the Ojibwa side—but not without some questionable editing. The new title, for one thing, is entirely her idea. *The Falcon* is a translation of John Tanner's Ojibwa name, *Shaw-Shaw-wa, be-na-se*. The 1830 edition bore no such title but was published simply as *A Narrative of the Captivity and Adventures of John Tanner (U.S. Interpreter at the Saut de Ste. Marie) during Thirty Years Residence among the Indians in the Interior of America*. Highlighting his return and his gainful employment in a government job, that original title put Tanner's narrative equally firmly on the Anglo side, a card-carrying member of the captivity genre.

That card-carrying identity is what Erdrich disputes. Paradoxically, to launch a counterclaim and turn the renamed *Falcon* into a Native genre, she must suppress one bit of information that would have certified Tanner's Indianness in no uncertain terms—namely, his inability to speak English at all when he first returned to the settlements. The 1830 book was dictated in Ojibwa and "prepared for the press by Edwin James, M.D.," as the title page acknowledged. It was published under James's name.

Edwin James, a physician and scientific explorer fluent in Ojibwa, would go on to write a primer on that language. In addition to transcribing Tanner's narrative into English, he wrote a thirty-four-page introduction to the 1830 edition as well as a 136-page "Part 2," a detailed catalog of Native American fauna and flora, customs, poetry, and music, including pictographic script accompanied by a glossary. The coauthored book, one of the most significant collaborations in the nineteenth century, "was one of the most valuable sources for the pictographic language of the Ojibway," Gordon Sayre notes in his review of *The Falcon* for *American Literary History*. This one-of-a-kind archive is now lost when that coauthorship is denied, when the Penguin edition "strips [James's] name and contributions from the book, creating the impression that Tanner wrote it himself in English."[17]

NEED-BASED HISTORY

Erdrich's compulsive editing adds a vexed twist to our understanding of "history." How to come to terms with her claim that John Tanner was purely Ojibwa and the measures taken to back up that claim? Or, differently put, how to come to terms with those not altogether fact-based editions of the past, produced by readers hungry for a history that seems not to have existed and doing what's needed to make it happen? Rather than settling for a single, definitive account of the past, Erdrich's newly edited version claims the mixed blessing of being still in progress. Its original chronological date is stamped with new dates, bearing the signatures of all those moments when it's revisited. How to conceptualize this process? Can we argue for a *directional parity*, a two-way traffic that allows the present to act on the past as much as the past on the present?

Such directional parity is especially notable in long-running genres spanning several centuries, evolving at every point, and bearing the compulsions of many users. Here, input does go back and forth, producing as many editions as there are connective nodes, recalibrating the potentialities of the past even as it resets the baseline for what's to come.[18] The captivity narrative is input-accepting in just this way. Rooted in hunger and running on deficit from the outset, it becomes in time a user-generated sequel, not stopping with official records and not shying away from conjectural claims—editions of history admittedly weak, though answering to a need all too real.

Such weak history can be understood as a need-based, virtual form, somewhat like the "twilight half-entities" proposed by W. V. Quine, with neither the solidity of physical things nor the force of full actualization, though not without an imperative of their own. Many meaningful entities in the world aren't absolutely verifiable, Quine points out. They're neither physically solid nor evidentially ironclad, neither fully formed in space nor fully articulated in time. Rather than discounting them categorically, or claiming for them an identity that cannot be sustained, "why not just accept them thus, as twilight half-entities to which the identity concept is not to apply?"[19]

Understood as some such "twilight half-entity," need-based history reclaims the past as an unforeclosed field, a subjunctive universe where the virtual isn't necessarily the antithesis of the actual. "The distinction between what happened and that which is said to have happened is not always clear," Michel-Rolph Trouillot points out.[20] Weak history further exploits that lack of clarity by opening its doors to many plausible candidates—all those events that could have happened even if there's no proof that they did. Lack of hard evidence is a problem, but such undocumented history makes up for it by grounding itself instead in the imperative of need. That imperative comes with a testimony—noise from the guts, so to speak—most clearly evidenced by patterns of interference in the historical field, resulting in different editions of the past reflecting the urges of those with different hungers.

NETWORK NOISE

These patterns of interference can be theorized by way of an online phenomenon: the IBN (internet background noise), an unwelcome but seemingly unavoidable part of net traffic. Consisting of rogue data sent to IP addresses not designed and not prepared to receive them, such noise amounts to an unauthorized use of the bandwidth. According to a report by the BBC in 2010, this "background hum of rogue data activity generates about 5.5 gigabits of data every second. Not enough to swamp the net's pipes but a sizeable hum nonetheless."[21]

Transposed onto the historical field, this hum points to a noise-rich environment, with built-in interference and distortion.[22] Early American literature would especially benefit from such analysis. Redescribed as user-generated input eliding supervision, the field becomes an actively cascading network, picking up noise at ever-greater distances from a signal's point of origin, a competition for bandwidth bound to multiply over time.

In his important book, *The Networked Wilderness* (2010), Matt Cohen invokes network analysis to theorize early American literature—in his case, to call attention to a world of alternative languages. Building on the work of James Axtell, Colin Calloway, Sandra Gustafson, Neal Salisbury, and others, Cohen challenges the conventional distinction between the oral and the literate and the relegation of Native Americans to a primitive orality. He highlights instead "multimedial" transactions between European and Native languages, by which he has in mind a much larger set of activities than the use of alphabetic scripts, done with nonverbal signs and gestures, with codified rituals and physical objects, originating from Native Americans and adopted by Europeans.[23]

Three other recent books have persuasively corroborated Cohen's argument and extended its scope: Birgit Brander Rasmussen's *Queequeg's Coffin* (2012); Jeffrey Glover's *Paper Sovereigns* (2014); and Sarah Rivett's *Unscripted America* (2017). Taking up the challenge issued by Walter Mignolo, Rasmussen points to a trilingual network based on the "interanimation" between European and indigenous languages across the Americas, from the use of wampum at a 1645 peace council between the French Jesuits and the Haudenosaunee to the mixing of Spanish and Andean literary conventions in Don Felipe Guaman Poma de Ayala's *El primer nueva corónica y buen gobierno* (1613). Glover, meanwhile, focusing on Anglo-Native treaties negotiated across the Atlantic World, against a background of English, Spanish, French, and Dutch rivalries, shows a truly eye-opening Native communicative network. From the great shout perfected by the English sailors as a ceremonial salute to Powhatan to the high diplomacy set into motion by an Anglo-Powhatan dynastic alliance—the marriage of Pocahontas to John Rolfe—Native rituals, gestures, and pictographs were accepted as viable alternatives to alphabetic script and responded to in kind by European nations. And Rivett, calling attention to missionary linguistics in New France no less than New England, makes a network of indigenous languages a fundamental reality in early America, crucial to the origins of the modern nations and the origins of Francophone and Anglophone literature both.[24]

Together, Cohen, Rasmussen, Glover, and Rivett make it clear that any conception of early American literature as "networked" would bring into relief Native languages, recasting the field as a polyglot environment with the potential for translation and collaboration.[25] That potential came to fruition neither in the seventeenth and eighteenth centuries nor in the nineteenth and twentieth.[26] Given those missed opportunities, Native "noise" in the twenty-first century is only to be expected, resulting, as we have seen, in something like a surge in unauthorized signals, a competition for bandwidth drowning out some existing sounds. The need-based history served up by *The Falcon* at the expense of Edwin James is an extreme case.

NON-ZERO-SUM GAME

Still, a zero-sum game isn't the only way to understand network noise. In fact, it's possible to experiment with the opposite, taking the bandwidth not as a fixed sum with strictly matching gain and loss but as a work in progress with expanded capabilities keeping pace with expanded vulnerabilities. Rewiring the input channels while broadening their reach, such a dynamic field meshes signal with noise to create an amplified sonic theater, a new threshold of the audible, less a field of attrition than a cascading free-for-all.

Writing before the advent of the internet, Thomas Greene, in *The Vulnerable Text* (1986), has already raised this possibility, arguing for a conception of literature as simultaneously unprotected and unsilenced, subject to ambient noise of all sorts, and acquiring richer tonalities in the process.[27] The "text does not exist which cannot be parodied," Greene says.[28] Hostile takeover is a fact of life for works of literature, a weakness that ends up giving these texts a continuous supply of variants. This is a case of "survival in spite of, or perhaps because of" known vulnerabilities,[29] for the text's ongoing propagation seems to correlate with its inadequate defenses. Unauthorized use of its bandwidth here allows previously existing signals to be boosted above their customary threshold, becoming newly and differently audible by virtue of this interference, a non-zero-sum game in which the gain of one party does not entail a corresponding loss on the other side.[30]

Louise Erdrich, in fact, offers a striking example of just such a non-zero-sum game in an earlier editorial effort, producing a variant of a still more celebrated captivity narrative, very different from the excisions visited on Edwin James. In 1984, shortly after the tercentenary of Mary Rowlandson's *Sovereignty and Goodness of God*, Erdrich wrote "Captivity," a poem published that same year in her collection *Jacklight*. Even though the tercentenary was a relatively minor event noted only in scholarly circles, its very occurrence spoke to the unwelcome longevity of this objectionable genre. An instant bestseller when it first came out in 1682, *The Sovereignty and Goodness of God* has gone through some thirty printings and is still commemorated three centuries later as a foundational text.[31] The affront was powerful enough, in any case, to jolt Erdrich into action. What results is a counterfactual rendition of *The Sovereignty and Goodness of God*, an indigenous rewriting of the captivity narrative, giving Rowlandson's seventeenth-century words a subjunctive twentieth-century plot.

SUBJUNCTIVE PLOT

Erdrich's poem opens with an epigraph attributed to Rowlandson and proceeds to chronicle her being captured, accepting food from her captor, and being won over by him. Then it tells of her restoration to Boston, where she hungers for her former life and longs to be with her Indian lover once again. The poem ends with these lines:

> I stripped a branch
> and struck the earth,
> in time, begging it to open
> to admit me
> as he was
> and feed me honey from the rock.[32]

The last four words are an almost verbatim quotation from *The Sovereignty and Goodness of God*, the concluding sentence of the Twentieth Remove. There, rejoicing at her deliverance, Rowlandson quotes Psalms 81:16, "But now we are fed with the finest of the Wheat, and, as I may say, with honey out of the rock." These words are now reproduced by Erdrich—and reproduced to yield an unrecognizable plot. There's now no mention of Psalms, not a hint that this is a biblical reference. And the emotional import of the cited words is turned on its head. For Erdrich, the restoration to Boston is the worst "remove" inflicted on Rowlandson, taking her away from her newfound companionship and the man at the center of it: the man who feeds her hunger as no one else can.

Erdrich seems to be flying in the face of Rowlandson's emphatic rejoicing at her deliverance: "I remember in the night season, how the other day I was in the midst of thousands of enemies, & nothing but death before me. It is then hard work to perswade myself, that ever I should be satisfied with bread again. *But now we are fed with the finest of the Wheat*, and, as I may say, *with honey out of the rock*. In stead of the Husk, we have the fatted calf."[33] How could a statement like that be made to say the opposite of what it seems to be saying?

ABORIGINAL SUSAN HOWE

And yet Erdrich isn't the only one to think there is room for doubt, or at least for wonder. In her celebrated and idiosyncratic *My Emily Dickinson* (1985), Susan Howe goes back to Mary Rowlandson to recover an overlooked past, beginning with the captivity narrative and in play since the seventeenth century, marked by "aboriginal anagogy."[34] Howe observes, "The captives who were ransomed and 'redeemed' knew what their neighbors dreaded to have thought."[35] Captives had to be objects of dread. How could they not be? Even relatively short sojourns among heathens—eleven weeks and five days in Rowlandson's case—might lead to some change of heart, never the most reliable organ to begin with.

Mitchell Breitwieser, Michelle Burnham, Christopher Castiglia, Kathryn Zabelle Derounian-Stodola, and Teresa Toulouse have all pointed to the psychic volatility of being among Indians.[36] Howe calls attention in particular to the ways firsthand knowledge of hunger might trigger that psychic volatility: the "captives [learned] that the hardships their captors endured were often the result of English inroads on their land and the subsequent depletion of their supply."[37] Knowing hunger as she never did, Rowlandson can't help knowing who caused that hunger, whose responsibility it was. Schooling of this sort makes these captives uniquely untrustworthy. Rowlandson has been "seduced" in this sense: knowing more than she should, more than is comfortable for her neighbors to find out. From here, it's a short step to lapses of another sort,

also having to do with food and equally worrisome—a sociality with her
captors too habitual and once again informed by too much knowledge:

> During my abode in this place, Philip spake to me to make a shirt for his
> boy, which I did, for which he gave me a shilling. I offered the money
> to my master, but he bade me keep it; and with it I bought a piece of
> Horse flesh. Afterwards he asked me to make a Cap for his boy, for
> which he invited me to Dinner. I went, and he gave me a Pancake, about
> as big as two fingers; it was made of parched wheat, beaten, and fryed
> in Bears grease, but I thought I never tasted pleasanter meat in my life.
> There was a squaw who spake to me to make a shirt for her *Sannup*, for
> which she gave me a piece of Bear. Another asked me to knit a pair of
> Stockins, for which she gave me a quart of Pease: I boyled my Pease
> and Bear together, and invited my master and mistress to dinner, but
> the proud Gossip, because I served them both in one Dish, would eat
> nothing, except one bit that he gave her upon the point of his knife.[38]

King Philip—or Metacom—appears in this narrative on a first-name basis,
and for good reason. This isn't the portrait of an abject captive clueless
among her captors. It's the portrait of a resourceful and sociable woman,
mingling with Indians with ease and relish. This woman admits to liking
the pancake fried in bears' grease, instinctively taking note of its size
and its ingredients. She gives and attends dinner parties. Even the one
catty remark here, directed at her mistress, seems prompted more by female rivalry than know-nothing racism. Rowlandson makes no mention
of the fact that this woman—Weetamoo—was the political and military
leader of the Wampanoag, much more powerful than her Narragansett
husband, Quinnapin, whom she married after her first husband, Wam-
sutta (older brother of Metacom), had died mysteriously after meeting
with the English. Suppressing all this information, Rowlandson here
domesticates Weetamoo in more senses than one, reducing her to a
nitpicking mistress with finicky eating habits, rightly chastised by her
spouse.

Rowlandson is subject to the same domestication herself. Back in
Lancaster, she had been *Mistress* Rowlandson. In captivity, however,
she quickly switches to a language appropriate to domestics, surrender-
ing her former title with little fanfare. That ease of surrender points to
a surprisingly transient form of belonging, not unlike the online signups

analyzed by Lee Rainie and Barry Wellman.[39] Reversible at a moment's notice, such belonging is weak and alarming for the same reason. Those who code switch so flexibly among Indians can presumably do the same when they go home, a no-fuss adaptability that bodes ill for the strength of allegiance and permanence of social forms.

CODE SWITCHING

Just how far did Rowlandson go in the other direction? The careful packaging of *Sovereignty and Goodness of God*, with a preface by Increase Mather, seems necessitated by the impossibility of ever knowing. Interestingly, Mather defends Rowlandson on just those grounds, highlighting the depths of her domestication among Indians to make vivid her unthinkable hardships to those who hadn't been through them: "None can imagine what it is to be captivated, and enslaved to such atheistical, proud, wild, cruel, barbarous, brutish (in one word) diabolicall creatures as these, the worst of the heathen, nor what difficulties, hardships, hazards, sorrows, anxieties and perplexities do unavoidably wait upon such a condition, but those that have tryed it."[40]

Surrounded by heathens, Rowlandson couldn't have survived without an exceptional ability to adapt, especially given by God. She must have made a special pact with Him. Mather was sure of it; and he was equally sure that it was this pact that was now driving her into something so unheard-of as publishing her work: "Deep troubles, when the waters come in unto thy soul, are wont to produce vowes: vowes must be paid. . . . Excuse her then if she come thus into publick, to pay those vows. Come and hear what she hath to say."[41]

It's an astonishing defense, and an astonishing attribution of motive. As far as the reading public was concerned, Mather needn't have worried. *The Sovereignty and Goodness of God* was an instant hit; the first edition in 1682 sold out so quickly that her publisher, Samuel Green Jr., had to enlist the help of his father, who produced a second and then a third printing that same year. Defense of Rowlandson, however, might not have been Mather's primary objective, if ever it was. Offered as an apology, his preface is perhaps less promotional than admonitory, a preemptive clearing of the air to remove any dangerous conjectures. In being so emphatic about her special vow with God, he dismisses out of hand any other ties vying for her affection. God, and God alone, was on her mind and in her heart while she was in captivity. His company was the only one she needed and the only one she kept.

That's how it should be, in theory. In practice it's an impossible order for Rowlandson, or indeed anyone else. Her narrative is a chronicle of the losing battle. In *The Sovereignty and Goodness of God* (a title no doubt gratifying to Mather), there are indeed no sexual liaisons of the sort conjured up by Louise Erdrich. But it isn't the case that God was Rowlandson's sole and exclusive companion. On the contrary, her daily socializing with Indians is such that on many occasions, *captors* and *captive* hardly seem the right words for that ease of association. Philip in particular is a gracious host, going out of his way to show his consideration for this special guest, soon to bring in a large ransom:

> Then I went to see King Philip, he bade me come in and sit down, and asked me whether I would smoke (a usual Complement now adayes among Saints and Sinners) but this no way suited me. For though I had formerly used Tobacco, yet I had left it ever since I was first taken. *It seems to be a bait, the devil lays to make men loose their precious time*: I remember with shame, how formerly, when I had taken two or three pipes, I was presently ready for another, such a bewitching thing it is; But I thank God, he has now given me power over it; surely there are many who may be better imployed than to ly sucking a stinking Tobacco-pipe.[42]

The invitation to smoke is not an attempt at seduction; Rowlandson is not suggesting it. Yet the fact that she's so excessively on her guard, and the equally excessive mitigating circumstances she feels called on to supply—explaining on the one hand that smoking is now a common practice, and on the other hand that of course she has foresworn the habit—makes it clear that this isn't a worry-free occasion. It's not for nothing that her protective gear, rhetorical and psychological, should be so fully on display. The resulting vignette amounts to an involuntary disclosure, a testimony to the hazards of code switching all the more telling for being unplanned. Ability to function in another language—the language of the enemy, no less—might have given Rowlandson a survival advantage, but it's a weakness when it comes to allegiance to one's native tongue. After all, an incident such as this ought to have been unremarkable. And it would have been unremarkable if Rowlandson hadn't made so much of it. Mather might insist that God was the only company she kept; her full defense mode suggests otherwise.

SHERMAN ALEXIE: LANGUAGE OF THE ENEMY

"Mary Rowlandson, it's true, isn't it? Tobacco and sugar are the best weapons," Sherman Alexie taunts her in "Captivity," his essay clearly inspired by Erdrich's poem. Alexie knows what he's talking about. Growing up on the Spokane Indian Reservation, he knows hunger firsthand and knows firsthand its peremptory urgings. "I wish I could draw a peanut butter and jelly sandwich, or a fist full of twenty-dollar bills, and perform some magic trick and make it real," he writes in *The Absolutely True Diary of a Part-Time Indian* (2007). "But I can't do that. Nobody can do that, not even the hungriest magician in the world." Hunger is an arithmetic familiar to all on the reservation: "Poverty = empty refrigerator + empty stomach." It's not all bad, though, Alexie goes on whimsically, for even though "sometimes, my family misses a meal, and sleep is the only thing we have for dinner," there's "nothing better than a chicken leg when you haven't eaten for (approximately) eighteen-and-a-half hours."[43]

In "Captivity," hunger becomes a shorthand for other felt needs. Foremost among these is a language of one's own, an ancestral tongue to pass on to descendants. An acute problem in the twenty-first century, it has an equally long and painful prehistory.[44] Nineteenth- and twentieth-century government schools, such as the Carlisle Indian Industrial School, took it upon themselves to "destroy savagery in this country" by removing Native children from their communities and immersing them in English. Richard Henry Pratt, Carlisle's founder, understood this process literally: English immersion meant "get[ting] them under" and "holding them there until they are thoroughly soaked."[45] Anything less would be a dereliction of duty. For Pratt, classroom and battlefield were one and the same, a military-pedagogic complex he illustrated with a gastronomic metaphor. Quoting Henry Ward Beecher, he said, "The common schools are the stomachs of the country, in which all people that come to us are assimilated within a generation. When a lion eats an ox, the lion does not become an ox, but the ox becomes a lion."[46]

The strong stomach of English immersion gives Alexie the idea for a twenty-first-century captivity narrative in which the always hungry Mary Rowlandson is now a language instructor, a "speech therapist." He comes up with several dates when this otherwise irreproachable woman might have gone too far, seduced by her appetite for language along with her appetite for tobacco and sugar: "Was it 1676 or 1976 or 1776 or yesterday when the Indian held you tight in his dark arms and promised you nothing but the sound of his voice? September, Mary Rowlandson, it was September when you visited the reservation grade school. The speech therapist who tore the Indian boy from his classroom, kissed him on the lips, gave him the words which echoed treaty. . . . Both of us force the sibilant, in the language of the enemy."[47]

Alexie is not writing in a vacuum—language instruction is front and center in indigenous revitalization in the twenty-first century. I'll be discussing these new developments, especially the resurgence of the Lakota tongue, in the afterword. In this chapter, I turn first to the other side of the problem, to the "language of the enemy," exploring it more broadly by reading the captivity narrative against the vexed landscape of language acquisition, in play since the eighteenth century.[48] The rhetorical force fields revolving around King Philip are especially helpful as points of entry, and William Apess, a compulsive participant, has much to tell us about the "speech therapy" coming from a language not one's own.

WILLIAM APESS AND DANIEL WEBSTER

Apess's "Eulogy on King Philip," written in 1836 to observe the 160th anniversary of Philip's death, was delivered twice in Boston and published the following year as a forty-eight-page booklet. Its objective couldn't be clearer: to set the record straight and convince the world that Philip deserved a place in the national pantheon, next to the "immortal Washington."[49] This was by no means a lone effort. Rehabilitation of King Philip was in full swing in the 1820s and 1830s. Beginning with Washington Irving's "Philip of Pokanoket" in *The Sketch Book* (1819) and followed immediately by J. W. Eastburn and R. C. Sands's *Yamoyden* (1820), an account of King Philip's War, it became a theater sensation with John Augustus Stone's *Metamora; or, The Last of the Wampanoags*. Starring Edwin Forrest as King Philip, the play premiered in New York in 1829 and remained popular for decades, turning the Indian king's dying words into nineteenth-century sound bites: "The curse of Metamora stays with the white man!"[50] Even the *North American Review*, ordinarily reserved but not so on this occasion, gushed that though defeated in the end, what Philip had done was surely enough "to immortalize him as a warrior [and] a statesman."[51]

In joining this chorus of voices, Apess made the decision that his eulogy would be a formal tribute, using conspicuously elevated language. Along these lines, Philip was "as active as the wind, as dexterous as a giant, firm as the pillars of heaven, and fierce as a lion, a powerful foe to contend with indeed, and as swift as an eagle, gathering together his forces, to prepare them for the battle."[52] Eulogy is of course a convention-bound genre; this one, written 160 years after Philip's death, was further conventionalized by its distance from its subject. Still, there's something about this compulsively lofty syntax that seems to exceed even the demands of the genre. This isn't a language of desperation, the language of a hunted, starving people. It's a stately, monumentalizing language, borrowed from Daniel Webster. Using the sonorous rhythms from the patriotic speeches Webster gave between 1820 and 1826, Apess set out to forge a new idiom for the downtrodden, those long without access to the written word.[53] But why this particular choice—why this magisterial "language of the enemy"—and why in 1836?

Apess, an Algonquian-speaking orator of mixed Pequot descent, had been an ordained Methodist minister and a champion of Native American rights ever since he published his autobiography, *A Son of the Forest*, in 1829. In 1833, to seek redress for the grievances of the Mashpee Indians, he helped organize what was known as the Mashpee Revolt (1833–34), in the course of which he was jailed for a month. With his popular base eroding, he gave the King Philip eulogy in 1836 in Boston as a final public lecture before moving to New York City and dying in obscurity in 1839 at the age of forty-one.

The eulogy was written under tremendous pressure, financial and psychological, with alcoholism setting in. It was haunted, above all, by the Mashpee Revolt, perhaps more of a goad to Apess than the exploits of King Philip in the seventeenth century. The effect of it, in any case, was to make a lofty, unassailable prose a kind of "speech therapy" for the user, a rhetorical constant in a life beset with uncertainty. By the late twentieth century, this rhetoric was no longer an option, its use of the "language of the enemy" alienating rather than inspiring. Erdrich and Alexie would have no truck with it. They've already forged a language of their own, an instrument sharpened by past harms and relentless in its

scrutiny of the enemy. Having socialized with her captors with such relish, what else might Rowlandson have done? How much of it is admis-
sible, and how much not? Is her narrative a full and complete record of
everything that transpired, or is it less than that, with significant details
left out?

LESS-THAN-FULL DISCLOSURE

Rowlandson herself seems to have anticipated such questions, baiting
her readers to some extent. At the end of the Twentieth Remove, just
before citing the book of Psalms, she makes this enigmatic confession:
"I can remember the time when I used to sleep quietly without workings in my thoughts, whole nights together, but now it is other wayes
with me."[54] What is it that keeps her awake? Without assigning specific
content to this teasing moment, we can say, at the very least, that less-
than-full disclosure seems to be a conscious strategy, here advertised by
Rowlandson herself. That strategy also happened to extend beyond this
particular phase of her life.

As is well known, Rowlandson had actually been Mary *Talcott* by
the time she published *The Sovereignty and Goodness of God* in 1682.
Her husband Joseph had died suddenly in November 1678 at the age of
forty-seven, and nine months later (a not uncommon interval of time) she
married Samuel Talcott, a wealthy landowner who represented Wethers-
field in Connecticut's General Court and who, during King Philip's War,
sat on that colony's War Council. Understandably, Rowlandson makes
no mention of these changes in her marital status, and no mention of
Samuel Talcott. The name Mary Talcott belongs to another narrative,
with a different beginning, a different ending, and perhaps a different
persona altogether, one incompatible with *The Sovereignty and Goodness
of God*.

Withholding information is of course a time-honored authorial pre-
rogative; the captivity narrative seems to have made good use of it. Not
least among its silences is the nondisclosure of forms of captivity inflicted by *white* captors—whether in the form of African slavery, Native
American slavery, or (less frequent but still common) white indentured
labor.[55] Ironically, Rowlandson's only public appearance as Mary Talcott was occasioned by a white-on-white captivity of that sort. In 1707,
she posted bond following the arrest of her son, Joseph Rowlandson Jr.,

charged by a long-missing brother-in-law of having gotten him drunk and sold him as an indentured servant to Virginia. Captives came in a variety of skin colors, many uncounted, unacknowledged. Just as the sale of enslaved Native Americans was an untold story of the seventeenth century, so the involuntary servitude of whites was likewise underreported. Highlighting the transience of group membership and the erratic constitution of the evidentiary field, the trial of Joseph Jr. would have been a distressing but fitting coda to Rowlandson's public career, putting a habitual dodger on the spot. Fortunately for her, death came in 1711, nine years before the court finally made its ruling in favor of her son's accuser.

"Every time the story is told, something changes. Every time the story is retold, something changes," Alexie writes.[56] Telling and retelling share the same morphology and blend into each other on the same continuum. Neither offers a pristine reality; each is already an edition, with necessary embellishments and lacunae. Alexie's and Erdrich's need-based histories must be seen against Rowlandson's own evasions and the weak constraints they exert over competing hypotheses. Less-than-full disclosure by the author makes it hard to rule out other scenarios. This is certainly the case with *The Sovereignty and Goodness of God*: the ratio between what was reported and what transpired and what might have transpired is anyone's guess. Edited as Rowlandson saw fit, this not entirely forthright document sets a precedent for the subjunctive constructs of Erdrich and Alexie, all three playing with evidence to some extent, telling stories less of what happened than of what could have happened.

MACRO AND MICRO

Erdrich and Alexie are in any case unapologetic, not least when they clinch their case with this epigraph, a supposed quotation from Rowlandson: "He (my captor) gave me a biscuit, which I put in my pocket, and not daring to eat it, buried it under a log, fearing he had put something in it to make me love him."[57]

As Yael Ben-Zvi points out, this stunning line is actually not from Rowlandson but from John Gyles's *Memoirs of Odd Adventures, Strange Deliverances*, published in 1736.[58] This could be an unintentional error— Erdrich getting her facts wrong and Alexie repeating her mistake—but given the tremendous mileage each gets from this misattribution, we must consider other possibilities as well. Gyles's narrative (contrary to the apparent thrust of the quoted words) in fact speaks not to the sexual titillation between captive and captor but to the political and religious drama played out among three sets of transatlantic players: the French and their Jesuit missionaries in Canada; English settlers, with their paranoia toward Catholicism; and Indians who were allies of the French. In 1689, when the Abenaki captured the ten-year-old John Gyles in Maine, his captors planned to sell him to a Jesuit missionary, Louis Pierre Thury. The transaction never took place, but it didn't stop Gyles from hyperventilating over the gift of the biscuit from Thury, or his mother from lamenting, "I had rather follow you to your grave or never see you more in this world, than you should be sold to a Jesuit; for a Jesuit will ruin you, body and soul!"[59]

Gyles's psychodrama speaks directly to the enmity between the two Atlantic empires, the attendant enmity between Protestantism and Catholicism, and the not insignificant role played by Indians in this tangle. *Memoirs of Odd Adventures, Strange Deliverances* is a text vividly illustrating what Jared Hickman calls "globalization and the Gods,"[60] religious conflicts as much geopolitical as doctrinal, played out through an axis of race extending across continents and oceans.

A number of factors contributed to this tangle of religion, psychology, and geopolitics: on a macro scale, shifting relations among the colonies and their parent countries, and on a micro scale, the complex diasporic identities of the European settlers themselves, making ties to Native populations increasingly volatile. Benedict Anderson and Ralph Bauer have framed the captivity narrative in terms of the creolizing forces extending across the Atlantic and the Americas.[61] Bridget Bennett emphasizes the importance of the "lost home" to Rowlandson.[62] Paul Baepler, Robert C. Davis, Nabil Matar, Gordon Sayre, Daniel J. Vitkus and Lisa Voigt, meanwhile, have made a case for the importance of North Africa to the captivity narrative, putting Barbary slavery squarely within its geopolitical, religious, and affective orbits.[63] This is the macro network underwriting the micro love stories told by Erdrich and Alexie. In this globalized world, such interracial love stories are not only thinkable but well-documented historical facts.

John Williams's *The Redeemed Captive Returning to Zion* (1707) tells just such a story. "Sir, if I thought your religion to be true, I would embrace it freely," Williams says to the Jesuit at Quebec who is trying to convert him, "but so long as I believe it to be what it is, the offer of the whole world is of no more value to me than a blackberry."[64] The Deerfield, Massachusetts, minister had been taken to Canada by the Mohawk during what was known as the French and Indian War, hostilities between the French and English colonies triggered by those between their parent countries, first during the War of the League of Augsburg of 1689–97 and then the War of the Spanish Succession in 1700.[65] Though Williams's own captivity was relatively short, what broke his heart was the fate of his daughter, Eunice, held by the Caughnawaga Mohawk, who refused to give her up even for a large ransom ("a hundred pieces of eight") offered by Governor de Vaudreuil of Quebec. Living among that tribe since age seven, Eunice would eventually marry an Indian and convert to Catholicism despite repeated attempts by her family and the Quebec authorities to bring her back to Deerfield.

This was by no means an anomaly. Adoption was a common practice of Native tribes to replace tribal members killed by war and by epidemics.[66] Colin Calloway notes that "among some of the Iroquois tribes to the west, adoption became such a practical way of replenishing the losses caused by war that adoptees came to outnumber pure-blooded Iroquois."[67] And many white captives were more than willing to be adopted. Wilcomb E. Washburn points out that "girls aged 7 through 15 were the most likely of all groups to be transculturated," and that "almost 54 percent of this group refused to return to New England compared with less than 30 percent of the boys in the same age group."[68] "No Arguments, nor Intreaties, nor Tears of their Friends and Relations, could persuade many of them to leave their own Indian Friends and Acquaintances," Cadwallader Colden fumed in 1747.[69] And even when redeemed, "unless they are closely watch'd," lieutenant governor Francis Fauquier of Virginia warned, "they will certainly return to the Barbarians," which was the case with two hundred white captives brought back in 1764 by Colonel Henry Bouquet through a treaty with the Delaware and Shawnee.[70] By the mid-eighteenth century, J. Hector St. John de Crevecoeur drily notes in *Letters from an American Farmer* (1782), "thousands of Europeans are Indians."[71]

Among these, none was more legendary than Mary Jemison. Captured in 1755 at age twelve by the Shawnee, she would spend the rest of her life among Native tribes, first marrying a Delaware and bearing him one child, then, after he died, marrying a Seneca and bearing him six children. She was with the Seneca Nation when it sided with the British during the Revolutionary War; she was there as well when the tribe was forced to sell its land to the United States afterward, skillfully negotiating more favorable terms at the treaty settlement at Geneseo, New York. Remembered as the "white woman of the Genesee," her fame would persist well into the nineteenth century. An 1844 elegy simply states that "she lov'd the Indian way of life."[72]

Eunice Williams had company. Like Mary Jemison, her micro love story is threaded through a formidable transatlantic network. "Where does the story begin?" John Demos muses in his book on her, *The Unredeemed Captive* (1994). Like Sherman Alexie, he calls up a number of dates, and a number of virtual scenarios:

> Perhaps it is in the old university town of Cambridge, England. In the summer of 1629. . . . Perhaps it begins in the villages of the Iroquois heartland (what is today upstate New York). In the decade of the 1660s. . . . Perhaps it begins in the Massachusetts town of Dedham. On May 22, 1670. . . . Perhaps it begins in the "borning room" of a particular house at Deerfield. In September 1696. . . . Perhaps it begins in the royal palace, in Madrid, center of the sprawling Spanish Empire. In the autumn of the year 1700.[73]

The Sovereignty and Goodness of God invites still other conjectures. Through the compulsive editing and subjunctive love stories told by Louise Erdrich and Sherman Alexie, we have an in-progress narrative, stamped with many dates and signed by many hands, extending from the seventeenth century to the twenty-first, with no end in sight. A need-based history to make up for what has yet to come to pass, it honors a world eloquent because deprived, ongoing because still hungry for sustenance.

2 · Almost Extinct

ELEGY, PASTORAL, AND SOUNDS IN AND OUT
OF THOREAU

This chapter is an attempt to bring together two looming prospects of nonsurvival: the possible nonsurvival of the humanities, and the already demonstrated though not always noticed nonsurvival of many species. Beginning with these shared hazards, I argue that by linking the fate of the humanities to these at-risk humans and nonhumans, we can face up to worst-case scenarios as scenarios all too close to home.[1] What might the humanities look like articulated through a future none of us would like to see?[2] Can a discipline self-recognized as weak, perhaps already set on a path to extinction, adapt in time to bounce back? And will it stay the same going forward, or morph into something different, shaped by the climate-endangered twenty-first century?

In what follows, I'd like to try out one such humanities scenario, acting out of its weak claim to existence and experimenting under duress. An emerging field, sound studies, is especially worth noting in this regard. Even on first showing, this largely ad hoc field, aligned with no single discipline, is making a virtue of that fact, assembling a network refreshingly unfamiliar—including music, linguistics, cognitive science, evolutionary biology, engineering, literary studies, and environmental studies. Here is a synthesis of arts and sciences outside the comfort zone of most of us but not absolutely beyond our capability. Pondering the tangled futures of the weak humanities on a weak planet through this network, and with a nudge or two from Thoreau, I begin with a recent book on the loss of biodiversity as a sonic phenomenon, Bernie Krause's *The Great Animal Orchestra* (2012).[3]

VANISHING SOUNDS

Krause is something of a cult figure to music fans: the last guitarist recruited by the Weavers to replace Pete Seeger, he teamed up a bit later with Paul Beaver to form the legendary synthesizer team Beaver and Krause, providing electronic music for films such as *Rosemary's Baby* and *Apocalypse Now*. For the past forty years, though, his work has been primarily in bioacoustics, focusing especially on the sound ecology of endangered habitats. Wild Sanctuary, his natural soundscape collection, now contains over four thousand hours of recordings of over fifteen thousand species.[4]

Krause tells us that animals consistently outperform us when it comes to sound: they both hear and vocalize better than we do and can do more with sound than we can. One example he gives is the sound camouflage perfected by the spadefoot toad. This amphibian species, like many animals in the wild, does not vocalize separately but does so as a group, "a synchronous chorus assuming a seamless protective acoustic texture."[5] Through this sound aggregation, these toads prevent predators such as foxes, coyotes, and owls from pouncing on one particular victim, since no single individual stands out.

Unfortunately, the complexity of this camouflage is such that any human interference is likely to disrupt it and undermine its working. Krause starts with the marvelous sound engineering of the toads, but by the time he's done it's no longer a happy story. When a military jet flew "low over the terrain nearly four miles west of the site," the sound camouflage was thrown off-kilter. It took the toads between thirty to forty-five minutes to rebuild their sound camouflage. Krause reports: "My wife and I watched from our nearby campsite as a pair of coyotes and a great horned owl swept in to pick off a few toads during their attempts to reestablish vocal synchronicity."[6]

The death of a few spadefoot toads is probably no major disaster, but the larger narrative coming out of *The Great Animal Orchestra* is disturbing in more ways than one. Something much larger, more systemic, and more destructive than military jets is preying on these sound ecologies, upsetting their delicate balance and making them less and less able to function as they used to. Almost half the habitats in which Krause made his recordings have now been seriously compromised or destroyed. His audio archives are all that's left of these once sound-rich environments.

ELEGY FOR THE PLANET

Bernie Krause is writing at a point in time when elegy is almost a default genre, one that speaks to losses sustained by the planet overall as well as to private and personal losses. While *elegy* is sometimes defined narrowly as a particular kind of lyric lamenting the death of a public personage or a loved one, historically its definition has been much broader: a meditation on nonsurvival, an *ubi sunt* tally of what was gone, common in Old English and in Norse, Homeric Greek, Hebrew, and Sanskrit.[7] At the same time, the genre has been understood from the very first to have implications for those still on this earth, left to do the mourning. "Elegies are for the living," Stuart Curran writes, "but how and why so can be a point of some dispute." And while the genre can be made to "cover any number of possible permutations," its principal charge is to speak for all humanity on the ground of our shared losses, to remind us that we're defined no longer by a "vital and buoyant present tense, but by what has been eroded from us and is left only in our memories, to taunt us with its inevitable absence."[8]

More recently, Timothy Morton has argued that elegy is a "quintessential mode of ecological writing," as much about the nonhuman as the human, to be found in the prose of Rachel Carson and the Dalai Lama no less than the poetry of Shelley and Keats. For elegy to become a genre on this scale—speaking for more than one species and addressing systemic rather than individual losses—it must do some adapting of its own. More complex verb tenses are needed to tackle such large-scale processes, potentially irreversible though open to some negotiation. Working with the subjunctive and the future perfect as much as the past and present, elegy brings a variety of time frames to bear on that negotiation. It "mourn[s] for something that has not completely passed, that perhaps has not even passed yet. It weeps for that which will have passed given a continuation of the current state of affairs."[9]

The Great Animal Orchestra is elegiac in all these senses, its future perfect looming ahead but not absolutely inevitable, and perhaps to be averted by retracing our steps, going back to a past not entirely behind us, not over and done with. Elegy in the twenty-first century is a conjecture about the future as much as a record-keeping backward glance. Neither the last act nor the last word, it calls for a sequel, a supplement. Turning from this already complex genre to the still more complex mix in *Walden* is both a journey back in time and a search for that sequel and supplement, a reckoning with the damage done, the better to go forward. Addressing the present-day crisis of the planet by retracing its prehistory two centuries ago might be one way to produce an experimental genre—I'm calling it the new pastoral—indebted to elegy but on its own in viewing mourning as a prelude rather than a coda. Intervening at a juncture just before extinction is final, it puts what could have been and what might yet be back into the realm of the thinkable, venturing into new pastures on just that basis.[10]

VERSIONS OF PASTORAL

There is no pastoral "unless there are serious forces at work," William Empson says in *Some Versions of Pastoral* (1974), where he also argues, famously and counterintuitively, that all "proletarian" literature is pastoral.[11] Faced with "human waste and limitation" while dreaming of peace and harmony, pastoral turns these opposing outcomes into "double plots," "tragi-comedy" pulling in opposite directions, never clearly telling the reader (or making up its own mind) whether the comic or the tragic is dominant.[12] Tracing these double plots back to antiquity, Raymond Williams argues that the classical form (e.g., Virgil's *Eclogues*) has always been double edged, driven by "living tensions." Pastoral goes hand in hand with counterpastoral, giving it an alternating rhythm: the idyllic yoked with its imminent collapse; "summer with winter; pleasure with loss"; the quotidian life of the farmer with the impersonal "observation of the scientist."[13] This alternating rhythm resurfaced in the seventeenth century as contrary intuitions: "the enjoyment of what seems a natural bounty, a feeling of paradise in the garden, is exposed to another kind of wit: the easy consumption goes before the fall."[14]

Equally struck by the inevitability of the fall, Paul Alpers argues that the version of pastoral that's most elegiac also "sum[s] up the whole genre." Pastoralism in general, like "pastoral elegy" in particular, takes "human life to be inherently a matter of common plights," a collective musing that confronts us at every turn with "the question of how the world continues after a loss."[15] In asking the most common and most inconsolable of questions, pastoral is "less a genre than a mode," deriving "its character not from its formal properties, as a genre does, but rather from a special perspective on human experience," Leo Marx controversially argues.[16] It is, in any case, a "cultural equipment that western thought has for more than two millennia been unable to do without," Laurence Buell observes.[17]

That longevity surely has something to do with its recurring sense of urgency, its habit, as Kenneth Hiltner says, of granting an endangered world "its belated emergence into appearance even as it disappears."[18] Pastoral owes its "staying power" to its long-running "covenant with life and the times," Seamus Heaney says, a covenant that under "extreme conditions" turns it into an "eclogue *in extremis*."[19] This is certainly the case with Andrew Marvell's "Upon Appleton's House," an eclogue in extremis for the seventeenth century updated now by the twenty-first, singing a dirge for nonhuman species as urgent today as it was back then:

> Unhappy Birds! what does it boot
> To build below the Grasses Root;
> When Lowness is unsafe as Hight,
> And Chance o'ertakes what scapeth spight?
> And now your Orphan Parents Call
> Sounds your untimely Funeral
> Death-Trumpets creak in such a Note,
> And 'tis the *Sourdine* in their Throat.

That dirge is a call to action as much as an act of mourning. "The very survival of our species depends upon" hearing it anew, Terry Gifford says.[20]

"ECLOGUE IN EXTREMIS"

Walden doesn't go quite so far. Still, it's an eclogue in extremis of sorts, not least when it's pastoral in what seems to be a naively idyllic sense— waxing eloquent on a bucolic present that harkens back to a golden past, as it does in this boisterous frog chorus:

> In the mean while all the shore rang with the trump of bullfrogs, the sturdy spirits of ancient wine-bibbers and wassailers, still unrepentant, trying to sing a catch in their Stygian lake,—if the Walden nymphs will pardon the comparison, for though there are almost no weeds, there are frogs there,—who would fain keep up the hilarious rules of their old festive tables, though their voices have waxed hoarse and solemnly

grave, mocking at mirth, and the wine has lost its flavor, and become only liquor to distend their paunches. . . . The most aldermanic . . . quaffs a deep draught of the once scorned water, and passes round the cup with the ejaculation *tr-r-r-oonk, tr-r-r-oonk, tr-r-r-oonk!* And straightway comes over the water from some distant cove the same password repeated.[21]

Repeated: this is the keyword here, perhaps the single most important word in this nineteenth-century report on the natural environment. Nothing spectacular, just the sense that there will be more, that whatever is happening now will happen again, a dilation of time that makes the future an endless iteration of the present. All this is suggested by the croaking of the bullfrog, so natural to that particular habitat and so reliable in its recurrence that it's unimaginable there would ever be a time when that sound wouldn't be there. The future of the planet seems guaranteed, and we, along with the frogs, can luxuriate in that fact.

It's a luxury, of course, to feel that way. There's no better measure of our distance from the nineteenth century than the evaporation of that assurance. Among the escalating changes to the environment that began with the Industrial Revolution, the loss of a reliable and habitable future must rank near the top. The now-familiar term *Anthropocene*, coined in the 1980s by ecologist Eugene F. Stoermer and atmospheric chemist Paul Crutzen, names human behavior as the chief cause of the drastically altered conditions for life on the planet, so abrupt and unprecedented as to constitute a new geological epoch. A sixth extinction seems well under way, the elimination of a "significant proportion of the world's biota in a geologically insignificant amount of time."[22]

THE SIXTH EXTINCTION

Such massive die-offs have happened only five times in the 3.6-billion-year history of life on the planet. Each time, it took millions of years for life to recover, starting from scratch with single-celled organisms such as bacteria and protozoans. The sixth extinction—if that's indeed where we're headed—promises to be even more cataclysmic than the previous five. The work of just one species, it has already resulted in 140,000 species disappearing each year, while half the life-forms on earth are slated for extinction by 2100, according to Edmund O. Wilson, writing in 2001.[23] Wilson's predictions have been borne out. In 2014, Elizabeth Kolbert reported that "it is estimated that one-third of all reef-building corals, a third of all fresh-water mollusks, a third of sharks and rays, a quarter of all mammals, a fifth of all reptiles, and a sixth of all birds are headed toward oblivion."[24] A new report by the UN Intergovernmental Panel on Climate Change, issued on May 6, 2019, warned that a million species will be extinct within the next decades.[25]

Frogs turn out to have been the first to sound the alarm. Since the mid-1970s, herpetologists from all over the world had begun to hear not their loud croaking but an eerie silence, a deafening absence of sound. Researchers from North America, the United Kingdom, Australia, and New Zealand started comparing notes, puzzled by the fact that in many of these cases, the disappearances were taking place apparently without encroaching human presence. There was no suburban development, no highways with life-threatening traffic. The frogs seemed to be dying out on their own.

What makes these extinctions especially worrisome is that the frog is one of the oldest species on earth. Its 300-million-year history is one hundred times longer than human history. Such a duration suggests that the evolution of amphibians is intertwined with that of the planet at every stage. Over their life cycles, they turn from tadpoles to frogs, moving from water to land and changing from plant-eater to insect-eater, so they have something to tell us about almost every kind of habitat. And because their skin is permeable, they are the first to register any environmental degradation, and to do so across the widest range of variables. It's for this reason that they're the proverbial canary in the coal mine: their well-being is also a measure of the well-being of the planet.

On December 13, 1992, "Silence of the Frogs" appeared on the cover of the *New York Times Magazine*, accompanied by a nine-page article by Emily Yoffe documenting the extinction or near extinction of many amphibian species. Sixteen years later, an article appeared in *Proceedings of the National Academy of Sciences*: "Are We in the Midst of the Sixth Mass Extinction? A View from the World of Amphibians."[26] The authors, David Wake and Vance T. Vandenburg, noted that although mass extinctions are unthinkably rare, based on the collective observations of herpetologists worldwide, they would have to conclude that the unthinkable was indeed about to happen. In 2009, PBS revisited the issue in a special episode of *Nature* entitled "Frogs: A Thin Green Line," showing that already one-third of all amphibian species had vanished.[27] In 2011, the *Guardian* reported that half the world's amphibians were in decline, and one third slated for extinction.[28]

In 2012, the *New York Times* reported that a killer had been identified: a fungus named chytrid, capable of wiping out entire frog populations in a matter of months. Ironically, the principal carrier for this pathogen appears to be Thoreau's bullfrog, itself resistant to the fungus and a popular food item, much in demand in the Chinatowns of New York, San Francisco, and Los Angeles. Human dietary habits, it seems, are responsible for the dissemination of this infectious agent, triggering mass extinctions as an unforeseen side effect.[29]

This isn't a future Thoreau could have imagined. And yet something does seem amiss in his archaic portrayal of the frogs: they are "wine-bibbers and wassailers," "quaff[ing] a deep draught" from the pond, accompanied by nymphs and the river Styx. These overdone classical allusions, rather than bringing Homer and Ovid into the modern world, underscore instead their distance, suggesting that frogs might be a relic both in the sense of hailing from the past and in the sense of being no longer viable in the present. Though still loudly croaking, they are in fact no longer what they once were. Try as they might to "keep up the hilarious rules of their old festive tables," the wine has "lost its flavor," and their own voices have grown "hoarse and solemnly grave." It's in such moments, when time becomes recessional and attritional, that the eternal present of *Walden* ceases to be eternal and becomes more like a finite endgame. Past and future are no longer one here. The terminal point is no longer a faithful replica of the starting point. Losses will be incurred that cannot be recovered, and points of no return will be reached from which there's no going back.

ANIMAL FABLES

If this is the case with Homer and Ovid, it's even more so with animal fables from the distant past. For an avid reader like Thoreau, these include not only fables from Aesop (620–560 BCE) but those from languages still more ancient. As Laura Gibbs points out, "The animal characters of Aesop's fables bear a sometimes uncanny resemblance to those in the ancient folktales of India collected both in the Hindu storybook called the *Panchatantra* . . . and also in the tales of the Buddha's former births, called *jatakas*."[30] Aesop's fables were first translated into English and published by William Caxton in 1484. The Indian Sanskrit stories were translated in 1775 as *Fables of Pilpay*.

In an undated entry in his commonplace book (what he kept before he started his journals), Thoreau pays tribute to these Greek and Indian fables, but then proceeds to tell an animal story of his own, pulling away from both:

> Yesterday I skated after a fox over the ice. Occasionally he sat on his haunches and barked at me like a young wolf. . . . All brutes seem to have a genius for mystery, an Oriental aptitude for symbols and the language of signs; and this is the origin of Pilpay and Aesop. . . . While I skated directly after him, he cantered at the top of his speed; but when I stood still, though his fear was not abated, some strange but inflexible law of his nature caused him to stop also, and sit again on his haunches. While I still stood motionless, he would go slowly a rod to one side, then sit and bark, then a rod to the other side, and sit and bark again, but did not retreat, as if spellbound.[31]

Pilpay and Aesop are mentioned by name, but there is in fact very little resemblance between Thoreau's encounter with the fox and the fable conventions these ancient authors put into circulation. Pilpay's and Aesop's animals typically talk, and typically do so inside a frame story, ending with morals that are clearly stated. Thoreau's fox does not. Rather than taking his place inside an edifying frame, this animal is out there running wild, moving according to a law of his own, one that makes no ready sense to humans. He is not the bearer of any morals, for he is himself a sealed book, an unyielding mystery. Yet the disturbance he's producing in the auditory field is such as to make this sealed book at once beyond our reach and impossible to ignore. With an intelligence unfathomable to humans, this fox seems to come from a sonic universe with a grammar of its own, a "language of signs" older than civilization and older than human language itself.[32]

Sound is crucial. For even though the fox isn't saying anything intelligible to humans, the auditory field here is in fact more electrifying than it would have been had he been capable of speech. Thoreau seems to go out of his way to create a sonic anomaly: this fox doesn't sound like a fox at all, his bark is like that of a young wolf. And he barks only when he's sitting on his haunches, while he's playing out a lockstep sequence with Thoreau. The man and the fox move strangely in tandem, two halves of the same ritual of speeding, stopping, and starting again, a dance of pursuit and flight, making humans and nonhumans part of the same rhythmic fabric.

And yet, this rhythmic fabric notwithstanding, the man and the fox are in fact not one, kept apart by a steadily maintained physical distance and by a temporal gulf still more daunting. "The fox belongs to a different order of things from that which reigns in the village," Thoreau says, an older dispensation that's "in few senses contemporary with" modern human life.[33] All that Thoreau can say about a creature so alien is that his bark is more wolf-like than fox-like, a sonic misalignment highlighting just how little the fox is attuned to us, acting out of a different place in time as well as a different rhythm in space.

SONIC MISALIGNMENT

There are good reasons why the fox should sound like a wolf to the ears of his pursuer. This animal is hunted, and though not to extinction, it has more than a little in common with the wolf that so vividly embodies that fate. As Christopher Benfey points out, "Among the first laws instituted by the Puritan settlers of the Massachusetts Bay Colony in 1630 was a bounty on wolves, which Roger Williams, who fled the colony for its religious intolerance, referred to as 'a fierce, bloodsucking persecutor.'"[34] According to the Massachusetts Office of Energy and Environmental Affairs, the gray wolf has been extinct in the state since about 1840.[35] Sounding eerily like that silenced species, the fox points to a world lost to humans, one our species has destroyed.

This isn't the only occasion when a lost world is hinted at through a mistaken sonic identity, a vanished sound reappearing as a persistent echo within a still living one. Thoreau's celebrated encounter with the loon in the "Brute Neighbors" chapter of *Walden* features another instance of such sonic disorientation. While Thoreau is single-mindedly pursuing this bird, his soundscape is once again strangely awry, haunted by what ought not to have been there. The "demoniac" cry of the loon, like the demoniac cry of the fox, breaks up the short-lived harmony of Walden Pond, letting in an intruding sound, alien because now ghostly:

[The loon's] usual note was this demoniac laughter, yet somewhat like that of a water-fowl: but occasionally, when he had balked me most successfully and come up a long way off, he uttered a long-drawn unearthly howl, probably more like that of a wolf than any bird; as when a beast puts his muzzle to the ground and deliberately howls. . . . At length having come up fifty rods off, he uttered one of those prolonged howls, as if calling on the god of loons to aid him, and immediately there came a wind from the east and rippled the surface, and filled the whole air with misty rain, and I was impressed as if it were the prayer of the loon answered, and his god was angry with me; and so I left him disappearing far away on the tumultuous surface.[36]

The wolf is here on Walden Pond strictly because of an aural conceit, a fancied likeness suggested by the ear. That likeness might not have occurred to everyone, but to Thoreau it's unmistakable. As in the earlier encounter with the fox, the sonic misalignment here changes the dynamics between sound and space and the relative distance between Thoreau and the loon. The intruding sound, as of a beast putting his muzzle to the ground and deliberately howling, let out at just the moment when the loon has "balked [Thoreau] most successfully," could in fact be quite unnerving. Even though it's meant to be a note of triumph, an undertone of ongoing hostility, perhaps even of remembered pain, seems to lurk just below the surface. It reminds us that the loon, too, is not unlike the wolf, headed for nonpeaceful noncoexistence with humans.

Indeed, by the end of the nineteenth century the loon would become locally extinct in eastern Massachusetts. Not till 1975 would a pair be sighted again, nesting at Quabbin Reservoir. Today, loons are listed on the Massachusetts Endangered Species Act list as a Species of Special Concern.[37] With remarkable prescience, Thoreau seemed to have anticipated all this. Through a sonic visitation, a haunting of the ear, he injects an edginess, an intimation of harm, into an otherwise idyllic setting. In *Walden*, though, this intimation of harm is both deliberately staged and just as deliberately allowed to subside. In this world, still relatively benign, miraculous deliverances do occur, and catastrophes do get averted. And the intervening force is literally a deus ex machina in the shape of the god of loons, signaling to Thoreau to leave the bird alone. This patently contrived happy ending is perhaps the point: this is meant to be whimsical rather than realistic. Any avoidance of harm resting on this whim is resting on an open fiction.

Here, then, is a story very different from those in Pilpay and Aesop. In those fables from antiquity, marked by a relatively harmonious continuum between humans and nonhumans, morals can be delivered, and death is instructive, not traumatic. In that clean, benign, and balanced universe, harm does occur but is fully rationalized by the concept of desert: it teaches its lesson and comes to an end when the fatal consequences of a misdeed are embodied without fail by the culprit. If harm were to befall the loon, it's likely to take a very different form; and the attendant response is also going to be shrill and unappeased, like that wolf howl, with nothing edifying to frame it, and nothing to hold it in check.

MAYA LIN: *WHAT IS MISSING*

Still, that wolf howl notwithstanding, climate-induced species loss wasn't a concept available to Thoreau, either to analyze large-scale changes in the soundscape or to spur individual and collective action in response. *Walden* is in that sense incomplete, a pastoral that hasn't quite finished its work, with more installments to be added in the centuries to come. As it happens, Thoreau's loon would play a key role in a current update—a multimedia project called *What Is Missing*, Maya Lin's "last memorial" to all the vanished and endangered sounds of the world. In progress since 2009, this project gathers and redirects the focus of Lin's Vietnam Veterans Memorial, turning from the finality of death to the hazards of living, and turning the black granite elegy into an experimental green pastoral.

"I am going to try to wake you up to things that are missing that you are not even aware are disappearing," says Lin in her interview with YaleEnvironment360.[38] Her project comes with this statement:

> We are experiencing the sixth mass extinction in the planet's history, and the only one to be caused by the actions of a single species—mankind. On average, every 20 minutes a distinct living species of plant or animal disappears. At this rate, by some estimates, as much as 30 percent of the world's plants and animals could be on a path to extinction.[39]

Bearing such grim statistics, *What Is Missing* sets out to "create, through science-based artworks," a virtual home for all those species "that have disappeared or will most likely disappear if we do not act to protect them."[40] More than a refuge, this virtual home is meant above all to be a launch site, proposing an alternate future for the planet. Thinking back to her Vietnam Veterans Memorial, Lin says that "the traditional war memorial always commemorates those who have died. I believe memorials are there to remind us and to remember the past, but in such a way that we're actively engaging the present and the future."[41] Her hope is to come up with "plausible future scenarios, what we call green print, which is really rethinking what the planet could look like."[42]

To maximize the chances of such green print becoming reality, *What Is Missing* exists not as a single, static monument but in multiple forms in multiple locations, and as an interactive website with many downloadable features to be continually added. The first installment, a listening cone of bronze and reclaimed redwood, opened at the California Academy of Sciences on September 17, 2009. With the help of researchers from the Cornell Lab of Ornithology, Lin was able to include recordings of common loons as well as humpback whales, prairie chickens, sea turtles, and coral reefs—all endangered species today.[43]

Since then, *What Is Missing* has celebrated Earth Day each year by adding a new feature to the website. In 2011, a *Map of Memory* was launched to give a sense of the biodiversity and sheer abundance of the past. This map comes with three types of clickable dots providing information on three different scales: dots that take visitors to personal testimonies and invite everyone to contribute; dots that open up literary and historical archives; and dots that offer macro timelines tracing the evolving pathways of humans and nonhumans across millions of years.[44] While the individual testimonies are "stories from around the world from everyday people," the project's partnership with the Cornell Lab of Ornithology means that "everything is deeply researched," notes John Fitzpatrick, director of the lab.[45] The personal stories are backed by high-resolution sound and image files documenting the species that have gone extinct. Buttons at the bottom of the map page allow visitors to switch between scales and to toggle between viewing the dots geographically (in map form) and chronologically (as time lines).

On Earth Day 2012, a new *What Is Missing* exhibit was mounted at

the Bloomberg Tower in New York City. It features video installations in
the tower atrium, with the elevators becoming miniature sound studios
filled with the haunting cries of the common loon and the humpback
whale. On the website, Lin simultaneously debuted "Conservation in
Action," showcasing more than four hundred success stories from environmental groups and local communities.[46] In 2016, another new feature, "What You Can Do," was added. Its suggested actions aren't pie-
in-the-sky fantasies but simple behavioral modifications, such as buying
fair-trade coffee that helps preserve indigenous habitats; using certified
wood products made by companies adhering to sustainable forestry
practices; and reducing the use of plastics to reverse our massive pol-
lution of the planet. Lin is now working on a curriculum for high school
students to foster such behavioral changes, once again teaming up with
scientists to create an actionable platform for informed citizenship. "We
need to stay really optimistic," she declares. "Because the alternative is,
what, we give up? The loss of species and habitats is all about land use
and resource consumption. We have to make species protection through
habitat conservation a huge priority because what we're doing right now
is spending our kids' and our grandkids' future."[47]

OLD TESTAMENT VERSUS CHARLES DARWIN

None of this, of course, is to be found in *Walden*: no sound recordings,
no interactive website, no behavior-modifying high school curriculum.
Still, though weak on the technology front, this nineteenth-century text
isn't without resources of its own when it comes to intervening in the
planet's future. As Stanley Cavell points out, the genre most useful to
Thoreau, the one closest to his temperament, might turn out to be that
good old standby in nineteenth-century America—the fiery lamenta-
tions of the Old Testament prophets, especially Jeremiah and Ezekiel.[48]
These are voices speaking in tongues, crying out in the wilderness, and
doing so because their faculty of hearing is exceptional, having received
in full what "the Lord said unto [them]." Prophesying is of supreme importance in the Old Testament, affirming the primacy of a sound-based
environment and providing the language, the rhetorical structure, and
above all the emotional fervor to mourn large-scale devastations already in our midst.[49] Here is Jeremiah: "For the mountains will I take
up a weeping and wailing, and for the habitations of the wilderness a

lamentation, because they are burned up, so that none can pass through them; neither can men hear the voice of the cattle; both the fowl of the heavens and the beast are fled; they are gone."[50]

Jeremiah talks only about all these species being "gone"; he doesn't use the word *extinction*. He couldn't have—the word first appeared in the sixteenth century. But the conceptual universe in which he operated was one in which that word would have meaning, one fully aware that the world was no longer what it used to be and would never again be the same. This sense of a process already well under way, unstoppable and nonbenign, is particularly striking if we compare it with the rhetoric of extinction that would later gain currency in the mid-nineteenth century.

Extinction was a word that loomed large in *On the Origin of Species*, especially the pivotal chapter 4, "Natural Selection." True to Charles Darwin's faith in a continuously self-regenerating world, it wasn't a word that caused him alarm. On the contrary, he was reassured by this phenomenon, glad that there was this long-standing and always reliable mechanism that would allow the world to update its inventory, getting rid of the obsolete and ill adapted. Natural selection would have been impossible without extinction, since this is the very means by which inferior species are eliminated to make way for superior ones: "The extinction of species and of whole groups of species, which has played so conspicuous a part in the history of the organic world, almost inevitably follows on the principle of natural selection, for old forms will be supplanted by new and improved forms." We shouldn't be unduly sentimental about species that die out, because it's to the benefit of all that "new and improved varieties will inevitably supplant and exterminate the older, less improved and intermediate varieties."[51]

Thoreau was an admirer of Darwin's. He had read *The Voyage of the Beagle* when its New York edition appeared in 1846, taking plenty of notes. When *On the Origin of Species* came out in late 1859, he was among the first to read and comment on it. And yet on one subject—the extinction of species—Thoreau was much less sanguine, much less convinced that it was a good thing, indeed much more in keeping with the lamenting spirit of the Old Testament prophets. On March 23, 1856, he wrote in his journal:

Is it not a maimed and imperfect nature that I am conversant with? As if I were to study a tribe of Indians that had lost all its warriors. Many of those animal migrations and other phenomena by which the Indians marked the season, are no longer to be observed. My ancestors have torn out many of the first leaves and grandest passages, and mutilated it in many places. . . . All the great trees and beasts, fishes and fowl are gone; the streams perchance are somewhat shrunk.[52]

OBSOLETE HUMANS

Already in the mid-nineteenth century, the world seemed like a damaged place, with vital parts of it gone and never to be recovered. Quite apart from the biblical tradition, where else could Thoreau get this idea: that there are losses not compensated for, not folded into a story of progress? The two references here to Native Americans—that the world once fully there for them is no longer there for us, and that these depletions in nature are related to depletions among these Native tribes—seem especially significant. After all, the fate of these indigenous populations was plain for all to see. Survival wasn't something they could count on, and neither could they count on the survival of the habitat in which they had been naturalized, in which they could flourish.

That much was clear. The question, though, was how to interpret this fact. Were Native Americans stand-alone casualties, collectively an exception and an anomaly, dying out for reasons peculiar to themselves? Did their long sojourn in the Americas, begun since time immemorial, make them obsolete by definition? Were they no longer fit for this world because they once had a self-evident claim to it?

Thoreau did occasionally embrace this line of thinking. "Ktaadn," the first essay in *The Maine Woods*, opens with a strangely cavalier remark about the "extinction" of Native Americans, taking it for granted. "The ferry here took us past the Indian Island. As I left the shore, I observed a short, shabby, washerwoman-looking Indian—they commonly have the woebegone look of the girl that cried over spilt milk. . . . This picture will do to put before us the Indian's history, that is, the history of his extinction."[53]

The word *extinction* stands out starkly, even though it's in fact encountered relatively infrequently in Thoreau. His preferred term was narrower in scope and policy specific—*extermination* rather than *extinction*—the outcome of a military campaign rather than impersonal natural selection.[54] His casual usage here seems not to register the gravity of the term, though this was hardly uncharacteristic of the mid-nineteenth century. It's helpful here to turn briefly to Washington Irving and Herman Melville to get a broader and contrasting sense of the assumed cause of the extinction, and the extent to which it was localized, indigenized, and taken for granted.

WASHINGTON IRVING AND HERMAN MELVILLE: INDIGENOUS EXTINCTION

Irving was by far the most outspoken on the subject, mincing no words about who was to blame. White society, he writes in *The Sketch Book*, has advanced on Native populations "like one of those withering airs that will sometimes breed desolation over a whole region of fertility."[55] He's especially outraged by the Mystic massacre in 1637, the burning of the Pequots' wigwams and the "indiscriminate butchery" that followed. Entering the swamps where the Pequot warriors had taken refuge with the women and children, the soldiers "discharged their pieces, laden with ten or twelve pistol bullets at a time, putting the muzzles of the pieces under the boughs, within a few yards of them," so that all were "despatched and ended in the course of an hour."[56]

For Irving, New World history was indeed one of mass extinction—accomplished not by the benign hand of natural selection but by the trigger-happy hand of war. It was atrocious, but it was also fait accompli. That fait accompli calls for a form of elegy dedicated to just one task: mourning. Native Americans "will vanish like a vapor from the face of the earth; their very history will be lost in forgetfulness."[57] Irving ends with the lamentation of an old Pequot warrior: "Our hatchets are broken, our bows are snapped, our fires are nearly extinguished: a little longer and the white man will cease to persecute us—for we shall cease to exist!"[58]

That path to nonexistence also seems to be taken for granted in *Moby-Dick*, though more offhandedly, in the form of a reminder about Ahab's oddly named ship: "The *Pequod*, you will no doubt remember, was the name of a celebrated tribe of Massachusetts Indians, now as extinct as the Medes."[59] The fate mourned by Irving as atrocity seems here to be no more than a casual aside. Yet that casual aside turns out to be premature (or deliberately misleading), for as we soon find out, the supposedly extinct are never absent from Melville's narrative. Beginning with the "old squaw, Tistig, at Gay-Head," who issues the veiled warning that

"the name [Ahab] would somehow prove prophetic,"[60] a surprisingly tenacious Native presence runs through the past, present, and future of
Moby-Dick, a web of tangled kinship ensnaring everyone, irrespective
of race.

In chapter 61, the first time a whale is killed, as the blood comes pour-
ing out, the "slanting sun playing upon the crimson pond in the sea, sent
back its reflection into every face, so that they all glowed to each other
like red men."[61] "Like red men": whites and Indians are no longer jux-
taposed in their contrasting fate but yoked together in their uncanny
resemblance. Stubb and his crew in the whaleboat are doing what sea-
faring Native Americans—the original Nantucketers—have done since
time immemorial. That resemblance is dramatized by the reflected crimson glow of the "slanting sun" on their skin. Could this shared skin
color—and the shared sunset—be the index to a future equally shared?
The ending of *Moby-Dick* seems to suggest as much. In the final scene,
as the concentric circles of the deadly vortex carry "the smallest chip of
the *Pequod* out of sight," the disappearance of that prophetically named
ship is accompanied by the most forceful reference yet to Native Americans persisting until the bitter end:

> But as the last whelmings intermixingly poured themselves over the
> sunken head of the Indian at the main-mast, leaving a few inches of
> the erect spar yet visible, together with long streaming yards of the
> flag, which calmly undulated, with ironical coincidings, over the de-
> stroying billows they almost touched;—at that moment, a red arm and
> a hammer hovered backwardly uplifted in the open air, in the act of
> nailing the flag faster and yet faster to the subsiding spar. A sky-hawk
> that tauntingly had followed the maintruck downwards from its natural
> home among the stars, pecking at the flag, and incommoding Tashtego
> there; this bird now chanced to intercept its broad fluttering wing be-
> tween the hammer and the wood; and simultaneously feeling the
> ethereal thrill, the submerged savage beneath, in his death-gasp, kept
> his hammer frozen there; and so the bird of heaven, with archangelic
> shrieks, and his imperial beak thrust upwards, and his whole captive
> form folded in the flag of Ahab, went down with his ship.[62]

Characteristically turning verbs into adverbs and nouns, Melville's idiosyncratic lexicon here seems to serve one specific purpose. Words like

whelmings, *intermixingly*, and *coincidings* mix together different parts of speech, a blurring of grammatical distinction that seems to play out as well on the level of narrative logic: in the end, everyone gets mixed together, a watery death uniting all. Ahab's flag, the imperial sky hawk, and the red arm and hammer all go down as one, folding the would-be conqueror in with the stubbornly unvanquished. *Moby-Dick*, in this sense, handily inverts the lamented but localized demise of Native Americans assumed by Irving. Mass destruction in Melville isn't race-specific; it's indiscriminate and across the board. With the exception of Ishmael, whose survival is belatedly added in response to skeptical English reviews,[63] there's no way out of that vortex. Fatality for one is fatality for all.[64]

ELEGY AND BEYOND

Here, then, is a version of elegy pushed to its tragic limits: austere, inexorable, and all-ensnaring in its catastrophe. Thoreau's approach is different. Though equally fatalistic about Native Americans, he concentrates nonetheless not on the sublime tragedy of the foretold end but on the day-to-day task of preserving what remains. Starting in 1847 during his stay at Walden Pond, he systematically compiled notes on indigenous peoples in North America and elsewhere, eventually amassing eleven volumes containing "2,800 handwritten pages or over 500,000 words," Richard Fleck tells us. These "Indian Notebooks," written "in English, French, Italian, Latin, and occasionally Hebrew," now housed in the Morgan Library and Museum in New York City, comprise the single largest Native American archive from the nineteenth century.[65] In 1853, when filling out the questionnaire and membership invitation from the Association for the Advancement of Science inquiring about the "Branches of Science in which especial interest is felt," Thoreau gave this response: "The Manners and Customs of the Indians of the Algonquin Group previous to contact with the white men."[66] Native American languages, along with material artifacts, creation myths, and animal fables, were constantly on his mind for the last fifteen years of his life.

These scientific inquiries suggest that another thought must have occurred to Thoreau, a sense that Native Americans might not be an anomaly at all but rather an advance warning to all of us, giving us a glimpse of our collective future in their present condition, a preview we ignore at our peril. His trips to the Maine woods in 1853 and 1857, marking his close companionship with his two Penobscot guides, Joe Aitteon and Joe Polis, were especially crucial to this alternative line of thinking.[67] An extraordinary passage from "Chesuncook," the second essay in *The Maine Woods*, shows a world with the tables turned and the axis of survival and nonsurvival reversed. Suddenly finding himself in a flourishing pre-Columbian soundscape entirely without meaning for him, Thoreau intuits for the first time that perhaps it isn't the Native Americans but he himself who is the alien and misfit:

> It was a purely wild and primitive American sound, as much as the barking of a chickadee, and I could not understand a word of it. . . . These Abenakis gossiped, laughed, and jested, in the language in which Eliot's Indian Bible is written, the language which has been spoken in New England who shall say how long? These were the sounds that issued from the wigwams of this country before Columbus was born; they have not yet died away.[68]

Listening to the sounds of the Abenaki language, Thoreau has a kind of negative epiphany: these sounds belong to these woods, and he does not. Native Americans, of course, were usually the ones made to feel that way. It says something about Thoreau that he's able momentarily to switch places with them and subject himself to that surreal sense of involuntary nonbelonging. In so doing, he makes vulnerability the baseline, the most widely shared and lowest common denominator for our species and other species. Listening to Native Americans in that way, he hears them for what they are: prophets in the wilderness and veterans of survival, speaking in tongues that have "not yet died away" and perhaps never will, tongues whose vital import is just becoming apparent.

INDIGENOUS PASTORAL

Here, then, is a new pastoral for the twenty-first century: a crisis-responsive genre, honed by disaster and able to project hope from that special knowledge. The sound tracks of now-legendary names in music—Charley Patton, Jimi Hendrix, Mildred Bailey, Robbie Robertson, Link Wray, and Redbone—featured in Catherine Bainbridge's award-winning film, *Rumble: The Indians Who Rocked the World* (2017), make up one strand of this indigenous pastoral.[69] The live performances at the National Museum of the American Indian make up another strand.[70] A record number of Native Americans winning congressional and state legislative seats in 2018 add a third.[71] The growing number of indigenous language programs adds still another, including the two-year master's degree program at MIT;[72] the eight-language offerings at Yale;[73] and the pioneering American Indian Studies Research Institute at Indiana University, which uses digital tools and online "talking dictionaries" to offer instruction in Arikara, Assiniboine, and Pawnee to elementary schools, high schools, and community colleges.[74] The NEH-funded Standing Rock Lakota/Dakota Language Project at Sitting Bull College, bringing together the last generation of native speakers to transcribe indigenous texts and make live recordings, suggests that this new pastoral might be far from its upper limits.[75]

Kyle Powys Whyte, Potawatomi philosopher, author, and activist, is especially helpful in linking these resurgent sounds to time-tested strategies of adapting and improvising. The massive disruptions we now associate with climate change—ecosystem collapse, species loss, involuntary relocation, and pandemics—have always been part of New World colonialism, Whyte argues. Newly seen as apocalyptic in the twenty-first century, they seem far less so to Native peoples, who have suffered under them and lived through them, emerging with a different relation to the nonhuman world and to ancestors and descendants both. Adaptation is key to indigenous communities, making them pioneers in a "forward-looking framework of justice." Honoring "systems of responsibilities" ranging from "webs of interspecies relationships to government-to-government partnerships,"[76] Native Americans are now on the forefront of climate activism, setting into motion a "green print" the rest of us are just beginning to rally to.

Indian reservations, taking up only 2 percent of the land in the United States, hold 20 percent of the nation's fossil fuel reserves, including coal, oil, and gas, worth some $1.5 trillion. Rather than privatizing and profiting from these reserves, Native Americans are among the most vocal opponents of fossil fuels. Deb Haaland, newly elected congresswoman from New Mexico, is committed to 100 percent renewable energy. "The fight for Native American rights is also a fight for climate justice," she says.[77] The National Caucus of Native American State Legislators, with eighty-one members from twenty-one states, has likewise made climate

change and renewable energy one of its key advocacies.[78] Sheila Watt-
Cloutier, chair of the Inuit Circumpolar Council and Nobel Peace Prize
nominee in 2007, has pushed for the same agenda in global governance,
working with Earthjustice and the Center for International Environmental Law to petition the Inter-American Commission to conduct
hearings on climate change and human rights.[79] The crucial presence of
indigenous tribes against deforestation in the Amazon both before and
during the devastating fires in 2019 is only the most recent example of
such climate activism.[80]

In the case of the Standing Rock Sioux Tribe, such activism managed to hold up the construction of the Dakota Access pipeline for three
years.[81] Even though the pipeline was eventually pushed through by the
Trump administration, the tribe monitored its oil leaks, filed a motion
against its proposed expansion[82] while continuing to oppose the Keystone XL,[83] and geared up for a new fight against yet another pipeline,
known by the innocuous name Line 3. Bill McKibben reports for the
Guardian:

> Winona LaDuke, a veteran Native American activist and remarkable
> orator, has led a series of horseback rides along the pipeline route. Last
> year a group of Native youth organized a 250-mile "Paddle to Protect"
> canoe protest along the Mississippi River, which will be crossed twice
> by Line 3.
>
> If you want to hear what the resistance sounds like, "No Line 3" by
> Native rapper Thomas X is a good place to start; if you want to get a
> literal taste of it, Native women have routinely brought traditional
> breakfasts like frybread with blueberry sauce to the various public hear-
> ings over the project, sharing the food with everyone right down to the
> pipeline lawyers. (If you'd like you can also order some wild rice from
> LaDuke's Honor the Earth, one of the premier indigenous environ-
> mental organizations on the continent.)[84]

Here, then, are the sights, sounds, and tastes of pastoral reborn. Schooled
by catastrophes and learning from experience not to be paralyzed, this
multimedia genre reaches beyond elegy to propose a way forward, keeping extinction a live prospect and a deferred end, always before us but
not so close as to silence the future.

3 · Less Than Tragic

C. L. R. JAMES, FRANK STELLA, AND AMITAV GHOSH DILUTE MELVILLE

How broad is the scope of tragedy, and how inevitable the catastrophe at the end? Is all the world under its jurisdiction, or are there some locales, some peripheral networks, outside its rule? What kind of future (if any) does it allow for? And what's the relation between the common adjective *tragic* and the highly developed, highly stylized dramatic form that flourished in Athens some two and a half millennia ago?

GENRE EXTINCTION

George Steiner celebrates the dramatic form in *The Death of Tragedy* (1961) but minces no words about its certified demise. According to him, the art that originated in fifth-century Athens is extinct, with no modern offspring. Tragedy belongs to the ancient world, where "man is taken to be an unwelcome guest," puny and disposable, that "the gods kill for their sport as the wanton boys do flies."[1] Steiner is quoting from *King Lear*, but for him tragedy among the Elizabethans was already "rearguard action" (292). After the seventeenth century, it would become less and less a living art and more and more a "relic in the museum of the moral past" (342), honored but discontinued.

What makes the extinction of this genre inevitable is its own relentless fatalism, for any account of "tragic drama must start from the fact of catastrophe" (8). This is its signature event, one that goes far beyond the ordinary unhappy ending. Any catastrophe worth its name must be absolute and arbitrary, "utterly out of proportion with the guilt of those" (8) subjected to it, as beyond human comprehension as it is beyond human control. The harm here is undeserved harm. It has nothing to do with poetic justice or moral desert, for doom here befalls many with no blame attachable. These people suffer, not because their culpable deeds call for it, but because a course of destruction, once launched, seems to have a will of its own, a life independent of human agency. This non-human force makes catastrophes what they are: self-propelled and self-escalating, not to be reasoned with or pleaded with, a chain of events deadly in its momentum and terminally lethal to humans. "Tragedy is irreparable" (8) for that reason, Steiner says. Just as the catastrophe cannot be averted, so, too, it cannot be set right. After the cataclysm, there's nothing more: no further development, no next episode, nothing that would make the stark ending less stark. This is a genre that comes with absolute force and zero distraction.

It's the zero distraction that commends the genre to Aristotle. In the *Poetics*, he says that of the six constituent elements of tragedy, the plot is the most important; and that the "heart and soul" of the plot is a "unified event," "an action complete and whole."[2] Merely having a single protagonist isn't enough, for "a large, indeed an indefinite number of things can happen to a given individual, some of which go to constitute no unified event." Only when a play is written with utmost fatalism can this all-important objective be met, for to be "both unified and complete, the component events ought to be so firmly compacted that if any one of them is shifted to another place, or removed, the whole is loosened up and dislocated."[3] Though Aristotle makes no specific mention of catastrophe as a means to unify and complete, the two emotions he famously associates with tragedy—pity and terror—clearly depend on the concentrated furor of this event, its brute finality, undiluted and nonnegotiable.

Tragedy, both as normatively defined by Aristotle and as regretfully reported as dead by Steiner, would seem to be the most powerful of genres: unappeasable, sovereign unto itself, coming always in maximum strength. Aristotle distinguishes between epic and tragedy on just this basis. Because of its size, epic is a weakly composite genre, pulled in different directions by its heterogeneous content, filled with unseemly details that would have been unthinkable in tragedy. His example is the long-drawn-out, one-on-one pursuit of Hector by Achilles, which "would appear absurd on a stage—the Achaeans standing there, not joining in the chase, and Achilles motioning to them to stay back."[4] Unity does not seem even to have been an objective in epic. It oscillates, it goes off in tangents, never settling down one way or another, hanging perilously here between calamity and farce.

Oscillations of this sort would never happen in tragedy, its unswerving teleology and no-holds-barred execution elevating it above all other genres for Aristotle. But is such execution sustainable across time, and is it a reproductive advantage? Steiner, faced with overwhelming evidence that tragedy as it once was no longer exists, reports that by the late sixteenth and early seventeenth centuries, the genre was no longer the relentlessly undeviating form it used to be. Even in the case of Shakespeare, with the exception of *King Lear*, the plays were already "tragi-comedy."[5]

Maximum strength might not be a good thing when it comes to the survival of genres. In the centuries to come, it was the weaker, watered-down versions that would go forward, their strength sapping at every turn and winning over new adherents in the process. "We come to tragedy by many roads," Raymond Williams writes in *Modern Tragedy* (1966), his tribute to the genre's current flourishing. For some, tragedy is "a body of literature, a conflict of theory, an academic problem." For others, it's a "common name . . . for other kinds of event—a mining disaster, a burned-out family, a broken career, a smash on the road."[6] Not always a stage performance and sometimes not even a finished script, tragedy could be any number of things that make life miserable for people, most of them falling short of absolute catastrophe and some downright amusing in stretching the definition of the term. Glenn Most and Adrian Poole have collected some of these, especially in the adjectival form.[7] Terry Eagleton has done the same, pointing out that "a suitably withering utterance of the word 'Tragic!' could trump almost any other comment."[8]

BESET BY COMEDY

This chapter argues for tragedy as weakened in modernity, no longer committed to catastrophe as a necessary ending and becoming input-accepting and user-amended as a result. Taking up residence in other genres, especially the novel, and entering into new networks and new conventions, it becomes an unruly composite—not unlike epic, in fact. Diverging from its normative path, it produces tangents of such abiding interests as to suggest an alternative reality, adding a flip side to the tragic plot in the foreground. Low comedy, unwashed and unchastened where tragedy is stringent and hidebound, is especially important as a tangent-producing force, useful to authors faced with new crises and refusing to accept catastrophe as a foregone conclusion. Putting off that outcome and contesting the very fatalism of the term, the influx of comedy changes the shape of tragedy, to the point where its signature ending seems less and less a given.[9]

David Hirst points to the emergence of a new hybrid genre, tragicomedy, at exactly the same moment that George Steiner names as the end of the Greek tragic form: the beginning of the seventeenth century. Giovanni Battista Guarini's *Compendio della Poesia Tragicomica* (1601), the first substantial treatise on this novelty, marked a century of experimentation, first in Jacobean England and then in mid-seventeenth-century France.[10] Still, as a freestanding genre, tragicomedy remains relatively limited. Rather than thinking about the synthesis of its two parent genres strictly within its confines, I'd like to explore instead a more complexly networked and less formally crystallized set of interactions while affirming the continued usefulness of the term *tragedy* to host such exchanges. Beset by comedy, modern tragedy moves further and further away from its antecedents but with enough residual connectivity to the Greek plays to remind us of their nonnegotiable endings.[11] In that form, it's uniquely suited to capture the large-scale harms of modernity, not bowing to them but putting them on the table all the same, highlighting their everyday normalcy and their tendency to spread and spiral, especially when undeserved.

DEMOCRATIZING HARM

Befalling those who aren't its rightful recipients, undeserved harm is a form of tragedy that has grown exponentially in modernity. Proverbs 26:2 tells us that such a thing doesn't exist, that "as the bird by wandering, as the swallow by flying, so the curse causeless shall not come." Yet modern writers and philosophers have observed otherwise. John Kekes sees undeserved harm as the mark of moral evil when inflicted on others.[12] Zygmunt Bauman, meanwhile, explores the concept by way of a popular military parlance—collateral damage—calling attention to adverse effects unintended but "nonetheless viewed as a risk worth taking," especially by those who are "not the ones who suffer the consequences." There's a "selective affinity between social inequality and the likelihood of becoming a collateral victim of catastrophes," Bauman says, since those who occupy "the bottom end of the inequality ladder" are often among the first to come in for their share of harm triggered not by their own deeds but by the misfire of others.[13]

This "selective affinity" between the unequal distribution of harm and other forms of unequal distribution helps pinpoint a new development in modern tragedy: its dissemination across a much broader demographic spectrum. As in ancient tragedy, the lack of correlation here between deed and consequence points to a world beyond human control; yet there does seem to be a fairly predictable pattern in where the harm falls and on whom. Secondary and marginal characters are far more likely to be on the receiving end, dying en masse and indiscriminately, noted only in passing. We might think of this as the nonrandomization of an otherwise random process, so much so that it could even be called a kind of "fate"—though fate updated by modernity, with mass casualties replacing single deaths as its effect. Stanley Corngold, writing about the staggering number of nonhuman deaths in W. G. Sebald, says that if "the survival of tragedy into the modern period" depends on the democratization of harm, now no longer vested in the "royal, the sovereign, the superior individual," it makes sense that Sebald would go one step further, "enlarging his frame to consider not only masses of ordinary men (the vast multitudes who have gone under) but masses of creatures as well—herrings and moths."[14]

The democratization of harm seems part of a twin development. Human casualties go hand in hand with a parallel occurrence on the nonhuman axis, with countless species, hitherto unnoticed, coming in for a bit of attention just before they are killed. In the nineteenth century, *Moby-Dick* is the prime example of this twin development, for the novel is very much a tale of collateral damage, with the entire crew of the *Pequod* perishing as a side effect of Ahab's monomaniacal quest. These human fatalities would never have happened had the *Pequod* not been a whaler to begin with. Melville updates the demographics of tragedy in two ways, enlarging its sphere of victimhood while renaming the nature of its nonhuman agency, a base modification crucial for the genre's survival into the nineteenth century. Given the economic dominance of whaling in this century, the nonhuman would no longer be the gods— it would be whales. And the catastrophe produced by an off-the-charts member of that species would fall not on royalty but on ordinary seamen. From this twin downshift, we can look forward to the industrial tragedies in the early twentieth century (such as Upton Sinclair's *The Jungle*), followed by war literature, and the tragedies of ecological disasters in the twenty-first.

But why democratize harm at all? Couldn't the ending of *Moby-Dick* have been different, offering a convincing demonstration of the whale's power but not at the expense of the *Pequod*'s crew? Or is there a necessary correlation between the power of the nonhuman and large-scale human fatalities? The jury is still out on this point. It's helpful, if only for this reason, to think of *Moby-Dick* (and indeed most modern tragedies) as not quite finished, not quite the last word. Not a sealed book, sealed by a sovereign author, it remains up for grabs, still accepting fresh data and still being tinkered with. What results is a volatile field of second look and second chance, user-amended sequels cascading unpredictably. Through this process, modern tragedy can reinvent itself in variously diluted forms, subject now to far-flung input networks and to the deflating pressures of the comic, branching out into genres and media less and less recognizable, and less and less tragic.

USER-AMENDED SEQUELS

Without further ado, then, let me turn to three figures—C. L. R. James, Frank Stella, and Amitav Ghosh—to demonstrate such less-than-tragic forms. I begin with James. No matter how we parse it, *Mariners, Renegades, and Castaways* (1953) is a strange book, a reading of Melville but not one Melville scholars would approve. James began writing this book on June 10, 1952, when he was arrested by the US Immigration and Naturalization Service, sent to Ellis Island, and detained for the next six months before being deported for passport violations. It was on Ellis Island, surrounded by the world's immigrant population, that the idea of the book came to him, a "natural and necessary conclusion," he says, to "the miracle of Herman Melville."[15] James writes:

> A great deal of this book was written on Ellis Island while I was being detained by the Department of Immigration. The Island, like Melville's *Pequod*, is a miniature of all the nations of the world and all sections of society. My experience of it and the circumstances attending my

stay there have so deepened my understanding of Melville and so profoundly influenced the form the book has taken, that an account of this had seemed to me not only a natural but necessary conclusion. This is to be found in Chapter VII.[16]

This was the plan. What transpired was a little different. The first edition, privately published in 1953, didn't sell well; of the twenty thousand copies printed, all but two thousand were returned to the author. That same year, negotiating with his British publisher, Frederick Warburg, James seemed already resigned to the excision of chapter 7, the very chapter he had previously taken pride in. Writing to a friend, "S," on August 12, 1953, he said he was hoping to "publish in England an edition of MRC, cutting out VII and rewriting VI to make it an embodiment of the ideas in the Leyda letter."[17] Chapter 7 was indeed left out of the 1978 Bewick edition and the 1985 Allison and Busby edition. It wasn't until 2001, when Donald Pease brought out a new edition from the University Press of New England, that the chapter was restored, and the book finally took the form that James had first envisioned.

What to make of this less-than-reassuring publication history? As a thought experiment, I'd like to side momentarily with the skeptical editors, seeing chapter 7 as they did—as weakly justified, nonessential, and unwarranted. How could James claim that his six-month sojourn on Ellis Island is organic to Melville's novel? Is it up to him to decide that this twentieth-century add-on is a "natural but necessary conclusion" for a text imagined by its nineteenth-century author to be already complete? And would he go so far as to say that any text must be *collaborative*, a form of work not executable by the author alone but requiring subsequent input from readers, done at multiple sites and at multiple points in time, in this case linking Ellis Island and Pittsfield, Massachusetts, as scenes of coproduction?

INTERMINABLE WORK

I put the questions this way—in terms of work and a sense of it as ongoing and unending—because this is what James himself seems to have in mind. The title of his book, *Mariners, Renegades, and Castaways*, is taken from *Moby-Dick* in the context of work, the habitual state of "the arm that wields a pick or drives a spike":

If then, to meanest mariners, and renegades and castaways, I shall
hereafter ascribe high qualities, though dark; weave among them tragic
graces; if even the most mournful, perchance the most abased, among
them all, shall at times lift himself to the exalted mounts; if I shall touch
that workman's arm with some ethereal light; if I shall spread a rainbow
over his disastrous set of sun; then against all mortal critics bear me out
in it, thou just spirit of Equality, which has spread one royal mantle of
humanity over all my kind.[18]

In one sense, this is a stirring apostrophe, a stirring tribute to the lowly
worker, lifting him up, claiming for him the "high qualities" traditionally
reserved for the wellborn. But of course the high qualities also happen
to be dark, woven with tragic graces, lit by a "disastrous set of sun." The
worker in Melville is deliberately elevated only to be brought low, hit by
a catastrophe guaranteed to happen.

James calls attention to this (one of his chapters is titled "Catastrophe"); he also insists on coming back to it, giving it renewed attention,
the benefit of a second look. It's important to do this, he says, since
Moby-Dick is not the same book the second time around. What we see
"at first sight" is indeed tragedy on a grand scale: "an industrial civilization on fire and plunging blindly into darkness . . . the world of massed
bombers, of cities in flames, of Hiroshima and Nagasaki."[19] But this is
not the only novel *Moby-Dick* could be, not the only future it has to offer. It's worth taking another look, because "when you look again, you
see that the crew is indestructible. There they are, laughing at the terrible things that have happened to them. The three harpooners are doing their work."[20]

"Doing their work." For James, there's a world of significance in that
phrase, in the form of the present participle, an action in the present carried on into the future. It is this verb tense and its work-based continuum that give him the idea that the apparently finished *Moby-Dick* is still
open to new input. It can be modified, extended, retrofitted for contexts
it couldn't have known about. This is a text entirely updatable. The feedback loop into it is never closed. This in-progress ontology gives work
its sense of primacy, efficacy, as well as comic relief. If texts are always
left in a state of incompletion, there's always more work, a lot more
work, for everyone to do.

Work, in short, is both the baseline condition of the crew on the

Pequod and the baseline condition that allows a succession of readers to have continued input into *Moby-Dick*, a text that is, mistakenly, imagined to be authored by just one person. For James, these two baseline conditions are one and the same: one implies the other and necessitates the other. The cross-mapping between these two suggests that there is no end to work, there being always a need for it. It suggests as well that what there is a need for is in fact its lowest common denominator, the least specialized, least glamorous part of it, what can be crowdsourced without difficulty and over and over again. Low-grade repeatability is its lifeline to the future, what guarantees its usefulness across time. And so, when it comes to work on the *Pequod*, we should not be surprised that there is no attempt on James's part to play up the nobility of the crew, to turn them into superworkers, superheroes. On the contrary, what is key here is just how ordinary these people are, lacking in distinction, lacking even anything that might make them noteworthy victims: "They are not suffering workers, not revolutionary workers, nor people who must be organized. . . . What matters to them primarily, as it does to all workers, and in fact to all people, is the work they do everyday, so many hours a day, nearly every day in the year."[21]

This description of work might seem less than thrilling, a regimen mindlessly routine. But for James, the routineness is the point. In dwelling on it, he also registers a significant departure from Melville, an implied critique as well as an alternative ending to *Moby-Dick* itself. In Melville, work is simply the background, the preexisting condition of those to whom something very bad eventually happens. As the background, it's not the main event, not a force actively shaping the ensuing drama. It has no power to determine the outcome, to avert disasters, to go forward into the future. It is static and non-evolving: the background, and never more than the background. In James's updated version of the novel, work has an entirely different status. Not just a given, it is a future-producing agency. The persistence of work, the continued need for it, suggests that workers have a durable place in the world, so long-lasting as to be virtually "indestructible."

SWITCHING GENRES

But is it indeed true that interminable work can give workers a claim to the future? Can this background condition become the main event? And

can it function as the equivalent of the present participle, which, even
if it doesn't absolutely shield the workers from harm, can nonetheless
give them an in-progress longevity conjecturally and not implausibly
suggested by the verb form itself?

There's no guarantee. What James has done, though, is to have introduced a slight wavering into *Moby-Dick*, undoing its severity, undoing
its closure, and, in so doing, also flipping the novel from the dominant
genre in the foreground to one weaker but fairly persistent, one that
takes a second look to detect. What was once tragedy on a grand scale
is now something less grand but also less tragic. It doesn't quite become
comedy, even though James seems to want to give it a push in that direction, going so far as to say that "almost every sentence" of the novel "can
be the subject of a comic strip."[22] He points to this passage from chapter 60 about the all-ensnaring coils of the whale line, and the habit of
mind that sailors develop as a result: "Yet habit—strange thing! What
cannot habit accomplish? Gayer sallies, more merry mirth, better jokes,
and brighter repartees, you never heard over your mahogany, than you
will hear over the half-inch white cedar of the whale-boat, when thus
hung in hangman's nooses."[23] For most readers, this might not seem
a pivotal moment. For James, it's absolutely crucial, so crucial that it
needs to be read more than once:

> Melville is so gay that at a first reading you can easily miss the signifi-
> cance of those last sentences for the world we live in. But re-read them.
> The humor and the wit of the mariners, renegades and castaways are
> beyond the cultivated inter-changes of those who sit around mahog-
> any tables. They have to be. Hangman's nooses hang loose around the
> necks of countless millions today, and for them their unfailing humor
> is an assertion of life and sanity against the ever present threat of de-
> struction and a world in chaos.[24]

In James's "second look" version—no longer pure tragedy—the humor
and the wit count as much as the nooses around the necks. The former
does not completely negate the latter; what it does, though, is make the
ending less certain, turning it from being the last word to something
considerably less and, in being less, in not quite achieving the finality
that tragedy calls for, slipping out from under it, bringing the flip side
into view.

This genre switching, this weakening dependency on one and half-accomplished migration into another, seems to rest on three things: first, the below-the-threshold potentiality of a text; second, the presence of readers also with this below-the-threshold potentiality; and finally, the crowdsourcing they participate in. This is the spin that James puts on what Ahab calls the "little lower layer." For him, that layer has to do, above all, with those mariners, renegades, and castaways who make up the background of the novel; it has to do with their work routine; and, when it does manifest itself, it takes the form of a humor that reverses the generic conventions of tragedy. But James isn't entirely clear—at least not yet—about why that might be the case. All he says is this:

> They are a world-federation of modern industrial workers. They owe allegiance to no nationality. There are Americans among them, but it is the officers who are American. Among the crew nobody is anything. They owe no allegiance to anybody or anything except the work they have to do and the relations with one another on which that work depends.[25]

James's "world-federation" seems to exist so far only as negatives: the workers are non-Americans; they are nobodies; they owe no allegiance to any nation. Together, they do add up to something, though what that is remains wishful, ill-defined. It is only from hindsight, with additional input from historians themselves inspired by James, that we can begin to see what this term might entail.

Peter Linebaugh and Marcus Rediker in their classic study, *The Many-Headed Hydra* (2000), have raised the possibility of just such a seaborne "world-federation," made up of "variously designated dispossessed commoners, transported felons, indentured servants, religious radicals, pirates, urban laborers, soldiers, sailors, and African slaves" united by their low opinion of high authorities and, when they saw fit, breaking out into strikes and mutinies that often took their superiors by surprise. Linebaugh and Rediker compare these insurrections to the "long waves" of the Atlantic, which, finally hitting the shore as breakers, might seem to have come from nowhere when in fact they have been a long time coming. The impact of each wave depends on "the length of its fetch, or the distance from its point of origin. The longer the fetch, the greater the wave."[26] The undercurrents of the Atlantic need significant distances to make themselves felt. Likewise, their human counterparts, what Line-baugh and Rediker call the "planetary currents" of the world's migrant workers, needed significant distances to do the same. Ocean voyages lasting for years gave their dormant capabilities a chance to form "new and unexpected connections," so unexpected that to the casual observer they must seem "accidental, contingent, transient, even miraculous."

This is the second time we are hearing that word and its cognate: *miracle, miraculous.* Tracing a developmental arc from James to Linebaugh and Rediker, it speaks to a felt need on the part of all three to name a phenomenon not yet fully understood but empirically observable, when hitherto unpromising players suddenly prove themselves capable of feats no one would have suspected. *Miracle* is a shorthand for this, for all those moments when, against all odds, people living all their lives in one genre suddenly slip out and make their way into another. James has always been interested in minor miracles of this sort, carrying no divine sanction and requiring only genre switching, the stuff history is made of.

THE BLACK JACOBINS

His earlier book, the now-classic *The Black Jacobins* (1938), is a tribute to just such genre switching. The slave population of San Domingo on the Caribbean island of Hispaniola, hitherto "trembling in hundreds before a single white man," suddenly and inexplicably turned into fierce fight-ers, successfully waging a twelve-year guerrilla war, defeating "the local whites and the soldiers of the French monarchy, a Spanish invasion, a British expedition of some 60,000 men, and a French expedition of similar size under Bonaparte's brother-in-law."[27] This was the only slave revolt that led to the founding of a state—the Republic of Haiti. And strangest of all was the transatlantic network these genre-switching slaves were able to forge, winning the support of the radical democrats during the French Revolution. James's chapter titles speak for them-selves: chapter 4, "The San Domingo Masses Begin"; chapter 5, "And the Paris Masses Complete." He marvels that "from indifference in 1789," the French Jacobins had by 1792 come to "detest no section of the aristocracy so much as those whom they called 'the aristocrats of the skin.' . . . Henceforth the Paris masses were for abolition, and their black brothers in San Domingo, for the first time, had passionate allies in

France."[28] All in all, "revolution moves in a mysterious way its wonders to perform."[29]

James himself is no stranger to such wonders; indeed, the very existence of *The Black Jacobins* is a testimony of sorts. The book was published in London in 1938, but it had been percolating in his head even before he left Trinidad six years earlier. Long impatient with histories featuring only the subjugation of slaves, he ordered books from France that had been written from a different perspective as soon as he arrived in London. Every day, he discussed these with Harry Spencer, owner of the tea shop he frequented. It was Spencer who urged him to write a book of his own:

> I told him that I had to go to France to the archives, I didn't have the money as yet but I was saving. He asked me how much money I would need and I told him about a hundred pounds to start with. He left it there but a few days afterwards put ninety pounds in my hands and said, "Onto France, and if you need more, let me know." As soon as the summer season was over (I was a cricket reporter), off I went and spent six months in France covering ground at a tremendous rate.[30]

Who would have thought that a colonial from Trinidad, born to a lower-middle-class family, traveling to England only because of his friendship with a cricket player who later became Lord Constantine, could produce a book like this? And who would have thought that the research for the book would be financed by the owner of an English tea shop? In its provenance no less than its argument, *The Black Jacobins* points to gut intuition as miracle working, a force in getting genres switched, and a much-needed ally in James's lifelong battle with Stalinism ("Night after night he would address meetings in London and the provinces, denouncing the crimes of the blood-thirsty Stalin, until he was hoarse," Frederick Warburg reported).[31] Against the formidable apparatus of the Communist Party and its claim to being the vanguard of revolution,[32] this gut intuition of the lower middle class is indeed contemptible, a weak phenomenon largely invisible to the world. All the same, it's the working knowledge for many, to be honored precisely because it's pre-institutional, not rising to articulate thought, limited in what it can do, and an alternative template for participatory democracy for just that reason.

WORKING KNOWLEDGE

Raymond Williams would later refer to this working knowledge as a "structure of feeling," not quite a philosophy or worldview but simply a "practical consciousness of a present kind, in a living and interrelating continuity." Practical consciousness of this sort, Williams goes on to say, "cannot without loss be reduced to belief-systems, institutions, or explicit general relationships, though it may include all these as lived and experienced, with or without tension."[33] It is this practical consciousness that James associates with the resilience of those who work every day, not so much as organized labor, as he is careful to emphasize, but simply as people thrown together by economic necessity and dependent on one another in their work routine. Just that, he says, is enough to create a bond, a pool of knowledge and a principle of connectivity, giving everyone a modest but functional place in the world.

In *Beyond a Boundary* (1963), James famously begins with the question, "What does he know of cricket who only cricket knows?"[34] A parallel question could be asked in *Mariners, Renegades, and Castaways*: What does he know of work who only work knows? The answer, in both cases, is Enough. Cricket, James says in *Beyond a Boundary*, has taught him to "fight the good fight with all my might. I was in the toils of greater forces than I knew. Cricket had plunged me into politics long before I was aware of it. When I did turn to politics I did not have too much to learn."[35] His epistemology is not one positing a sharp break between gut intuition and objective truth, with the latter categorically superior to the former. On the contrary, it is gut intuition, especially when it comes from work, that instills in workers a baseline knowledge that allows them to navigate the world.

In an essay entitled "Every Cook Can Govern," James notes that in ancient Greece, the work of government was rotated among all its citizens, randomly picked each time by sortition, or lottery. Greek democracy was founded on an "extraordinary confidence" in the "ability of the ordinary person, the grocer, the candlestick-maker, the carpenter, the sailor, the tailor," trusting that each, when "chosen by lot" to govern collaboratively, would be able to do so.[36] The same confidence should be placed in sailors who know their ships, the seas, and the seaborne planet. These people are "federated by nothing. But they are looking for federation."[37] They'll always be here, with a work-based claim to the future.

This is what Melville has overlooked. In taking work to be an inert background, he has granted it no dynamic relation to time. That dynamic relation creates consequential actors out of those we would otherwise imagine to be without agency. Melville is wrong, then, not to take these people more seriously and not to give serious consideration to the question, Why doesn't the crew revolt? Clearly, there's another story to be told. And here is where Ellis Island comes in, for James's own experience there, mingling with others coming through it—the twentieth-century descendants of Melville's mariners, renegades, castaways—has given him just the working knowledge to add another chapter to *Moby-Dick*, putting its background population in the foreground and switching genres in the process. Not everyone could agree, of course.[38] But at least one other reader of Melville would.

BACKGROUND TO FOREGROUND

Frank Stella, creator of a long-running *Moby-Dick* collage series, is not the most obvious reader. Working with visual and sculptural forms rather than words, he is known for having turned the art world upside down not once but twice: first with his minimalism of the early 1960s, then with the maximalism of the ensuing decades. As a young painter, Stella had been indebted to the abstract expressionism of Jackson Pollock, Mark Rothko, and Willem de Kooning; but impatient with these artists' lingering attachment to representation (or "illusionism"), he had come up with a series of abstractions far more thoroughgoing. His *Black Paintings* series of 1957-61—featuring monochrome black stripes produced with cheap house paint and filling the entire canvas—are organized only by parallel or perpendicular relationships. Eliminating all distinctions between content and medium, between representational figures in the foreground and perspectival space in the background, these paintings were instead canvases uniformly and stubbornly flat, with no receding dimensions, no pretense at being anything other than canvases. Stella famously said, "My painting is based on the fact that only what can be seen there is there. . . . What you see is what you see."[39]

There was a context for such paintings. While some of them had been started at Princeton University, most were produced after Stella had graduated and moved to New York, where for the first six months he worked as a house painter three to four days a week. Since his boss,

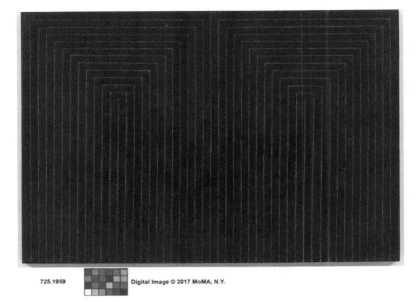

Fig. 3.1 Frank Stella, *The Marriage of Reason and Squalor* (1959). © 2019 Frank Stella / Artists Rights Society, New York. Photograph: © The Museum of Modern Art / Licensed by Scala / Art Resource, New York.

J. Husiash of Astoria, Queens, charged unusually low fees, many of the painting jobs were in the slums, where the courts had been ordering landlords to repaint. As William S. Rubin points out, "The ambience of these jobs is directly connected with the titles of the Black Paintings."[40] *The Marriage of Reason and Squalor* (1959) (fig. 3.1)—bought by the Museum of Modern Art after Stella's 1959 debut exhibition—typifies these low-cost, low-key, low-affect paintings, taking poverty in stride and without illusion, "marrying" it to a form of pictorial intelligence as close to geometry as possible.

Still, these monochrome, two-dimensional paintings seemed not to have satisfied Stella entirely. Beginning in the 1970s, he would take the art world by surprise again, first with an explosion of color, then with a resolute return to three-dimensionality—not through perspectival space, however, but through what would become a lifelong preoccupation on his part: a dedicated creating, assembling, and sculpting of various material forms as surfaces for paint. What links these non-canvas-based collages to the early *Black Paintings* is the continued flipping of fore-ground and background. Just as the two-dimensional canvases had col-lapsed the two in their thoroughgoing flatness, so the three-dimensional collages now did the same by refusing to assign primacy to the content of the painting over and against the material medium on which it is ex-ecuted. Rather, the material medium is as interesting to Stella as anything else, full of surprises and the ground for experimentation, so much so that his later works are almost never regular paintings but rather painted reliefs, painted sculptures, or even painted architectures, as Paul Gold-berger has argued—paint applied to dimensioned spaces that are them-selves part of the drama and part of the point.[41]

Crucial to this parity between medium and content is Stella's col-laboration with printmaker Ken Tyler, "one of the great partnerships in American art history," Robert Hughes has noted.[42] It began in 1967, when Stella moved to California to start teaching at the University of California, Irvine, only to be denied the job upon his refusal to sign the required state loyalty oath. Jobless, he accepted Tyler's invitation to work with lithography at the newly founded Gemini G. E. L. (which became Tyler Graphics in 1974).[43] Ever since, printmaking has offered Stella alternative resolutions for seemingly intractable problems en-countered in painting. Indeed, the very organization of his paintings into the series format reflects his habit of mind as a printmaker, since seriality is especially salient with prints, where permutations of shape become immediately discernible. Furthermore, whereas paintings ex-ist as dust-free products, prints retain their connection to the workshop, an artisan's space, a world of preliminary studies, multiple drafts, and leftover scraps.

By the time of the *Swan Engraving* series (1982), Stella's prints were no longer mere copies of the paintings. They were autonomous creations, equal to the paintings and with continual input into them. Stella says that he would work on both "concurrently, almost simultaneously. A tremendous feeling of freedom was triggered by the realization that I didn't have to make prints after the paintings . . . in the sense of being a copy or reproduction of the painting. I could work on prints as I was working on the paintings. The prints and the paintings would share the same ideas, but each could develop in its own way." He added, "I see the future of painting through the eyes of printing," for "without really

noticing, I have absorbed printing—a printmaking way of thinking—
into the pattern of my normal thought process. . . . Printing and printmaking have infiltrated my psyche to such an extent that I simply will
have to learn to live with them."[44]

"ABSTRACT ENOUGH"

The *Moby-Dick* series bears the signature of a printmaker. Beginning
in 1985 in conjunction with his *Wave* series and then with two other series, *Beluga* and *Irregular Shapes*, Stella produced prints, metal reliefs,
sculptures, murals, and large-scale installations loosely based on the
135 chapter titles of Melville's novel, over three hundred of them at
this point, with a projected goal as high as fifteen hundred.[45] These are
mostly mixed-media works, using cardboard, fiber, plywood, aluminum
sheets, stainless steel, and scraps lying around on the shop floor ("debris
d'atelier," Stella calls them),[46] leftover bits and pieces from other projects with already etched surfaces. Recycling these scraps allows Stella
to produce multilayered and multi-textured collages of unprecedented
complexity, a print aesthetics in turn transposed onto his paintings. As
Philip Leider points out, "Ideas of palimpsest, superimposition, frag-
mentation and juxtaposition previously developed in Stella's printmaking finally came tumbling into" these collages. His unique achievement
as an artist is just that: a "steadily and inexorably achieved parity" between printmaking and painting.[47]

   Two geometric shapes are especially noticeable in this regard: on the
one hand, curvilinear waves, and on the other routinized grids akin to
drawings for ornamental rain gutters Stella had found in a turn-of-the-
century catalog of cast-iron manufacturers.[48] What results are swirling,
churning shapes superimposed on an enormous disk near the center of
these pieces: a disk sometimes concave and sometimes convex, often
missing part of its arc, imprinted with Chinese lattice designs. These
works aren't about *Moby-Dick* in any obvious way. Other than the titles
assigned them, there are few demonstrable links between Melville's
novel and these extravagant abstract shapes. Driven by a new synergy
between printmaking and painting, they are instead a testimony to
Stella's working belief that despite the persistence of representational
art, "the future belongs to surface and color, self-generating and self-

sustaining abstractions bound together in an undeniable presence that makes itself felt as art."[49]

Stella himself says that the initial inspiration for him was visual rather than textual, based on physical movements in space rather than words on a page:

> The idea of the wave and its various permutations is what drives the new series. Once I started on the wave shape, I saw it began to look like a whale—a combination of wave and whale. I got the idea for the shapes at the aquarium, particularly from watching the way the Beluga whales move. The idea of the whale reminded me of *Moby-Dick*, so I decided to go back and read the novel and the more I got into it, the more I thought it would be great to use the chapter headings of the novel for the titles of the pieces.[50]

Siri Engberg points out that the "titles are almost always assigned to the work after the fact,"[51] which suggests that *Moby-Dick* might have been an afterthought from beginning to end. And in any case, Stella's upbeat view of the novel might not square with that of most readers. According to him, "There is no depression in it; every line is up."[52] Philip Leider argues that the *Moby-Dick* series is less a reading of Melville's novel than a self-delighting celebration of Stella's own "working space"—the title of his Charles Eliot Norton Lectures (1983–84)—an homage to abstraction featuring such illustrious forebears as Picasso, Kandinsky, and Jackson Pollock mixed in with a record of his own labor, with many of his previous works making whimsical cameo reappearances. Its "bouncy, buoyant" forms and "irrepressible comic energy" come from Stella's "realization that he was, at the end of his third decade as one of the most important American artists, about to embark on the best work of his career."[53]

The connection of the series to *Moby-Dick* is no doubt weak, with less than what the chapter titles promise. Still, it is worth thinking about the switch from tragedy to comedy in Stella's hands. Robert K. Wallace, who has spent almost two decades studying these works, argues that it is here that Stella became comically resigned to being less than 100-percent abstract. In 1995 Stella had told him, "It's pretty impossible to have truly abstract painting, even if you begin with an abstract, nonfigurative base, which I actually do." What got in the way was "two things happening": "living in the world, so associational things come through," and "relat[ing] to the history of the past, so even though you started with abstraction, figuration comes back in from the other side."[54]

Abstract art is by nature vulnerable, it seems. Referential content is always sneaking in through the back. Open to everyday associations and to our collective histories, such art is defenseless against unauthorized incursions of meaning. It can try hard to be no more than a canvas with paint on it, but that purity is hard to maintain, and viewers often have other ideas. Ironically, juxtaposition and superimposition, two techniques honed through printmaking, are now the conduits for such semantic invasions. And the content-laden *Moby-Dick*, with its encyclopedic histories and a plot all too tangible, is spearheading the process, making it impossible for Stella not to be referential at some point. Faced with this unstoppable deluge, the artist himself seems to give in somewhat—not all the way but enough to suggest that abstract art need not be maximum strength. A weaker version would do just fine.

In a lecture at the University of Michigan in 1997, thinking back to two shows he had seen the previous year—*Splendors from Imperial China* at the Metropolitan Museum and *Abstraction in the Twentieth Century* at the Guggenheim—Stella mused that "in the right hands representational art can be abstract enough."[55] It's not surprising that the Chinese paintings should be the occasion for this thought, for a degree of abstraction has always been part of Chinese visual language, never fully representational and never fully abstract but enough of each. Those lattice designs that Stella has been using throughout the *Moby-Dick* series testify to just such minimum-strength admixtures.

MINIMUM STRENGTH

He had found those lattices in a book by Daniel Sheets Dye.[56] They are uniquely suited for his multilayered, collage-driven aesthetics. Themselves geometric and abstract, they are not so strict as to repel nonabstract meanings that end up being deposited on them. There is nothing ritzy or showy about these lattices. They are just there: routinized and endlessly repeated but reliable, durable. Chinese artisans have been using them for hundreds of years. In the hands of Stella, they become something of a manifesto, or rather, a counter-manifesto, challenging the illustrious forebears here gathered, making it known that there is another, less exalted side to his art. Coming from the workshop and the anonymous routine of the artisan, these lattice designs are his signature as a printmaker. They are hardly the main event, but they aren't in the background either, not subordinate, a low-key but recurring affirmation of manual labor, linking the artist to all those on the *Pequod*.

"Ahab's Leg" and "Ahab and the Carpenter" are exemplary here. Coming near the end of the novel and featuring a half-comic, half-ominous exchange, these chapters pit their sublime protagonist against a humble, all-purpose workman. The carpenter's "brain, if he ever had one, must have early oozed into the muscles of his fingers," Melville tells us. He's like a pocket knife "but containing, not only blades of various sizes, but also screw-drivers, cork screws, tweezers, awls, pens, rulers, nail-files, countersinkers," giving him a "crutch-like, antediluvian, wheezing humorousness" toward all mishaps that need to be fixed.[57] Ahab has summoned the carpenter because his ivory leg (replacing the flesh-and-blood one carried away by Moby-Dick) has been damaged and needs a replacement. The carpenter obliges, using one of the whale bones always on hand.

In *Ahab's Leg* (1989) (fig. 3.2), the mood is set by Ahab's unrelenting fatalism. To this tragic hero, all "mortal miseries shall still fertilely beget to themselves an eternally progressive progeny of griefs beyond the grave," a genealogy of such "archangelic grandeur" that it "carries us at last among the sourceless primogenitures of the gods."[58] Stella renders this genealogy of griefs with graphic vividness: to the left, we can quite clearly see Ahab's boot, but just one. The missing one is indicated to the right by long red streaks and what looks like dripping blood, a wound forever unhealed and festering. The Chinese lattice pattern, meanwhile, is central but also recessional in this painting: the carpenter is making another ivory leg, but while the focus is on Ahab's one-leggedness, both he and his work must take a back seat.

In *Ahab and the Carpenter* (1990) (fig. 3.3), that distribution of foreground and background is reversed; the lattice pattern is now front and center. The carpenter's handiwork will save the day in this chapter: Queequeg's unused coffin is being recycled, made over into a replacement life buoy. Stella, who knows a thing or two about recycling himself, is no

Fig. 3.2 Frank Stella, *Ahab's Leg* (1989). © 2019 Frank Stella / Artists Rights Society / New York. Photography by Jason Wyche. Photograph: Courtesy Frank Stella Studio.

doubt indulging in a private joke. Ahab, of course, sees nothing to joke about. Nothing will distract him from his single-minded path to catastrophe: "A life-buoy of a coffin! Does it go further? Can it be that in some spiritual sense the coffin is, after all, but an immortality-preserver? I'll think of that. But no. So far gone am I in the dark side of earth, that its other side, the theoretic bright one, seems but uncertain twilight to me. Will ye have done, Carpenter, with that accursed sound? I go below; let me not see that thing when I return again."[59]

Stella takes that soliloquy and redistributes it into a very different kind of pictorial dynamics, the "other side" to Ahab's darkness. His *Moby-Dick* series stops short of being entirely comic, to be sure; but it

Fig. 3.3 Frank Stella, *Ahab and the Carpenter* (1990). © 2019 Frank Stella / Artists Rights Society, New York. Photography by Steven Sloman © 1990. Photograph: Courtesy Frank Stella Studio.

also stops short of being entirely tragic, just as it stops short of being entirely abstract. In *Ahab and the Carpenter*, this interlaced, minimum-strength aesthetics honors the work of an artisan, the sole member of the crew who could look the catastrophe in the eye and wrest from it a small piece of its victory. Ahab might never see the coffin/life buoy again. But Ishmael will.

<h2 style="text-align:center">INDIAN OCEAN ENGLISH</h2>

Still, such gestures notwithstanding, Stella's commitments remain over-whelmingly to abstraction; it's virtually impossible for his geometric forms to provide the clear-cut alternative ending to *Moby-Dick* that C. L. R. James wants. It takes a third reader, firmly in the nonabstract camp, to add one other sequel, housed in the twenty-first-century novel and giving tragedy an even more comic home.

Amitav Ghosh's connection to Melville is shaky like Stella's, hard to decipher in his case, with a degree of equivocation intriguing to behold. On the one hand, he is on record as saying that of all nineteenth-century authors, he is indebted to "Melville most of all," that *Moby-Dick* is "inexhaustible in its inspiration." In a November 19, 2008, interview with Christopher Lydon on *Open Source*, a WBUR radio talk show, Ghosh said he would "love to recapture the cosmopolitan vision" of "Obama's true precursor." He went on:

> One of the most wonderful things about Melville is that he was just about the only one of the nineteenth century nautical writers who paid enough attention to the world of the sea to write about Indian sailors. . . . It is so rare actually to find a believable representation of an Asian. . . . You remember, in *Moby Dick*, the 40th chapter, all of the sailors sing in different languages, and then suddenly you discover that this ship, which is a Nantucket whaling ship, actually has forty different nationalities on board, including Indians.[60]

A very different picture emerged, however, in his essay, "Of Fanas and Forecastles," published just a few months earlier, in the Mumbai-based *Economic and Political Weekly*. In this essay Ghosh gives nineteenth-century literature only a cursory glance, his primary focus being the nonliterary world of "indigenous sailors from the Indian Ocean areas—

Arabs, Chinese, East Africans, Filipinos, Malays, and South Asians," collectively known as the lascars. This often overlooked group populated the oceans with "the Laskari language," drawn from "English, Malay, Hindustani, Chinese, Malayalam and the entire Babel of languages spoken on board."[61] How this tongue fares in Melville's hands is indicative of the failure of Western authors to come to grips with this remarkable linguistic form. Turning to the very same *Moby-Dick* chapter, chapter 40, he would single out for praise on the WBUR show, Ghosh here observes that among the polyglot crew on the *Pequod*, "there is of course a token lascar, whose contribution to the merriment consists of: 'By Brahma! Boys, it will be douse sail soon. The sky-born, high-tide Ganges turned to wind! Thou showest thy black brow Seeva!' "[62]

Melville isn't even trying and failing here; there's simply no attempt on his part to have the lascar's speech sound the least bit like Laskari. This abysmal performance makes *Moby-Dick* not so much a precursor as an irritant. Ghosh's commitment to Indian Ocean languages, like Stella's commitment to abstraction, thrives on its weak connection to Melville's novel, claiming it, in this case, as a template meager enough to be negatively inspiring. The *Ibis* trilogy that results, beginning with *Sea of Poppies* (2008), followed by *River of Smoke* (2011), and ending with *Flood of Fire* (2015), retraces *Moby-Dick*'s voyage, crossing the same three oceans—the Atlantic Ocean, the Indian Ocean, the South China Sea—but offering passage to a very different linguistic universe and stopping at places the *Pequod* never visited.

Ghosh gives us, in fact, not a single Laskari tongue spoken by the entire floating population from one end of the Indian Ocean to the other but at least four variants, showcased at different stages in the trilogy. *Sea of Poppies* gives us Laskari perhaps in its purest form (if this isn't a contradiction in terms), spoken by the crew's leader, Serang Ali. Here, under the guise of translating for Jodu, another Lascar sailor, Ali offers made-in-Indian-Ocean marital advice about Paulette Lambert, daughter of a deceased botanist, now eating "big-big rice" on the estate of Benjamin Burnham, ship owner and opium trader:

"Launder say father-blongi-she go hebbin. That bugger do too muchi tree-pijjin. Allo time pickin plant. Inside pocket hab no cash. After he go hebbin cow-chilo catchi number-two-father, Mr. Burnham. Now she too much muchi happy inside. Eat big-big rice. Better Malum Zikri

forgetting she. How can learn sailor-pijjin, allo time thinking ladies-
ladies? More better keep busy with laund'ry till marriage time."
    The malum took unexpected umbrage at this. "Hell and scissors,
Serang Ali!" he cried, springing to his feet, "Don you never think of
nothin but knob-knockin and gamahoochie?"[63]

While one would expect Ali to talk the way he does, Zachary, the second
mate (known to the sailors as Malum Zikri), born and bred in Maryland,
seems to be learning fast, developing a version of Indian Ocean English all his own, with African American syntax and phonetics thrown
in. Ghosh is not interested in pristine languages. It's the mixing, the
bastardization of tongues, that preoccupies him, a vernacular spectrum
changing with the scenes of action encountered.
    River of Smoke, the second in the trilogy, opens with a "mixture of Bhoj-
puri and Kreol" (as we are told up front) spoken by Deeti, an Indian woman
from Ghazipur now living on the island of Mauritius: "Revey-te! È Banwari,
è Mukhpyari! Revey-té na! Haglé ba?" But this vernacular form quickly
gives way to yet another, this time the pidgin English spoken around the
city of Canton (Guangzhou today), especially in Fanqui-town, the foreign
enclave. Bahram Modi, leader of the Parsi merchants from Bombay (now
Mumbai), and Chi-mei, the Chinese woman he ends up having an extended affair with, seem to be having fun conversing in this language:

> When she tried to pull off his sacred waist-strings he whispered: "This
> piece thread blongi joss-pidgin thing. No can take off."
>   She uttered a yelp of a laugh. "What Joss-pidgin thread also have got?"
>   "Have. Have."
>   "White Hat Devil have too muchi big cloth."
>   "White Hat Devil have nother-piece thingi too muchi big."[64]

Pidgin English is not a debased form of English in the *Ibis* trilogy. It is
a language unto itself, with a working grammar, and a colorfully improvised vocabulary used to good effect by the two speakers. It is a lingua
franca as no pure language can be.
    In fact, it's the disappearance of this shared tongue in *Flood of Fire*,
the last volume of the trilogy, that signals the end of an era. Featuring
the run-up to the First Opium War followed by massive bloodshed, this

novel is dominated throughout by the rigid hierarchy among the sepoy ranks making up the British forces, a backlash against the two preceding volumes. Kesri Singh, a sepoy in the Bengal Native Infantry, defends his sister Deeti in Hindustani, in complete sentences, strictly unadulterated: "Aur ham tohra se achha se jaana taani! And I know her better than you!" His superior, Subedar NirdhaySingh, responds in kind: "Abh hamra aankhi se dur ho ja! Now get out of my sight, Kesri Singh! I never want to set eyes on you again."[65] The need for translation speaks for itself. Pure Hindustani is incomprehensible to anyone not knowing the language. Pidgin English, on the other hand, though initially a challenge, is accessible by all and hospitable to all, a common tongue crucial to the vitality of this polyglot world. There is no better accompaniment to the First Opium War than the silencing of this tongue.

WATERED-DOWN TRAGEDY

The stage is set for a maximum-strength tragic ending; yet this is just what Ghosh avoids. In an inspired revamping of the tragic form, the catastrophe in *Flood of Fire* is not concentrated at the end but scattered throughout the entire second half of the book, with Chinese civilian casualties and the discreetly reported but no less harrowing deaths of two main characters happening relatively early on. When the novel finally comes to an end, it's on a very different note. Before it closes, *Flood of Fire* circles all the way back to the previous volume of the trilogy, to the opening pages of *River of Smoke*. Picking up on Deeti's point-by-point explication of the painting in her shrine, known as *The Escape*, it offers this account of miraculous deliverance, rendered in her signature mix of Bhojpuri and Kreol:

"Ekut. Ekut!" Deeti would cry, and that great horde of bonoys, belsers, bowjis, salas, sakubays and other relatives would follow her finger as she traced the path of Jodu's sampan as it edged across the bay, from the Kowloon side, to draw up beside the *Ibis*, which was all but empty . . .
There vwala!
Her finger would come to rest on Serang Ali: You see him, this grankoko with a head teeming with mulugandes? This is the great burrhuriya who had once again thought up the plan for their escape.[66]

The *Ibis* is the means of deliverance for Jodu and for Maddow Colver, formerly Kalua, driver of an oxcart in Ghazipur and now a gun lascar for the East India Company, but destined to become the patriarch of the La Fami Colver here assembled. The *Ibis* is not sucked into a vortex, like the *Pequod*. Ghosh's only concession to Melville is by way of another ship, the *Anahita*, which, thanks to the three thousand chests of opium it's carrying, is no doubt a better candidate for that tragic fate.

And the *Anahita* does meet its end in a manner distinctly reminiscent of *Moby-Dick*. The *Pequod* has gone under, spinning in a contracting spiral: "And now, concentric circles seized the lone boat itself, and all its crew, and each floating oar, and every lance-pole, and spinning, animate and inanimate, all round and round in one vortex, carried the smallest chip of the *Pequod* out of sight."[67] The *Anahita* also spins around and around but with a crucial difference: "A whirlpool took shape around the stricken ship, and as she was vanishing into it, the spinning whorls seemed to race towards the longboat. But then a wave took hold of the boat and carried it away, pushing it towards East Point."[68] Unlike the all-engulfing vortex in *Moby-Dick*, this one destroys the ship but not the lifeboat. The destructive agent here, after all, is not a super-intelligent whale but a regular typhoon. This is not a tale of vengeance in which all perish but one in which a wave happens to come along to give everyone a lucky break.

The *Ibis*, meanwhile, is undamaged. As it's spirited away from Hong Kong, it's manned by a crew of six representing both sides of the Opium War, including Serang Ali and Jodu fighting on the Chinese side and Kesri and Maddow Colver on the side of the British. The pivotal role of Serang Ali is telling and to no one's surprise. He has seemed savage at first glance (with a "mouth that was constantly in motion, its edges stained a bright, livid red: it was as if he were forever smacking his lips after drinking from the open veins of a mare"),[69] but a second look reveals that the mouth in question is stained with no more than betel juice. Looking initially like one of Fedallah's "tiger-yellow" crew in *Moby-Dick*, Ali proves to be the comic heart of the *Ibis* trilogy, afloat in an ocean utterly beyond his control but surviving, at least for the time being, with skill, luck, and working knowledge in a bastardized tongue. Gone now are the sublime drama and unrelenting fury of Ahab's end. What Ghosh offers instead is weak tragedy, as watered-down and mixed-up as the Lascari it speaks. C. L. R. James would have been elated.

Part Two
Rebuilt Networks

4 · Contagiously Irish

COLM TÓIBÍN, W. B. YEATS, AND GISH JEN INFECT HENRY JAMES

Colm Tóibín plays host to Henry James, entertaining the latter for 338 pages in *The Master* (2004), though probably not in a way the latter would have liked. Hosting is of course a complicated activity, as Jacques Derrida has reminded us: never simply benign, indeed not unrelated to hostage taking, opening up vulnerabilities on both sides and exposing both to unforeseen hazards.[1] So there's no telling what sort of accommodations Tóibín's novel would be, what effects it might have on the two authors in question, and on American literature and Irish literature as a jointly globalized ecosystem, facing newly arisen risks but perhaps also poised for new feats of endurance.

The Master begins with the toughest moment in James's life: January 5, 1895, the opening night of his play *Guy Domville*. The London literati were all there for the performance at the St. James's Theatre, but the novelist couldn't bear to sit through it. Too much was hanging on this potentially life-changing debut. So he had the "ingenious thought" of playing hooky instead at the nearby Haymarket Theatre, where a new Oscar Wilde play, *An Ideal Husband*, was drawing a crowd.

A month later, he wrote to William and Alice James about that play: "so helpless, so crude, so bad, so clumsy, feeble and vulgar" that it filled him more with apprehension than with disdain. "How *can* my piece do anything with a public with whom *that* is a success?"[2] Mercifully, that opening was two days earlier, so only the general audience would be there now. And "most consoling of all," Tóibín adds, "there was no sign of Wilde himself, loud and large and Irish as he was."[3] The crowd seemed to love every minute. After many curtain calls, James had to go back to his own play—in time for the hoots and jeers and catcalls from the orchestra pit, drowning out the applause from the invited guests.

Guy Domville was without question a vocational crisis, the end of any crossover hopes James might have harbored. Doors seemed to have slammed in his face. A playwright he would never be; theater and fiction were destined never to mix in his case. *Guy Domville* was replaced on February 14, 1895, by Wilde's *The Importance of Being Ernest*, with the entire cast simply signing on to the new play. For James, the shame was long lasting and all consuming, "a bitterness of every hour, ramifying into every throb of one's consciousness."[4]

HOSTING AND INFECTING

The Master plays host to that bitterness, but the rawness and feverishness of the episode suggest that Tóibín's novel might not have started out in pristine health, without a temperature of its own. In fact, the accommodations it provides might turn out to be signally unsafe for its guest, coming as it does with a preexisting condition, possibly infectious and possibly nonbenign. Such a host (*The Master* is hardly alone) puts literary history in conversation with two other viral forms: the runaway spread of cultural information on social media and the runaway spread of genetic information in infected cells.[5] Immunity breakdown, survival networks, and the ever-shifting dynamics between the beneficial and the harmful—these are only some of the more interesting phenomena that open up when texts are imagined as contagious sites in globalized ecosystems.

Tóibín is the first to admit that this is the case—that his hosting of James is overheated, overdetermined, not altogether benign. There's in fact a more immediate context for *Guy Domville*. Along with the nineteenth-century one centered on James, there's one very much in the present, centered on Tóibín's own ordeal in the here and now, "still raw, still preying on my mind." Tóibín is speaking of the trauma of the Booker Prize. His novel *The Blackwater Lightship* was shortlisted in 1999. Of the award ceremony, he wrote:

> There are six cameras and sets of lights in the vast ballroom, one camera is focused on each author. It seems as though each of us have

won . . . the cameras come closer, right into your face, as the name is about to be read out. . . . And then the name is read out and it is not yours. Within an instant, the lights are turned off and the cameras packed up and no one is looking at you. You feel a strange guilt and shame. . . . You are an outsider in London.[6]

There is a degree of sadism to all award ceremonies, the Booker Prize probably more so than others. What makes the sadism so contagious, spreading with such ease, is that textual boundaries seem to pose no barriers: James's century-old play, nested in Tóibín's novel, would now be fair game. *The Master* is, in this sense, both host and parasite, breaking down the immunities of those lodged within it, subjecting them to an involuntary family resemblance. J. Hillis Miller speaks of this host/parasite dialectic as the "double antithesis" of "viral infection": an "osmotic mixing" that reprograms the occupied entity, turning it into evermultiplying copies of the infectious agent.[7]

What are we to make of such reprogramming? It seems to be the unavoidable side effect of any interactive proximities. Any live culture, human as much as microbial, would have some such side effects. In literary ecosystems, such reprogramming suggests, at the very least, that we should stop thinking of causation as singly and antecedently given, located in the past and by now safely concluded. For better or worse, a live culture isn't likely to have an end date. Viral action opens up contagious sites linking past, present, and future, the passage of time generating new vulnerabilities but also new survival networks. We can think of this as a globalized and coevolving risk ecology: a double helix of continually emerging hazards matched by continually emerging adaptations, especially worth noting in an age of climate-related pandemics.[8]

GLOBALIZED RISK

In literature, the equivalents of pandemics are likely to be runaway semantic contagions, spreading rapidly in this case across the entire James corpus, reprogramming all his language as induced effects. This process subjects James's novels—no less than his plays—to an immunity breakdown at multiple junctures. Mediated by Tóibín—an author who wears his Irishness and queerness on his sleeve—ethnicity and sexuality

suddenly become contagious sites in James: open to symptomatic reading, most often as spiraling vulnerabilities but occasionally also as networked resilience.

James has always been read as Anglo-American rather than Irish, yet
Irishness is a prominent fact in his biography. William James, the novelist's grandfather, had come from County Cavan, Ireland. Leon Edel's
five-volume biography begins, in fact, with this Irish patriarch and his
subsequent career in the United States.[9] It's a story of spectacular up-
ward mobility, an immigrant making good and leaving his mark on his
adoptive country. Edel tells us about the towns, Albany and Syracuse,
with streets that bear the James name. The towns on the other side of the
Atlantic haven't been in the picture thus far. Thanks to Tóibín, they now
surface with a vengeance.

The Master devotes a good twenty-five pages to James's Irish trip,
which happens within days of the *Guy Domville* debacle. James is hosted
by the British military establishment: he stays first at Dublin Castle with
Lord Houghton, the new lord lieutenant, and then at the Royal Hospital at Kilmainham with Lord Wolseley, commander in chief of the British forces in Ireland. Even though his privileged lodgings seem secure
enough, this doesn't stop him from being dislodged from time to time by
symptomatic readers who wouldn't allow themselves to forget his family
origins. One of these is Webster, a member of Parliament, relentlessly
clinical about James's "Irish kinsmen":

> "What was the name of the place, Lady Wolseley? Bailieborough, that's
> right. Bailieborough in County Cavan. It is where you will find the seat
> of the James family."
>
> Henry noticed Lady Wolseley blushing and keeping her eyes from
> him.[10]

Rather than being immunized by his lordly surroundings, James is vulnerable here to something like a double exposure, the effect of the clinical inspection on the part of his hostess and the English MP. They have
put him under the microscope, looked into every detail the least bit sus-
picious. Not only was his grandfather originally from Bailieborough, but
the author himself, at this very moment, is in danger of being sent back
to the social equivalent of that ancestral home.

Immunity breakdown of this sort isn't limited to *The Master*. In fact, what emerges here is a symptomatic field of global proportions, spreading retroactively from Tóibín to James and making hitherto unmarked phenomena suddenly marked. There is, for instance, that small detail in the opening pages of *The Golden Bowl*, suddenly salient now, raised above the threshold of legibility, inviting and indeed compelling diagnosis. Prince Amerigo is introduced here for the first time: "his handsome face, constructively regular and grave, yet at the same time oddly and, as might be, functionally almost radiant, with its dark blue eyes, its dark brown moustache and its expression no more sharply 'foreign' to an English view than to have caused it sometimes to be observed of him with a shallow felicity that he looked like a 'refined' Irishman."[11]

What does it mean for a face to be "functionally almost radiant"? Interesting as it is, the phrase is just a tease, a prelude to the spectacularly convoluted last leg of the sentence. The twice-removed causation and double passive voice make the entire description seem strangely remote, as if it were some generic scenario that has to do with no one in particular. On its own, the sentence would probably have gone unnoticed for most readers. Thanks to the globalized contagion of Tóibín, it suddenly becomes impossible to overlook. Perhaps the generic Englishman *is* in fact some kind of double passive voice, an impersonal gaze that, with a "shallow felicity," is in turn capable of an agentless reduction, performing the operation first on the Irish and now extending it to the Italian prince, both being generic inferiors within the colonial taxonomy of the British Empire. James is not ordinarily subject to this kind of reading; Tóibín's company makes it almost unavoidable.

INDUCED VULNERABILITY

There's no better example of globalized risk. Induced vulnerability here spreads not only across space but also across time, reversing the flow of causation, going backward from the twenty-first century to the nineteenth, turning the hitherto unscrutinized Henry James into a diagnostic object. Fanning out into a symptomatic field, it features at least three or four carriers doing active duty, targeting gender no less than ethnicity, the British Empire no less than the James family. Sexuality is, not surprisingly, a key index, joining ethnicity and coloniality as prime infectious sites.

Tóibín is an openly gay author; James was not, though his queerness is increasingly highlighted in the critical literature.[12] Infected by Tóibín, queerness is now front and center, not an isolated fact but linked vulnerabilities featuring several other communicable traits. All of these come to a head in the person of Hammond, a servant in the Wolseley household specifically assigned to take care of James. Hammond is a servant, but he seems always to be on the verge of becoming something more. He could be two different things, with two different relations to this American author who, on his end, also seems to be oscillating in exactly the same way, neither one nor the other, without the security of full membership or full resolution:

> Hammond was Irish, though he spoke with a London accent, having been taken to England when he was a child. He seemed to like lingering over his tasks and talking as he cleaned. He apologized as he came and went. Henry made it clear that he did not mind the interruptions.
>
> "I like the hospital, sir, and the old soldiers," he said. His voice was soft. "They've mostly been in the wars and some of them fight their wars all day, sir. They think the windows and doors are Turks and Zulus or whatever and want to charge at them. It's funny here, sir. It's half Ireland and half England, like myself. Maybe that's why I feel at home."[13]

The Royal Hospital at Kilmainham is indeed a funny place. For one thing, this seems to be the ground zero of colonial warfare, impossible to forget even in this sexually charged moment. The phantom presence of the Turks and Zulus reminds us that the British military establishment in Ireland has an extensive prior history. And the historical Lord Wolseley was in fact a pillar of the British Empire, fighting in the second Burmese War, the Crimean War, the Indian mutiny, the second Opium War, the Anglo-Ashanti War, and the Anglo-Zulu War. Colonial ventures of this sort, indexed along with ethnicity and sexuality, put the entire James corpus within the reach of a symptomatic network. No novel is immune, least of all *The Golden Bowl*. This novel is now infected by a new strain of the imperium, extending from the Tiber to the Thames and onward across the Atlantic in the twentieth century, featuring carriers coming from the New World, newly dominant on the world stage.

Guy Domville isn't immune either, though its vulnerability runs on a somewhat different axis. Given its plot of monastic celibacy, the globalized contagion of Tóibín means that symptomatic queerness for this novel is all but inevitable. James's accidental run-ins with Oscar Wilde now seem telling in more ways than one. With the latter's homosexuality an open secret and soon to be on trial, the psychodrama besetting *Guy Domville* suddenly becomes more than just a vocational crisis. Its feverishness has still other meanings.

SYMPTOMS AND BEYOND

There's almost no limit to such a symptomatic field. Even though the contagion starts out as a specific effect between Tóibín and James, it's now overtaken and overshadowed by the larger-than-life and infinitely more toxic Oscar Wilde. The effects unleashed by such a viral agent are everywhere visible. Diagnosis is easy, but with that ease often comes a clinical overreach, what Fredric Jameson calls "premature immediacy and the establishment of unreflected unities." Jameson's own emphasis on "mediation" as a constraint on symptomatic reading that short-circuits its phenomena, that reduces "distinct realities to a common denominator," is especially pertinent here.[14] To see James and Tóibín (or anyone else) only as symptoms is to grant them no alternate life, no ability to turn those overdetermined scripts into scripts of their own making.

That short-circuiting is all too tempting for James, perhaps never more so than in a letter to Edmund Gosse. Dated April 8, 1895—three months after the *Guy Domville* debacle, and two days after Wilde was indicted under Section 11 of the 1885 Criminal Law Amendment Act, denied bail, and thrown into London's Holloway Prison—the letter shows just what this fallen rival had meant to James:

> It has been, it is, hideously, atrociously dramatic and really interesting—so far as one can say that of a thing of which the interest is qualified by such a sickening horribility. . . . But the *fall*—from nearly twenty years of a really unique kind of "brilliant" conspicuity (wit, "art," conversation, "one of our two or three dramatist, etc.") to that sordid prison-cell and this gulf of obscenity over which the ghoulishly public hangs and gloats—it is beyond any utterance of irony or any pang of compassion! He was never in the smallest degree interesting to me—but this hideous human history has made him so—in a manner.[15]

From the sloppiness of the syntax to clunky words such as "horribility," the prose here sinks under James's gloating, even as he projects that unseemly sentiment onto a vulture-like public. The transparency of the psychology speaks to the short emotional leash, the short step from injury to revenge. This failed playwright did not have to wait too long, after all. His hitherto triumphant rival—Irish and gay—got his comeuppance sooner than anyone might have thought. Things have come full circle. There's satisfaction in that; but loops and tangents that are less tidy would have been interesting as well, and perhaps more fruitful in the developmental arcs they afford.[16] There is such a thing as ending too quickly and too summarily, opting for the muscularity of the punch line over non-muscular forms less preoccupied with symptoms than with what comes after symptoms: a future-building network, dedicated to survival and turning globalized risks into adaptive variants.

ADAPTIVE VARIANTS

To go some way toward the latter, a lesson could perhaps be gleaned from the behavior of actual viruses and their adaptive survival through the production of variants. Learning from these often deadly creatures isn't as odd as it might seem. Viruses are, after all, our oldest companion species. Human DNA contains roughly 100,000 pieces of viral DNA, making up about 8 percent of the human genome. Some of this viral DNA has been there since time immemorial. In July 2017, scientists investigating a mysterious substance in the human embryo discovered a protein called Hemo, jointly produced by the fetus and the placenta, and descended from the viral DNA that entered our ancestors' genomes 100 million years ago. Other viral DNA in humans is still more venerable, dating back to perhaps as early as 450 million years ago.[17] Most of this comes from one particular group: retroviruses, infectious agents that adapt to their environments by inserting their genes into the host DNA. If an egg or sperm happens to be infected, the viral DNA can potentially be reproduced along with the human DNA, fused with the latter and coevolving from generation to generation.

"I love the fact that human genomes can be found in only about 10 percent of all the cells that occupy the mundane space I call my body; the other 90 percent of the cells are filled with the genomes of bacteria, fungi, protists, and such, some of which play in a symphony necessary to my being alive at all," Donna Haraway writes.[18] The symphonic role played by viruses is especially interesting. Even though these creatures are too small to count as organisms, incapable of existing on their own and without even the benefit of a protective membrane, such vulnerabilities have only made them veteran survivors, adapting to changing environments by diversifying both themselves and their hosts.

Much more so than humans or other organisms, viruses can mutate to good effect, producing variants that manage to resist or evade the search-and-destroy operations of immune systems and antiviral drugs. While mutations in humans occur at a rate of one in every million nucleotides per generation, in viruses the rate is about one in every thousand per generation. This much higher frequency is partly because, compared to the human reproductive time span of about thirty years, viruses can reproduce in a day or two, doing so without any proofreading to hold errors in check. Every time a virus infects a cell, its DNA or RNA may be copied thousands of times, throwing up several mutant viruses with each round of infection. "This high mutation rate in viruses is their lifeline; in some, it is essential for their survival," Dorothy H. Crawford notes.[19] While some of the mutants are nonviable, others enjoy an adaptive advantage over their siblings, in time remaking entire populations. Some of the most successful viruses are such virtuoso mutants. Measles, around for two thousand years, exists now in a form that emerged only two hundred years ago. And HIV, reigning infectious agent and single largest killer in Africa today, wreaks devastation because of its unfailing ability to adapt, to bounce back with yet more drug-resistant strains, a recombined DNA continually mutating and perennially indestructible.

RECOMBINED DNA

While measles and HIV are without question pathogens, the remarkable capacity of all viruses to recombine DNA has led scientists to look more closely at their often harmful but also quite necessary role as catalysts and mediators, channeling genetic material across species boundaries and producing adaptive variants, a process beginning with gene swapping among related viruses, known as reassortment.[20] "Viruses are the unseen but dynamic players in the ecology of Earth. They move DNA between species, provide new genetic material for evolution, and regulate vast populations of organisms. Every species, from tiny microbes to large mammals, is influenced by the actions of viruses," Judy Diamond and Charles Wood write.[21] Newness, for good or for ill, comes into the world thanks to them.[22] These border-crossing mutants are "inventors" by necessity, Michael G. Cordingley points out. Coevolving with their hosts and reconfiguring the latter's DNA, they produce a "metagenome the sheer volume and diversity of which overshadow all other genetic information in the biosphere."[23]

Rather than thinking of viruses simply as life-threatening harms, it might be helpful to think of them also as life-diversifying conduits, recombining gene pools by channeling fresh input into all species. In a 2017 article, "Symbiosis," M. J. Roossinck and E. R. Bazan make just that argument. Highlighting immunity breakdown as the basis for an evolving planet, they urge us to explore the reciprocal diversification resulting from the contact between viruses and hosts. "Ultimately, symbiosis can lead to symbiogenesis, or speciation through fusion," Roossinck and Bazan conclude. Biodiversity owes everything to these invaders doubling as DNA carriers. Over time, "the presence of large amounts of viral sequence in the genomes of everything from bacteria to humans, including some important functional genes, illustrates the significance of viral symbiogenesis in the evolution of all life on Earth."[24]

Here's an example from the natural world worth pondering, a form of contagion that turns shared vulnerabilities into shared plenitude. What might literary history look like imagined as a parallel process? Taken as an ecosystem with weakly defended borders, and with adaptive variants as not always benign but fairly routine outcomes, viral symbiosis points to immunity breakdown as experimental paths to the future. Opening up potentially risky exchanges on multiple fronts, it turns literary history into a history of nonsolitary acts. Discrete texts give way here to input-bearing networks, collective DNA culled across space and time. Such collective DNA, still under threat but newly connected and recombined, does seem to have a shot at the future.

RISKY SYMBIOSIS

As it happens, Colm Tóibín himself has already pointed us in this direction. *The Blackwater Lightship*, his 1999 novel that failed to win the Booker Prize, revolves around just such a risky symbiosis, triggered by the immunity breakdown wrought by the HIV virus. Featuring several gay friends, a grandmother living in her former boardinghouse, and a mother and daughter who haven't spoken for seven years, this symbiotic network, gathered around a terminally ill AIDS patient, is anything but reassuring. But no death occurs under its watch, and the estranged mother and daughter, uneasily reconciled at the end of the novel, are able to speak as a "we"—newly recombined, its fate uncertain, but not shy about laying claim to the future tense: "We'll go and see Declan later, but we'll sleep for a while first; we'll sleep for a while."[25] A risky "we" matching a risky future, but symbiotic enough to avert disaster for now.

Other books by Tóibín, notably *House of Names* (2017), a retelling of the story of Clytemnestra, also experiment with risky symbiotic forms.[26] Oprah.com says that the novel combines the "restraint of classical art with the frenzy of a Pollack painting."[27] Recombined DNA of this sort looks beyond a single author, a single medium, while opening up corresponding hazards. In a *Washington Post* online discussion, Tóibín was asked if he planned to "write a similar novel about Oscar Wilde" as a sequel to the one hosting Henry James. His answer: "I won't write another novel about a writer, I hope."[28] And he was right: so far there's been no such *novel*, though this would hardly be the end of his attempts at hosting. Drawn as he is to risky symbiosis, another try is bound to show up, if in a different genre.

The publication of *The Master* also marked the opening of Tóibín's play, *Beauty in a Broken Place*. Hosting some of the brightest lights in the Irish firmament, this parallel venture is conducted in a medium still more dangerous. Writing the play had begun while writing the novel. The commission had come at an inopportune time, but Tóibín couldn't afford to turn it down, for the simple reason that the play was already "in my novel. It gave me a chance to be a character in my novel."[29] Besides, this would be his first play, debuting at the Abbey Theatre, no less. A chance like this might never come again. There's no venue more hallowed. The risks as well as the benefits of being hosted by such an institution weren't lost on Tóibín; indeed, his play dramatizes that very subject. Beginning with the riots occasioned by Sean O'Casey's play *The Plough and the Stars* (1926)—a less-than-hagiographic account of the 1916 Easter Rising—*Beauty in a Broken Place* is in turn a less-than-hagiographic account of the Abbey Theatre, featuring a cast as iconic as Dublin can offer.

POETRY CROSSED WITH THEATER

Maude Gonne MacBride and Hanna Sheehy-Skeffington, widows of the Easter Rising, are front and center on Tóibín's stage, going all out to shut down *The Plough and the Stars* at the Abbey. W. B. Yeats, the Abbey's cofounder and guiding spirit, is front and center as well, going all out to foil them. Not quite an alter ego but very much an institution, here is a larger-than-life presence, dangerous for Tóibín to play host to, but whose DNA he probably wouldn't mind carrying.

"Yeats was like a cross between the President of the Executive Council running Ireland and Michael Collins running a guerrilla war," Tóibín's O'Casey tells us. He "hires men to carry sandwich-boards advertising the play, he speaks to them as though his own life depended on the message they carry. He spends a fortune on posters and puts big ads in the papers." No one, not even "the King of England or Julius Caesar or the Kaiser himself," would have defied the poet.[30] That isn't quite true: Yeats is in fact shouted down by the crowds. The following day, however, it's revealed that he foresaw this reaction and has already gone "to the newspapers with copies of his statement so that he didn't need to be heard. The whole country heard him in the morning. It made the headlines. He had it all ready."[31]

At the Abbey Theatre, high modernist poetry could combine quite handily with low theatrics. A cross between such extremes, though unsafe, had been something of a tradition here: dreamy-eyed poetics and not-so-dreamy-eyed politicking had always been part of Yeats's risky symbiosis since the founding of the theater in 1898.[32] The Abbey was meant as a showcase for Yeats's own plays and those by other Irish writers. But it was also a hard-nosed business proposition: the London theater scene, the new theatrical prospects in Germany, the challenge of putting on Irish plays—all these issues were on the table from the outset.[33] Yeats spoke of the theater as a "small stock company."[34] To survive financially, it needed above all a paying public from the full political spectrum, a point repeated several times in its manifesto.[35] In 1924, Yeats and Lady Gregory, the two cofounders, offered the Abbey to the Irish Free State, but they were initially turned down. The following year, however, Minister of Finance Ernest Blythe arranged for an annual subsidy of 850 pounds, making the Abbey the first publicly funded theater in the English-speaking world.

The public had reason to feel entitled; it acted accordingly when provoked.[36] And Lady Gregory was ready for it. When riots broke out in 1907 over J. M. Synge's *The Playboy of the Western World*, a "nephew at Trinity College" was asked to bring along "a few fellow athletes" to repel any attack on the stage. "Every night protestors with their trumpets came and raised a din. Every night the police carried some of them off to the police courts. Every afternoon the papers gave reports of the trial before a magistrate who had not heard or read the play and who insisted on being given details of its incidents by the accused and the police."[37]

CROSS-GENRE HYBRIDITY

For Lady Gregory as for Yeats, all this came with the territory. This wouldn't be the only time when the police was brought in, nor the only time, as Tóibín points out in *Lady Gregory's Toothbrush*, when "the founders of the Abbey Theatre reverted to their Ascendancy and Protestant backgrounds."[38] Switchable allegiances such as these weren't a fluke, a distraction from Yeats's true calling. They were the lifeblood of his risky symbiosis, his mix of poetry and theater, alternately lyricizing and grandstanding, speaking to the Ascendancy no less than to the nationalists and the Irish Republican Brotherhood. His poem "Easter 1916" is a masterly example of just such a switchable act:

> This other man I had dreamed
> A drunken, vainglorious lout.
> He had done most bitter wrong
> To some who are near my heart,
> Yet I number him in the song;
> He, too, has resigned his part
> In the casual comedy;
> He, too, has been changed in his turn,
> Transformed utterly:
> A terrible beauty is born.[39]

John MacBride, leader of the Easter Rising and Maude Gonne's estranged husband, is here "a drunken, vainglorious lout," the unsurprising fate of someone in the hands of a vindictive foe. Yet by the end of the poem, it is this reviled figure who delivers the famous last line:

"A terrible beauty is born." How could this be? Yeats, it seems, has partly rescinded his earlier verdict by hybridizing the political insurrection, combining it with a different genre. Seen as *theater*, the Easter Rising is not half bad. This is what redeems MacBride; and he is redeemed, above all, because the play in question happens to be "casual comedy." This genre has always been kind to the ignominious. Its conventions have always favored happy endings. Even drunken, vainglorious louts can bring terrible beauty into the world.

Yeats knew something about these comic conventions himself. His high-sounding words, his behind-the-scenes machinations, the over-the-top fanaticism of his on-site performance, all combined to produce a comic theater of one, every bit as riveting as what transpired on stage. Dominating the Abbey Theatre with the hybrid force of the poet and the stage manager, Yeats acted out a risky, cross-genre symbiosis, claiming for theater the same license that was poetry's birthright.

HENRY JAMES, W. B. YEATS, AND WORLD WAR I

How much poetic license could be exercised by the Abbey as a publicly funded theater, and what were its rights and obligations?[40] The poet-as-stage-manager thought he knew; the theatergoing public had other ideas. Some pushback from the audience was only to be expected. Still, for Yeats there was no question that such cross-genre hybridity would ever be discontinued. Against this unsafe symbiosis, Henry James's repertoire might seem tame; yet Yeats's reckless experimentation is not without a parallel in the novelist.

Ezra Pound, a longtime James admirer, brought out a special issue of the *Little Review* honoring him two years after his death, highlighting a genre crossing every bit as formidable as the Irish poet's: "There was emotional greatness in Henry James's hatred of tyranny," a greatness emerging from "the momentum of his art, the sheer bulk of his processes, the size of his fly-wheel." We are seriously mistaken, Pound says, if we think of James only as a miniaturist. He experimented with genre on the world stage. Indeed, we should "rest our claim for his greatness in the magnitude of his protagonists, in the magnitude of the forces he analyzed and portrayed."[41]

Writing in 1918, Pound was no doubt thinking of World War I, a genre populated by forces of hitherto unknown magnitude. James did indeed act nontrivially if equivocally in this genre, again not unlike Yeats. As Leon Edel has documented in some detail, when the war broke out James agreed to serve as chairman of the American Volunteer Motor Ambulance Corps and, in that capacity, acted very much like a seasoned lobbyist, paying frequent visits to the American Embassy in London to pressure the US government to do more for the Allies.[42] He also made a special effort to reach out to Yeats—whom he had met when both men were on the Academic Committee of the Royal Society of Literature[43]— asking him to contribute a piece to *The Book of the Homeless* (1916), a volume of essays, art, poetry, and music put together by Edith Wharton as a fund-raiser for Belgian refugees.

Yeats responded with a poem, "A Reason for Keeping Silent." The accompanying letter to James read as follows:

Dear Mr. Henry James: I have sent your friend these verses:

> "A Reason for keeping silent"
> I think it better that at times like these
> We poets keep our mouths shut; for in truth,
> We have no gift to set a statesman right;
> He's had enough of meddling who can please
> A young girl in the indolence of her youth
> Or an old man upon a winter's night.

It is the only thing I have written of the war or will write, so I hope it may not seem unfitting. I shall keep the neighbourhood of the seven sleepers of Ephesus, hoping to catch their comfortable snores till bloody frivolity is over. Yours sincerely, W B Yeats[44]

Keeping silent wasn't always a top priority for Yeats. When it came to the "bloody frivolity" that was World War I, however, it seemed to be an absolute necessity. Yeats was Anglo-Irish, with a Protestant and Ascendancy background, as already noted. He was also married to an Englishwoman and spent time regularly in London. Yet when it came to the wars of Great Britain, a fierce apathy took over. Later, Yeats would write no fewer than four poems on the death of Robert Gregory (son of Lady Gregory), speaking from the standpoint of the volunteer soldier and alternating between being caught up in the war and being utterly indifferent. It's the latter that we hear in "An Irish Airman Foresees His Death," in which Robert Gregory, more Irish in death than in life, seems to be speaking for the poet, also more Irish at this point in his uneasy symbiosis:

> Those that I fight I do not hate,
> Those that I guard I do not love;
> My country is Kiltartan Cross,
> My countrymen Kiltartan's poor,
> No likely end could bring them loss
> Or leave them happier than before.[45]

Published in 1919, "An Irish Airman Foresees His Death" belatedly explains why Yeats himself couldn't warm to a war not Ireland's, why hybrid poets like him had to "keep our mouths shut" for the duration of World War I, a strategic disability he apparently thought the American author wouldn't understand.

STRATEGIC DISABILITY

Contact with Yeats, however, seems to have brought out in James a strategic disability of his own. While serving as chairman of the American Volunteer Motor Ambulance Corps, James granted an interview with Preston Lockwood for the *New York Times*, published on March 21, 1915, and ending with an up-front request for money, for checks made out to the Ambulance Corps and sent to Brown Brothers, 59 Wall Street, New York City. But that wasn't quite the whole story. In this interview—which, as Leon Edel tells us, was actually written by James, not Lockwood[46]—there are some odd tangents, with the "fly-wheel" flying off the handle.

Given that this was an attempt to drum up war support, it was odd that James should also have *this* to say about war and its crippling effects on the English language: "The war has used up words; they have weakened, they have deteriorated like motor car tires; they have, like millions of other things, been more overstrained and knocked about and voided of the happy semblance during the last six months than in all the long ages before, and we are now confronted with a depreciation of all our terms, or, otherwise speaking, with a loss of expression through increase of limpness, that may well make us wonder what ghosts will be left to walk."[47]

This might sound like a variation on *A Farewell to Arms*, where Hemingway famously complained about "abstract words such as glory, honor, courage, or hallow" becoming "obscene" under conditions of war.[48] But James's emphasis was actually a little different—not the danger of obscenity but the danger of incapacitation, the danger of being "weakened" by exposure to contagious war rhetoric. Lacking immunity from such bombast, words suffer a semantic "limpness," a "loss of expression." "Overstrained" and "depreciat[ed]," they become ghosts of their former selves, in danger of being crippled for good, never able to walk as they once did.

This wasn't the first time James fretted over the immunity breakdown suffered by language. In a letter to Edith Wharton on March 5, 1915, and commenting on what she was doing on the French front, he wrote, "I unutterably envy you these sights and suffered assaults of the *maxima*—condemned as I am by doddering age and 'mean' infirmity to the poor mesquins *minima*."[49] On March 24 he wrote again, returning once more to the "assaults of the *maxima*" but putting a new spin on it this time, taking considerable pride now in his disabled tongue, disabled on purpose: "I put forth not the slightest pretension to measure. In fact, I think I am not measuring anything whatever just now, and not pretending to—I find myself, much more, quite consentingly dumb in the presence of the boundless enormity."[50]

THE SEMICOLON

Like Yeats, Henry James had been struck dumb, a disability apparently as strategic as the Irish poet's. One would not expect it from the chairman of the American Volunteer Motor Ambulance Corps. But a *minima* faced with the "boundless enormity" of war seemed to have no choice. And the only way this *minima* could regain some semblance of speech was, paradoxically, by standing up for something even smaller—punctuation, for instance. In response to Preston Lockwood's question, "Are you not famous, Mr. James, for the use of dashes?" James's first response was, "Dash my fame!" But he then went on in earnest about the "representative virtue" of punctuation, especially the semicolon, a small dot over the comma, so seemingly trivial yet so important to our perspective on the world. "A fine sense for the semicolon," he said, "like any sort of sense at all for the pluperfect tense and the subjunctive mood, on which the whole perspective in a sentence may depend, seems anything but common."[51]

Punctuation, verb tense, and grammatical mood—where do these three meet up? The pluperfect moves the narrative action to a more distant anterior, conjuring up a time that can't be encompassed by the simple past, while the subjunctive goes even further, conjuring up recesses of time still more remote, populated by events not actualized, not part of documented reality, yet not consignable to oblivion either. This ever-active and ever-shadowy penumbra stretches the known world a hundredfold. There are many backstories here, forking structures at various removes from what did happen. For James, these forking structures are also the essence of the semicolon. They make room for alternative forms of locomotion, alternative maps of what might yet come to pass, allowing a sentence to walk itself back, possibly going forward again, possibly heading off in a different direction, a tangent-producing nexus giving disabled authors a chance to turn their strategic dumbness into articulate speech.

Yeats was an aficionado of the semicolon perhaps for that very reason.[52] The semicolon is front and center in both "Easter 1916" and "An Irish Airman Foresees His Death." In the former, it appears twice in the four pivotal lines chronicling Yeats's change of heart toward John MacBride:

> Yet I number him in the song;
> He, too, has resigned his part
> In the casual comedy;
> He, too, has been changed in his turn

In the latter, the semicolon mediates the two faces of Robert Gregory: his flatly stated indifference to World War I and his equally flatly stated, reflexive attachment to Ireland:

> Those that I fight I do not hate,
> Those that I guard I do not love;
> My country is Kiltartan Cross,
> My countrymen Kiltartan's poor.

The semicolon is a push and pull on the rope of affect, roping in sentiments yoked together, yet each insisting on a sharp edge of irreducibility with respect to the other. Important to James and Yeats apparently for the same reason, this humble mark points to the limits of naturalization, the limits to how far an ecosystem can integrate and assimilate its conflicting loyalties. Most of us would have associated this incomplete naturalization only with the Anglo-Irish Yeats; it now appears that James is likewise susceptible.

INCOMPLETE NATURALIZATION

Early in June 1915, Henry James applied to become a British citizen. His decision was partly prompted by his discovery that as a noncitizen (categorized as a "friendly alien"), he wouldn't be able to travel to Lamb House, his home in Rye, without a certificate of permission from the government. To put a speedy end to that annoyance, James asked prime minister Herbert Asquith to serve as one of the four required witnesses attesting that he was a "respectable person" capable of "speaking and writing English decently."[53]

After his naturalization was finalized on July 26, James placed a statement in the London *Times* explaining why he chose to become a British citizen at that moment. He had been living in England for almost forty years, he said, and had formed "long friendships and associations." But it was the German atrocities in Europe that cemented his "desire to throw his weight and personal allegiance, for whatever they may be worth, into the scale of the contending nation's present and future fortunes."[54] It was just the explanation everyone was looking for. Rudyard Kipling, out of touch for years, responded instantly: "You don't know what it means or what it will go on to mean not to the Empire alone but to all the world of civilization that you've thrown in your lot with them."[55]

Still, James hadn't thrown in his lot with the British Empire to such an extent as to be fully assimilated to its cause. Against the war fever of Kipling, his coolheaded assessment becomes all the more striking. Leon Edel gives a vivid account of a particularly clear-eyed meeting with a mastermind of the war. In January 1915, James was invited to Walmer Castle, the prime minister's weekend retreat. Among those present was Winston Churchill, only forty years old but already the First Lord of the Admiralty. James had met him a month earlier, but this second encounter wasn't a happy one. Churchill had never been able to read James; he was impatient with the slow and convoluted speech of this old man; he interrupted those long sentences before James could finish them. As for James, upon his leave-taking he said to Violet Asquith, the prime minister's daughter, that it was a "very encouraging experience to meet that young man. It has brought home to me very forcibly—very vividly—the *limitations* by which men of genius obtain their ascendancy over mankind."[56]

What were the limitations of Churchill? James never elaborated, but two other authors, also not fully assimilated to Britain's cause, serve as unwitting hosts and carriers for him as they revisit Churchill over the course of a century. Propelling James's critical judgment into theaters of action well beyond his biological life span, they grant him vicarious life, a kind of assisted survival. Hosted by these two, neither of whom he could have foreseen, James's incomplete naturalization becomes part of our collective DNA, extending from the early twentieth century into the twenty-first, and with consequences for the carriers as much as what they carry. In what follows, I explore this risk ecology of time-borne contagion, adding a longitudinal axis to the standard definition of the term to highlight a future-building network, especially important here as a sustained alternative to war.

TIME-BORNE CONTAGION

I begin with Nicholson Baker. An author of small books on small things, Baker has devoted an entire chapter of his book *The Size of Thoughts* (1996) to the history of punctuation. But he has also written a book that, at 566 pages, is on the opposite side of the spectrum—*Human Smoke: The Beginnings of World War II, the End of Civilization* (2008). Reviewing the book for the *New York Times*, Colm Tóibín notes that "Baker has not done this as a literary exercise, nor as a new way of amusing himself and his readers, but because of a passionate view of how the war against Germany was conducted by Britain under Winston Churchill."[57]

Baker goes back to World War I and Churchill's decision in 1914, as First Lord of the Admiralty, to run a blockade of Germany. He justified his action with these words: "The British blockade treated the whole of Germany as if it were a beleaguered fortress, and avowedly sought to starve the whole population—men, women, and children, old and young, wounded and sound—into submission."[58] For Baker, the "end of civilization" began with that statement. And he quotes many others, the most remarkable all coming from Churchill, whose directives were carried out by the British military around the globe throughout the 1920s and 1930s and with maximum intensity during World War II. In his *New York Times* review, entitled "Their Vilest Hour," Tóibín reproduces several of these, above all this key summation of Britain's commitment to aerial bombing, a blanket infliction of harm targeting civilians as much as military installations. "One of our great aims," Churchill wrote in July 1941, "is the delivery on German towns of the largest possible quantity of bombs per night."[59]

The "limitations by which men of genius obtain their ascendancy over mankind," intuited by Henry James back in 1915, crystallized in World War II as a maximum-strength militarism, blind to any consideration other than a brute show of force. Championed by Churchill and nightly executed by the all-important Bomber Command of the Royal Air Force, blanket bombing sealed the fate of millions of civilians, in Berlin, Dresden, Hamburg, and Munich and indeed all over Europe.[60] James, of course, had been in the grave for twenty years by the time that policy was systematically enforced. Through long-distance carriers, however, his DNA has persisted beyond his biological end, a spreading gene pool turning time itself into a contagious theater.

The part Colm Tóibín plays in this DNA transfer is especially interesting. Not on record as feeling one way or another about Churchill, he becomes a vocal critic by hosting others, carrying their genes—an art congenial to him and experimented with across a range of genres, spreading from novel to play to book review. Left to his own devices, he's judiciously noncommittal about Britain's war atrocities, but he's entirely within protocol reproducing many self-incriminating Churchill quotes while reviewing *Human Smoke*. As a contagious theater, the book review is second to none. So it's not surprising that Tóibín should also reproduce this quote from a member of Churchill's own cabinet, who as early as 1914 had written, "Bombing does NOT affect Germany's morale; let's get that into our heads and not waste our bombers on these raids." And before wrapping up, he adds one more from Lord Trenchard, father of the Royal Air Force, who admitted that "the percentage of bombs that hit the military target at which they are aimed is not more than one percent."[61]

ANTIWAR IRELAND

Carrying such DNA from Baker, more potent than any direct commentary from himself, Tóibín turns his own corpus into an antiwar gene pool, allowing each of his works to be contagiously touched by *Human Smoke*. The prominent role he assigns Hanna Sheehy-Skeffington in *Beauty in a Broken Place* is especially significant in this context.

Appearing in the play as an Easter Rising widow determined to shut down the Sean O'Casey production at the Abbey Theatre, Sheehy-Skeffington was in fact a great deal more. As a suffragette and a co-founder of the Irish Women's Franchise League, she was Ireland's most prominent feminist and most vocal opponent to World War I, under surveillance by the British on both counts. In April 1915, she was prevented from attending the International Congress of Women, held at The Hague. In 1916, Francis Sheehy-Skeffington, Hanna's husband, was executed without trial by Captain John Bowen-Colthurst, even though he wasn't part of the Easter Rising and was on the street to stop the looting. Hanna refused the compensation of ten thousand pounds offered by the British government and was eventually able to force the Royal Commission to open an inquiry, leading to the conviction of Bowen-Colthurst. In December that year, she embarked on a two-year lecture tour of the United States, meeting with president Woodrow Wilson and serving as Ireland's sole representative to the League of Small and Subject Nationalities, held in New York City. Upon her return in July 1918, she was arrested and held in Holloway Prison in London. Her book, *British Militarism as I Have Known It* (1917), based on her lectures, was banned in Britain for the duration of the war.

It is this outspoken critic of World War I who emerges as the most credible symbiotic force in *Beauty in a Broken Place*: an Irish pacifism tested by fire and fused with an international feminism, a form of hybridity very different from Yeats's but, like his, at once future-building and steadily anchored to the here and now of Dublin. When Sheehy-Skeffington voices her outrage against a play that "held up to derision and obloquy the men and women of Easter Week," painting "not only the wart on Cromwell's nose" but also adding "carbuncles and running sores in a reaction against idealization,"[62] her objections aren't taken lightly: not by Tóibín's Sean O'Casey and not by Tóibín himself. Instead of getting up to refute her, as he has been planning to do, O'Casey simply says, "Oh I sat down, I don't know why I sat down."[63]

Henry James has no relation whatever to Hanna Sheehy-Skeffington, except for the fact that *Beauty in a Broken Place* was written at exactly the same time as *The Master*. Mediated by Tóibín, this less-than-fully-naturalized British citizen meets the feminist-pacifist and her adversary, the Anglo-Irish poet, in a contagious field with new entries still being added. Reproduced in all those not fully assimilated to the cause of war, such a long-distance gene pool sets into motion a subjunctive future, a road not yet taken but noteworthy all the same as an alternative to maximum-strength militarism. For Tóibín, as for Sheehy-Skeffington and Yeats, being "Irish" is shorthand for such a subjunctive future, a hoped-for world to be cherished for being so far unrealized.

SUBJUNCTIVE FUTURE

Henry James is "Irish" also in this sense, a contagious effect rather than a secure national heritage. He arrives at this weak form through being carried by others, an assisted survival giving him no more than a vicarious future, but not meaningless at its moment of inception and not without fresh input since then. James, needless to say, has nothing to say about Irishness of this sort. But even here he has help, and from the most surprising quarter.

In a short story entitled "Who's Irish?" Gish Jen offers what amounts to a gloss on induced Irishness, with little to do with one's nationality and everything to do with the company one keeps. The narrator in this story is an old Chinese woman, now taking up residence in the United States and speaking her own hybrid English. For a while she stays with her daughter and her son-in-law, John Shea, but she is being hosted now by her Irish in-law, Bess, John's mother. She could go back to China. But why should she? She has a far more interesting future here, subjunctively Irish, materializing through the words of Bess:

> The Shea sons hang around all the time, asking when will I go home, but Bess tell them, Get Lost.
> She's a permanent resident, say Bess. She isn't going anywhere.
> Of course, I shouldn't say Irish this, Irish that, especially now I am

become honorary Irish myself, according to Bess. Me! Who's Irish? I say, and she laugh. All the same, if I could mention one thing about some of the Irish, not all of them of course. I like to mention this: Their talk just stick. I don't know how Bess Shea learn to use her words, but sometimes I hear what she say a long time later. *Permanent resident. Not going anywhere.* Over and over I hear it, the voice of Bess.[64]

Irish words that "just stick"? One could say that about Gish Jen herself.[65] One could certainly say that about Hanna Sheehy-Skeffington, Colm Tóibín, and W. B. Yeats. And one could also say that about Henry James, creature of words who sticks around with the help of others, laying claim to a future more populous for being subjunctive.

5 · Vaguely Islamic

HENRI MATISSE, JAMES JOYCE, EZRA POUND, AND LANGSTON HUGHES, WITH PAUL BOWLES

Could a case be made for a weaker form of what is otherwise a "strong" religion? One of the strongest today is Islam—the world's second largest, with almost 1.57 billion followers, many visibly set apart in ritual and apparel. It draws a clear line between itself and other faiths, not to say secular life.

And yet Islam hasn't always been strong in this way but messier, variant rich, permeated by its millennium-long contact with cultures around the world. Robert Irwin speaks of the emergence of an "Islamic world system" between the years 1000 and 1500 CE, stretching at one point from Spain to India and China.[1] This world system was multilingual and multicultural from the first, a cacophony of local practices, with foreign converts only partially assimilated and fueling its growth through uneven hybridization. The military success of Islam, for instance, was largely due to the Turkish-speaking "steppe barbarians," who adopted the Muslim faith but kept their own language while furthering the cause of jihad with their battle prowess, creating increasingly divergent forms of the religion in South Asia, North Africa, and central and western Europe.[2]

Even before these military victories, Islam had already been expanding—and unevenly hybridizing—in its religious base. Spearheading this development was Sufi mysticism, a popular form of Islam emerging around the eighth century and emphasizing the direct experience of God outside the Ulama, the state-sponsored clerical orthodoxy. The Sufi followers—*faqirs* in Arabic and *darwish* in Persian—organized themselves into small groups, each led by its own spiritual leader, called a *shaykh* in Syria and Iraq, *pir* or *musrhid* in Persia and India, and *muqaddam* in

Africa. As is clear from these polyglot incarnations, Sufism had many local names. Operating well below the power of the state or the clergy, it spread rapidly for just that reason, mixing lessons from the Qur'an with folk practices borrowed from every religion in sight: "Christian, Jewish, Gnostic, and indeed Buddhist and Zoroastrian," according to Fazlur Rahman. By the ninth century, Islam was hybridized to the point where it was a religion less of the zealous than of the "half-converted and nominally converted."[3]

Marshall Hodgson has coined a new word, *Islamicate* as opposed to *Islamic*, to describe these weak, hybrid formations.[4] I won't be using the neologism in this chapter, though the literary phenomenon I call "vaguely Islamic" is very much part of that process, exemplified here by Henri Matisse, James Joyce, Ezra Pound, and Langston Hughes. These four remain perched on the outer edges of Islam (if they have even made it that far), looking at it sometimes intently and sometimes absent-mindedly, for reasons of their own, and through the illuminating but fraught lens of Morocco, which two of them never visited. Seen through that lens, Islam is often no more than a cipher—abstract, atmospheric, barely there. These vague allusions, perhaps deliberately vague, are nonetheless not trivial or without some far-reaching implications.[5] Indeed, as I will argue, fuzzy portraits such as these might turn out to be "subjunctive futures" of sorts (as I've been calling them throughout this book): risky experiments making room for alternative realities, not bothered by their slim chances of materializing, their no doubt weak resemblance to existing facts.

Still, Matisse, Joyce, Pound, and Hughes aren't reliable guides on their own. Their vague accounts become significant only through a mediating collectivity, only when seen against contrary efforts by others. I'll begin not with them but with Paul Bowles, an antithetical figure: making his home in Morocco, witnessing its turmoil firsthand, and taking the full measure of Islam in a way that both amplifies its explosive tensions and raises the stakes for the weaker forms offered by Matisse, Joyce, Pound, and Hughes.

SERIOUSLY MOROCCAN

When Bowles died in 1999, he had been living in Tangier, Morocco, for fifty-two years. He had first visited that city and port in 1931 in the company of Aaron Copland, a stay of a few months that made it clear just what an extraordinary place it was: a trading hub since the fifth century BCE, first settled by Phoenicians and Carthaginians and surviving into the twentieth century with a dizzying mix of languages and religions, with Berbers and Arabs living uneasily alongside the Spanish and the French.

Bowles was by no means the first Westerner to arrive. If anything, he was a latecomer. Morocco had been a destination for diplomats and spies, writers and painters since the nineteenth century. The first overseas property owned by the US State Department was the American Legation Building in the medina of Tangier, a Moorish mansion presented to the United States in 1821 by sultan Moulay Sulliman in celebration of the 1786 Moroccan-American Treaty of Friendship. Mark Twain showed up just after the Civil War and found enough material to fill a couple of chapters in *Innocents Abroad* (1869). Kaiser Wilhelm II showed up as well, landing in Tangier on March 31, 1905, in an ostentatious bid for dominance. Known as the First Moroccan (or Tangier) Crisis, it had the effect of lining up Britain, Russia, Spain, Italy, and the United States behind France—a slap in the face for Germany and a dress rehearsal for World War I. France, meanwhile, acting on its own and sending troops far inland, precipitated the Second Moroccan (or Agadir) Crisis, with an unsurprising outcome: the Treaty of Fez (1912) ended the independence of Morocco, dividing it into French and Spanish protectorates.

Westerners now started arriving in large numbers. Edith Wharton came during the final days of World War I at the invitation of the French resident general, Hubert Lyautey, and dedicated her *In Morocco* (1920) to him. Matisse visited several times in 1912 and 1913 and produced many Morocco-inspired works, including landscapes such as *Vue sur la baie de Tanger* (1912); portraits such as *Le rifain debout* (1912); and architectural paintings featuring iconic buildings, such as *Le marabout* (1912/13). It was Matisse who persuaded Gertrude Stein and Alice B. Toklas to make the trip, and Stein who in turn persuaded Bowles and Copland, reassuring them that the Hotel Villa de France was excellent, with a piano to be had for the asking.

Bowles returned to the Maghreb all through the 1930s and early 1940s, tumultuous decades, with Morocco once again as its epicenter. Though Tangier had been designated an international zone since 1923 and administered by a committee of eight nations,[6] this did not stem the anticolonial tide, on the rise since the 1912 Fez riots and erupting once again into the open during World War II. Spanish troops under General Francisco Franco occupied the city on June 14, 1940, the same day German troops entered Paris. This all-out war among the colonial powers further inflamed Moroccan nationalism. In January 1944, the Istiqlal Party issued a manifesto demanding independence for Morocco, national reunification, and a democratic constitution, all of which the French rejected out of hand.

It was during this latest crisis that Bowles returned once again in 1947, this time to remain. In December 1952, a riot broke out in Casablanca over the murder of a Tunisian labor leader. The following year, France exiled sultan Muhammad V to Madagascar, replacing him with the unpopular Mohammed Ben Aarafa, a move that made a united front out of the warring Moroccan political parties. In 1955, riots broke out in Tangier itself. Faced with this escalating violence and with similar violence in Algeria, the French finally gave in, restoring Muhammad V and agreeing to negotiations for independence. Tangier was returned to Moroccan rule in 1956.

Bowles lived through all these crises apparently unfazed. From 1959 to 1961, he traveled across North Africa, making field recordings of Moroccan music for the Library of Congress. In the 1960s, he began collecting and translating the tales of oral storytellers, especially Mohammed Mrabet, Larbi Layachi (Driss Ben Hamed Charhadi), Mohamed Choukri, and Ahmed Yacoubi.[7] He remained a US citizen, but the permanence and primacy of his tie to Morocco were never for a moment in doubt.[8]

That was his chosen life and his fatal limitation, according to his obituary in the *New York Times*. Rather than forging ahead, Bowles had "retreated to Tangier and become a collector of Arabian stories and songs." Moving ever "farther away from the world of publishing and society toward an unknown destination," he had become "an artist whose name evoked an atmosphere of dark, lonely Moroccan streets and endless scorching deserts, a haze of hashish and drug-induced visions."[9] The *Wall Street Journal* was still more damning with its obituary. "A Nihilist's Wasted Talent," the headline read. Succumbing to a "life of kif and stupor," Bowles had allowed Morocco to "make him a victim of himself."[10]

Perhaps the best example of what it takes to be seriously Moroccan, Paul Bowles will be an intermittent but indispensable presence in this chapter. For while the focus here is on four other figures, it is only against his example—and those of Twain and Wharton—that the fraught attempts of Matisse, Joyce, Pound, and Hughes become correspondingly instructive. These four never set out to be advocates or conduits of Islam. A claim could be made on their behalf only when those tasks are broadly distributed and borne by others, a mediating network with many entry points, most at some distance from Islam and complementing one another in just that capacity.

JAMES JOYCE'S GIBRALTAR

Joyce's entry point is of course not Morocco but at still another remove. It's the military outpost across the strait, with its own complicated relations to Spain and to North Africa, that offers the first glimpse of Islam. Gibraltar, Molly's girlhood home, is a surprisingly conspicuous presence in *Ulysses* (1922) almost from start to finish. As Richard Brown points out, in quantitative terms roughly "a fifth to a quarter" of the novel's "Penelope" episode is set here, making it the novel's significant "other" locale.[11] It's odd that in a novel so focused on Dublin and circumscribed by Ireland, the last chapter should have this unexpected foray, vaulting to a place so far outside that orbit.

Robert Martin Adams shows that Joyce had done his research with customary thoroughness, reading up on details of streets and names of shops in the *Gibraltar Directory*, just as he had done with *Thom's Dublin Directory*.[12] Never to visit Gibraltar himself, Joyce also drew heavily from Henry Field's *Gibraltar* (1888) and repeated some of its errors, including its tendency to make too much of a good thing. Field emphasizes, for instance, the magnificent vistas opening up from Gibraltar. An officer on duty can, "with his field-glasses, sweep the whole horizon, north and south, from the Sierra Nevada in Spain, to the long chain of the Atlas Mountains in Africa."[13] Joyce recycles this information and makes the views still more breathtaking by equipping Molly with a borrowed spyglass, which enables her to "see over to Morocco almost the bay of Tangier white and the Atlas mountain with snow on it."[14]

As field guides go, *Ulysses* seems less informative than most. It also happens to be factually incorrect. As Don Gifford drily observes, "On a clear day, Molly could easily see Morocco, but Tangier, 35 miles through the straits to the southwest, would be masked by headlands, and the snowcapped Saharan Atlas Mountains in Algeria, 375 miles to the south-east, are clearly out of range."[15] Joyce's account of Morocco is both heavily mediated, in this case compounding the prior errors of others, and descriptively vague, with the snowcapped "Atlas mountain" and the "bay of Tangier white" the only landmarks in sight, the whiteness of the sea shading into the whiteness of the snow in a monochrome continuum.

Not a city but a body of water, Joyce's "bay of Tangier white" is an integral part of the Mediterranean. And it's Mediterranean in another sense as well. Seen from a distance, it's idealized as Gibraltar is idealized—as a cultural as well as a geographical counterpoint to Dublin, open and vibrant where Dublin is inbred and insular.[16] These are the sights and sounds Molly recalls: "the Spanish girls laughing in their shawls and their tall combs and the auctions in the morning the Greeks and the jews and the Arabs and the devil knows who else from all the ends of Europe."[17] Jews and Arabs might have been expelled from Andalusia according to historical record, and Spain and Britain might have been at each other's throats for centuries, but Molly notices no trace of such hostilities. Her girlhood home is a garrison town seen as a teeming bazaar, with all the ethnicities of the Mediterranean converging but not colliding. Islam is both present and absent here, disappearing into an ambient backdrop, a helter-skelter crowd, nonsectarian, nonspecific.

MARK TWAIN, EDITH WHARTON, AND PAUL BOWLES: COLONIALISM'S PALETTE

Mark Twain's *Innocents Abroad* offers a revealing contrast here. Gibraltar, the first place to greet Twain's eyes after his passage across the Atlantic, is an unforgettable sight, but unforgettable mostly as an armed-to-the-teeth "walled town" built on a rock, where "everywhere you choose to look, is clad with masonry and bristling with guns."[18] Upon landing, even more unforgettable are the underground fortifications "the English have blasted out in the rock," with cannons sticking out of portholes at short intervals: "There is a mile or so of this subterranean work, and it must have cost a vast deal of money and labor. The gallery guns command the peninsula and the harbors of both oceans, but they might as well not be there, I should think, for an army could hardly climb the perpendicular wall of the rock anyhow."[19]

As befits a garrison town, Gibraltar is defined by its guns. These in turn are set against a riot of colors, making *Innocents Abroad* the opposite of the monochrome *Ulysses*. Along with the "red and blue" uniform of the British soldiers and their "undress costumes of snowy white," we also see the dark-skinned Spanish girls; "veiled Moorish beauties (I suppose they are beauties) from Tarifa"; "turbaned, sashed, and trousered Moorish merchants from Fez, and long-robed, bare-legged, ragged Muhammadan vagabonds from Tetuan and Tangier, some brown, some yellow and some as black as virgin ink—and Jews from all around."[20] Twain is clearly describing the same mix of English and Spanish, Moors and Jews that Molly so fondly recalls, but what is striking here is how many more North African locales are mentioned, and how emphatic those brown, yellow, and black "Muhammadan vagabonds" are, not vague at all but hotly clamorous, all but drowning out the red-blue-and-white.

The monochrome palette in Joyce's "bay of Tangier white and the Atlas mountain with snow on it" is shared by no other author. Even Edith Wharton, determined to show that Morocco had achieved unprecedented peace and prosperity under the French, is struck by the not-to-be-ignored presence of "three swarthy musicians" at a dance, set into relief by the "celestial snow . . . where the Atlas floated above mists." Tacitly, she recalibrates the meaning of the scene she is witnessing:

> It was a grave static dance, such as David may have performed before the Ark; untouched by mirth or folly, as beseemed a dance in that somber land, and borrowing its magic from its gravity . . . only when, one by one, the performers detached themselves from the round and knelt before us for the *paseta* it was customary to press on their foreheads, did one see, by the moisture which made the coin adhere, how quick and violent their movements had been.[21]

The Atlas is a constant for all authors, but the accompanying colors can't be more different. Joyce's snowcapped mountain flows into the "bay of Tangier white" with no break, no indication of distance between the two, and nothing to suggest any intervening complication. Wharton's mountain, on the other hand, serenely white as long as it stays above the snow line, is greeted by the swarthiness of the musicians and the dark "gravity" of the dance the moment it hits the ground, producing enough heat and sweat to make a coin stick to the foreheads of the dancers. That coin, the *paseta*, belies the claim that the dance is "customary," as ancient as King David. Ancient it might be, but local dancers receiving the Spanish coin while kneeling before a foreign audience speak volumes about Morocco's present. The dance has been countersigned by colonialism and stamped with its palette, its clash of colors.

Even to Wharton, modernity meant at least that much. To Paul Bowles, on-site witness to the trauma of decolonization, modernity and the clash of colors are inseparable. "A Distant Episode," (1947) one of his best-known stories, is a stark reminder of how Europeans fare when left to the mercy of the locals. As for the Atlas mountain, it's everywhere in his work, and never without a jarring colonial accompaniment. *Their Heads Are Green and Their Hands Are Blue* (1957), his oddly hued account of prewar travels from French Morocco through Algeria and into the Sahara, seems to cast modernity itself as a surreal palette, recent in its provenance but seemingly timeless in its lasting effects. "One is inclined to forget that the French began to settle in Morocco only at the time of World War I," Bowles writes. "Xauen, whose mountains are visible from the terrace of my apartment in Tangier, was entered by European troops for the first time in 1920. Even in southern Algeria, where one is likely to think of the French as having been stationed for a much longer time, there are war monuments bearing battle dates as recent as 1912." And "south of the Grand Atlas it was 1936 before 'pacification' came to an end."[22] No celestial snow for this Atlas mountain: it's mired in the blood and gore of geopolitics. Bowles himself, traveling "over the Grand Atlas to Ouarzazat, full of excitement at the prospect of seeing the Casbah there with its strange painted towers," was stranded at a truck stop for three days and then sent "straight back to Marrakech, having seen nothing but Foreign Legionnaires, and having heard no music other than the bugle calls that issued every so often from the nearby camp."[23]

FUZZY KNOWLEDGE

For Bowles, the modernity that glows like a surreal palette can quickly turn into a regimented khaki when colonialism snaps into focus. That snapping into focus is what *Ulysses* resists, as it also seems to do with the global capital that Fredric Jameson and Enda Duffy see as overtaking

Dublin.[24] And yet colonialism and capitalism, though never directly on exhibit, are never entirely absent either, giving the novel an expanding list of consumer goods as well as war dead, putting even the Atlas mountain and the Bay of Tangier into a blood-soaked color field:

> I went up windmill hill to the flats that Sunday morning with Captain Rubios that was dead spyglass like the sentry had he said hed have one or two from on board I wore that frock from the B Marche Paris and the coral necklace the straits shining I could see over to Morocco almost the bay of Tangier white and the Atlas mountain with snow on it and the straits like a river so clear Harry Molly Darling I was thinking of him on the sea all the time after at mass when my petticoat began to slip down at the elevation weeks and weeks I kept the handkerchief under my pillow for the smell of him there was no decent perfume to be got in that Gibraltar only that cheap peau despagne that faded and left a stink on you more than anything else I wanted to give him a memento he gave me that clumsy Claddagh ring for luck that I gave Gardner going to South Africa where those Boers killed him with their war and fever but they were well beaten all the same.[25]

Frocks from Paris department stores (and, no doubt, better perfumes in the future) go hand in hand with a globe-trotting military, with its fortified bases, constant troop movements, and many casualties. This is the moment when we get a glimpse of a gun-clad Gibraltar spilling out into the rest of the world. But it's just a glimpse, fleeting, wrapped in a sensory and mnemonic overload, and quickly passed over, because it happens to be mediated and circumscribed by the consciousness of Molly, who isn't thinking about colonialism at all but rather about the various men from various points in her life: Harry Mulvey, her first love, the one who gave her the claddagh ring, now dead; Captain Gardner, the new recipient of the ring, later killed in the Boer War; Captain Rubios, her beau for the occasion who loaned her the spyglass, now also dead; and of course Leopold Bloom, thankfully still alive, but mixed up with all the others.

This tangle of men, whose distance from one another is deliberately not specified, not measured with any numerical precision, collapses space and time into the same liquid solvent, a sensory pool and refracting medium for events both large and small, magnifying some and mini-mizing others in an across-the-board scalar indeterminacy. It's not just that the Boer War is now roughly the same size as the claddagh ring. The concentrated attention given to this ring—the initial gift of it and the death of its final bearer—creates a significant degree of foreshort-ening, so much so that everything between those two points, Gibraltar and South Africa, is either emptied out or dissolved into a kind of atmo-spheric haze. Morocco, in this hazy rendition, is simply the place on the other side of the Strait of Gibraltar. It's not depopulated, but much of the trauma that had historically convulsed that population is barely present, accessible only as fuzzy knowledge.

Of course, Molly would not be the one to tell us that there was a long and fraught history between North Africa and Spain, that the word *Moor* still conjured up unquiet specters long after 1492, when Granada, the last of the Islamic cities, fell to Ferdinand and Isabella, and Andalusia once again came under Christian rule. Even though she herself is probably of Jewish descent from her mother, Lunita Laredo (as Phillip Herring, Marilyn Reizbaum, and others have argued),[26] she might not know that Jews were banished along with the Moors after the Reconquista, and that the 1712 Treaty of Utrecht, by which Spain formally ceded Gibraltar to Britain, carried an explicit clause prohibiting Jews as well as Arabs from settling in the city. And since the narrative present for her is the Dublin of 1904, and she's thinking back to her girlhood in Gibraltar in 1884–85, the 1905 Tangier Crisis, the 1911 Agadir Crisis, and the 1912 Treaty of Fez are all in the future, out of reach for her. She wouldn't know any of these things. But Joyce most certainly did.[27]

"This very instant," Leopold Bloom famously laments in the "Cy-clops" episode, Jews are being "Plundered. Insulted. Persecuted. . . . Sold by auction in Morocco like slaves or cattle."[28] While Jews techni-cally weren't slaves in Morocco in 1904, they were subject by law to "compulsory service," made to perform menial tasks even on the Sab-bath.[29] Jewish refugees arriving in Tangier, meanwhile, were harassed and eventually massacred by the sultan's troops between November 16 and December 7, 1903.[30] Joyce seemed to have this incident in mind in singling out Morocco as the epicenter of anti-Semitism. Still, this is an unusually emphatic moment; elsewhere in *Ulysses*, historical trauma is almost always fuzzy knowledge: abstracted, rescaled, put through the filter of a deliberately constrained palette.

HENRI MATISSE'S COLOR FIELD

Henri Matisse's Moroccan paintings offer an interesting parallel here: like Joyce's snow-covered Atlas mountain and Bay of Tangier white, many of these works are monochrome or nearly so, more compositional than representational in their use of color, and able to render fuzzy knowledge into a sustained visual effect. While Joyce's Morocco is mostly white, many of Matisse's Moroccan works are blue green. In each case, the narrow range of the palette produces a stylized, washed-out effect, at once geometrizing and idealizing the subject.

Le marabout (1912/13) is a case in point (fig. 5.1). Painted during Matisse's first trip to Morocco, it represents an actual site in the Casbah of Tangier: the Marabout de Sidi-Berraïsoul, the tomb of a Muslim saint.[31] Inspired by the black-and-white postcards and photographs of the time and by the muted tones in the Tangier paintings by Matisse's friend Albert Marquet, this painting is likewise muted, with serene blues and greens covering almost the entire canvas. This unusual tonality is all the more notable because the actual color of much of the architecture in

Fig. 5.1 Henri Matisse, *Le marabout* (1912/13). Private Collection.

Fig. 5.2 Anon., Postcard (n.d.). Tangier, Casbah Marabout de Sidi-Berraïsoul. Aga Khan Program for Islamic Architecture and the Visual Collections of the Fine Arts Library, Harvard University.

Tangier, and especially the Marabout de Sidi-Berraïsoul, is not blue green but white (fig. 5.2).

This nonrepresentational palette is still more striking in *Le rifain debout* (1912) (fig. 5.3), another blue-green work, featuring a wary-looking Riffian with a hard stare. The Riffians, Berbers from the northeastern

Fig. 5.3 Henri Matisse, *Le rifain debout* (1912). State Hermitage Museum, St. Petersburg.

part of the country known as the Rif, have often been taken to symbol-ize an undefeated, precolonial Morocco.[32] Marcel Sembat, reviewing the painting at the 1913 Galerie Bernheim-Jeune exhibition and noting the young man's "angular face" and "ferocious build," was directly reminded of Islamic threats from the past: "How can you look at this splendid bar-barian without thinking of the warriors of days gone by! Such a fierce expression—just like that of the Moors of The Song of Roland!"[33]

Threat was very much in the air. Matisse had barely left Morocco in April 1912 when soldiers mutinied on the seventeenth, angered by the Treaty of Fez and the annexation of their country as a French protector-ate. Sixty-six Europeans, forty-two Jews, and some six hundred Moroc-cans died in the ensuing violence. The Riffians were hardly an isolated case in that context. Not foreseeing this, Matisse seemed nonetheless to have gone out of his way to downplay the supposed ferocity of a poten-tial insurgent. Rather than zeroing in on the weapon the Riffian is carry-ing, much of the painting is devoted instead to the green wool *djellaba* worn over the weapon, making its wearer shapeless and impassive. This *djellaba*, in turn, is part of a larger composition, a lengthwise division of the background into a rectangle of loosely brushed blue and one of loosely brushed green, a light, vegetal palette that tempers the reputed bloodthirstiness of the subject.

As Pierre Schneider points out in his catalog essay for the 1990 exhi-bition at the National Gallery of Art, Matisse began a "process of bota-nization" during his stay in Morocco, turning humans into blue-green geometrical shapes.[34] In *Le rifain debout*, this blue-green geometry be-came the basis for what the artist would call, after World War II, an art of "refuge"—though he was quick to add, "I came to realize that there was no refuge and that one must live with one's robe of Nessus."[35] He had already been experimenting with such art in many of his Moroccan works. *Vue sur la baie de Tanger* (1912) (fig. 5.4) is another example, offer-ing a somewhat different ratio of blue to green and perhaps a hint of the "robe of Nessus" lurking just beyond.

Painted during Matisse's first visit to Tangier, this work presents a panorama of the city, ringed by hills and the bay to the left, drawn in wiry lines with pen and ink. While the dominant color here is ochre—a thin wash of it covering much of the beach, with a deeper, more solid pig-ment on a large building to the left and a corresponding patch of earth to the right—the dynamics of this composition rest not on this color alone

Fig. 5.4 Henri Matisse, *Vue sur la baie de Tanger* (1912). Musée de Grenoble.

but on its interplay with three others. The blue and green are here but dark, leaden, the color of the overcast sky and the storm-threatened sea. The color white is here as well, on the domed portion of the marabout. Finally, still more striking is the presence of the color black: hooded figures in burqas gathered around the marabout in the foreground, a reminder of the local dress code and the local faith, not quite blending with the beach scene. These vertical black figures are echoed by horizontal shapes—black boats in the dark-blue sea. Together, they give the painting an intimated future in which Islam is a force to reckon with, and storm is a distinct possibility.

That intimated future notwithstanding, the black figures are nonetheless part of an ochre ambience for the time being, a composition played out without incident among its constituent colors. Islam's presence here is painterly rather than doctrinal. As embodied by these black figures, it exists as a pictorial ingredient rather than a coded menace, a surface effect rather than a hidden interior with unknown motives. *Vue sur la baie de Tanger* remains what it sets out to be, a relaxed scene of

Fig. 5.5 Henri Matisse, *Les Marocains* (1915–16). Museum of Modern Art, New York.

everyday enjoyment, done with a light touch and covered only in the thinnest washes of pigment, an exposed canvas with no room for any version of Islam other than a "weak" one: lacking in intrigue, lacking in militancy, with no sensational appeal and no political threat to speak of.

Unlike the French Orientalists—Jean-Léon Gérôme among others, who had traveled to North Africa since the early nineteenth century and produced titillating portraits of exotic customs and nude women bathing—Matisse painted instead fully clothed and minimally rendered figures standing or sitting at ease. He concentrated on the designs of buildings and textiles, and most of all the quality of light, played out as always through color and through geometry.[36] After his return to France, he began to experiment with the color black as a tribute to the shadow-casting brightness of the tropical sun. When he produced his last Moroccan painting, *Les Marocains* (1915–16) (fig. 5.5), three years after his stay in North Africa and meant indeed as art of "refuge" during the dark days of World War I, he said he was trying to "use pure black as a color of light and not as a color of darkness."[37]

Far more abstract than Matisse's other Moroccan paintings, *Les Marocains* follows a tripartite division. At the top left is a glimpse of the dome of the marabout, seen here as white, and a pot of disklike blue-and-white flowers sitting on the corner of a balcony. Underneath, at the bottom left, are four yellow melons amid large green leaves. Both of these, set against an intense, opaque black, are relatively easy to decipher. What we find on the right is far more puzzling: a rectangle of pink with a group of seated Moroccans, apparently at prayer but bare and enigmatic, in sharp contrast with the legible forms of architecture and still life on the left. The only recognizable figure here is a blue-clad priest in the foreground with his back to us, wearing a white turban; but the oval shapes in the middle distance and the angular planes at the top are barely rendered as human forms.

Many critics have been struck by this and by the lack of transition in this tripartite canvas. Each component part is "isolated, hemmed in," Pierre Schneider writes.[38] Still, the almost cubist abstraction of the painting could itself be a thread of continuity: Alfred Barr and Jack Flam argue that the repetition of rectangles and ovals, circles and half circles creates the "visual equivalents of assonance, rhyme, and alliteration."[39] Above all, it's the color black—thick, primal, nonnegotiable, and clashing with the pink, the green, and the yellow—that gives the painting its own distinctive syntax. If black is indeed "as luminous as the other colors,"[40] as Matisse insisted, a "color of light and not . . . a color of darkness," that light is defined nonetheless by the shadow it casts, by a constitutive darkness now emphatically in the foreground. *Les Marocains* is the opposite of *Vue sur la baie de Tanger* in this sense, reversing the color ratio of the earlier painting, its opaque and unmodulated black now dominant and bringing with it an Islam equally so.

That kind of black has perhaps always been implicitly there in most of the Moroccan paintings, even when the blues and greens are in the foreground. Yet black isn't the color most emblematic of Matisse, nor is it one that would end up taking over his corpus. Indeed, at the very end of his life, especially the signature year 1952, the outpouring of paintings would once again be in blue and green.[41] The color black, potent but held on reserve, in abeyance, is underutilized in much of Matisse, not unlike the underutilization of knowledge in John Rawls's "veil of ignorance."[42] Like Rawls's information-withholding and justice-facilitating veil, these paintings keep their contours fuzzy, not fleshed out in any way that would have crystallized the outcome. What results is an Islam invoked but also held in suspense, not pushed through to any definitive conclusion. While the white dome of the marabout and the white turban of the priest echo each other and set up a diagonal that cedes two-thirds of the painting to that religion, the sketchy outlines of the worshippers leave that space as space, barely occupied, barely articulated. I call this low-resolution Islam Matisse's Calypso effect.

CALYPSO EFFECT

Calypso (1935) (fig. 5.6) is one of the six etchings Matisse produced in 1934 for a special illustrated edition of James Joyce's *Ulysses*.[43] While eager to take on the assignment (which came with five thousand dollars from the American publisher George Masey), Matisse apparently never bothered to read Joyce's novel, basing his work solely on the six episodes from Homer's *Odyssey*. In that epic poem, Calypso is the daughter of Atlas, a sea nymph who keeps Odysseus holed up on her island, Ogygia, shielding him from the wrath of Poseidon but also delaying his journey home by a good seven years. In Matisse's *Calypso*, this thin line between refuge and prison is minimally rendered, featuring several intertwined figures with no facial features and barely sketched bodily details, locked in a tangle of limbs and motions, possibly companionable and possibly adversarial. True to the etymology of her name (from Καλυψώ, meaning "to cover," "to conceal," or "to hide"), Matisse's figure of Calypso is a soft blur, its either-or vagueness never resolved, occupying both ends of a low-resolution spectrum.

A spectrum of that nature is equally interesting to Joyce, though for reasons probably somewhat different from Matisse's. "Calypso," the fourth episode of *Ulysses* and the first in which Leopold Bloom appears, also happens to feature a religion, in the foreground but noticeably out of focus, sketchy to a fault. Reversing the westward journey of the marital bed, shipped to Dublin "all the way from Gibraltar," Bloom finds himself transported east in a flight of fancy, to some distant locale vaguely North African or even Middle Eastern, with Islam prominently if imprecisely invoked: "The shadows of the mosques along the pillars: priest with a scroll rolled up. A shiver of the trees, signal, the evening wind. I pass on. Fading gold sky. A mother watches from her doorway. She calls her children home in their dark language. High wall: beyond strings twanged. Night sky moon, violet, colour of Molly's new garters. Strings. Listen. A girl playing one of these instruments what do you call them: dulcimers. I pass."[44]

On the scale of verisimilitude, "Calypso" probably scores even lower

Fig. 5.6 Henri Matisse, *Calypso* (1935). © Succession H. Matisse / Artists Rights Society, New York. Harvard Art Museums / Fogg Museum, Gray Collections of Engravings Fund. Photograph: © President and Fellows of Harvard College.

than the "Penelope" episode. Bloom himself says as much, musing, "Probably not a bit like it really. Kind of stuff you read: in the track of the sun. Sunburst on the titlepage."[45] Islam for Bloom is low-resolution because secondhand, derived in this case from a travelogue, Frederick Diodati Thompson's *In the Track of the Sun* (1893). Vague to the point of parody, there's nonetheless something to be said for such scattered illumination—"sunburst on the titlepage" and perhaps not much else, but sunburst nonetheless. When Joyce began work on his next book, *Finnegans Wake* (1939), immediately upon the completion of *Ulysses*, Islam would once again be there, also book derived, with bits and pieces taken from the Qur'an and many secondary works and subject this time to the scrambling that Joyce has made his signature.

PORTMANTEAU RELIGION

James Atherton, in his pioneering study, *The Books at the Wake*, says that "Joyce was probably talking about himself when he made his Shaun say of his Shem: 'I have his quoram of images all on my retinue, Mohammadhawn Mike' (443.1)."[46] The portmanteau *Mohammadhawn*—at once a Mohammedan and a *homadhaun*, Irish for "a lout"—is a counterintuitive but not unfitting description of the author of *Finnegans Wake*, far more versed in Islam since his last book. The very fact that the Qur'an is encoded as "quoram" and equipped with a retinue/retina makes it clear that Joyce's starting point is no longer Gibraltar but some place closer to home, a bookish haven. The reference here is to the first European translation of the Qur'an, a Latin text by one "Robert of Retina," a detail Joyce no doubt picked up from Thomas Hughes's *Dictionary of Islam*, where the translator in question, Robert of Cheshire, is referred to in this way, and the Koran is always given its transliterated Arabic spelling, *Qur-an*.[47]

Joyce began writing *Finnegans Wake* in 1922. By 1924, installments of this new work began to appear in serialized form in two Parisian literary magazines, the *Transatlantic Review* and *transition*, under the title "fragments from *Work in Progress*." The actual title was not revealed (and perhaps not even decided on) until May 4, 1939, when these pieces were published under one cover. During the seventeen years it took to write the book, Joyce filled some fifty notebooks with entries he jotted down and took great care to preserve, mostly passages from books or newspapers he was reading, followed by his own comments.[48] Entries on Islam are especially abundant in notebooks 24, 31, and 45.[49] Among these are references to a French translation of the Qur'an by J.-C. Mardrus (a copy of which Joyce owned, though only the first thirty-three pages were cut),[50] along with excerpts from the articles "Mahommedan Religion,"

"Mahomet," and "Mecca" in the *Encyclopædia Britannica*;[51] *The Speeches and Table-Talk of the Prophet Mohammad* by Stanley Lane-Poole;[52] *The Story of Mohammed*, a 1914 biography by Edith Holland; and Sir Richard Burton's *The Book of the Thousand Nights and a Night*, with extensive notes on the doctrine and practice of Islam in Joyce's own marginalia, running from 1922 through 1939.[53] When a given Notebook entry was incorporated into *Work in Progress*, he would cross it out with a colored crayon. The pages with references to Islam are among those most heavily crossed out: they can be deciphered only when viewed through a filter tinted orange-red, the color of the crayon Joyce used in deleting the entries.

Color is important to *Finnegans Wake* in other ways as well. This novel is nothing if not data-flooded when it comes to Islam, overflowing with what most readers would consider arcana, made still more arcane by an unfamiliar palette wrought by the portmanteaus. We see this almost as soon as the novel begins, in one of its most iconic sentences: "Our cubehouse still rocks as earwitness to the thunder of his arafatas but we hear also through successive ages that shebby choruysh of unkalified muzzlenimissilehims that would blackguardise the whitestone ever hurtleturtled out of heaven."[54]

The "cubehouse" is a reference to the Kaaba, a cube-shaped building at the center of the holiest mosque in Mecca, al-Masjid al-Haram, linked here to the other icon of Islam, Mount Arafat, where the prophet Muhammad gave his sermon on the essence of the Muslim faith. The Kaaba is marked by a stone, said to be white when first descended from heaven but darkened—"blackguardised"—over the ages by human sin. So far, the color iconography of the sentence seems in keeping with doctrine, though not entirely, for the blackguards here are not sinners in general but a more puzzling group: "that shebby choruysh of unkalified muzzlenimissilehims." "Choruysh" could refer to the Kuraysh tribe that ruled Mecca, Muhammad's own kinsmen who treated him badly, as Roland McHugh has suggested. But it could also be a "chorus," and a shabby one, made up not of credentialed Muslims but of those unqualified—"unkalified muzzlenimissilehims"—two more portmanteaus that seem to have packed in *muezzin* (whose job it is to call worshippers to prayers), *him* (litany of Qur'anic verses), and "missile," the stones thrown by pilgrims as they perform their ritual circling around the

Kaaba, as well as a non-Islamic word with an edge to it, "muzzle." An author who calls himself *Mohammadhawn Mike* could well be one such *unkalified muzzlenimissilehim*.

AUDITORY OVEREXPOSURE

Portmanteaus, Joyce's signature creation in *Finnegans Wake*, bring a new sensory dynamics—and a new kind of vagueness—to bear on Islam. Since *muezzin*, *him*, and *muzzle* all have to do with sound, and are themselves combined and recombined through the scrambling of phonemes and morphemes, words like *muzzlenimissilehim* are aural phenomena above all, marked by the uncertain boundaries of sound, much more so than ordinary English words. As befits a novel featuring a family of Earwickers, the cubehouse bears not eyewitness but "earwitness," a far less trustworthy source of information, raising the possibility that the religion here might be no more than hearsay. After all, the sacred "thunder" from Muhammad's sermon comes through the same sensory faculty as the "thunder fart."[55] The auditory field is perhaps always overexposed, vulnerable to what comes unbidden, with every conceivable echo and proximate sound drifting in. An Islam accessed through this noisy medium is largely defenseless, reverting to a noise-filled chaos, in turn scrambled by the *Mohammadhawn Mikes* of the world.

Hitching a ride on this weak religion, Joyce will make his way circuitously back to Dublin, taking in the "lokil calour and lucal odour,"[56] paying his respects to the river Anna Liffey and her namesake, Anna Livia Plurabelle, or ALP. ALP has written a "mamafesta" commemorating her disappeared husband, Humphrey Chimpden Earwicker:

In the name of Annah, the Allmaziful, the Everliving, the Bringer of Plurabilities, haloed be her eve, her singtime sung, her rill be run, unhemmed as it is uneven!

Her untitled mamafesta memorializing the Mosthighest has gone by many names at disjointed times. (104.1–5)

Meshing the Islamic *basmala* ("in the name of Allah") with the Lord's Prayer, this chant is dedicated to neither Jehovah nor Allah but a mongrel "Annah," "maziful" rather than merciful, gathering in one person the Labyrinth of Crete; the labyrinthine Rome of Livia Drusilla, wife of the emperor Augustus; and the veil-donning, shape-shifting Maya of the Vedic scriptures, the "Bringer of Plurabilities."

To such a deity, our prayer would not be to "Our Father who art in heaven," since the addressee is unlikely to be an all-powerful, heaven-dwelling god, but rather a disheveled goddess with unhemmed skirts, as vulnerable as her creations and glad to have everything in tolerable working order. Her mamafesta is written on the reverse side of a chatty letter from Boston, ending up in a mound of trash until dug up in a scarcely legible form by the hen Belinda. Itself without a title, this document has "many names it has gone by at disjointed times," including a name culled from Islam, "by the Stream of Zemzem at the Zigzag hill" (105.7–8); one taken from the Egyptian Book of the Dead, "Of the Two Ways of Opening the Mouth" (105.23–24); and one from the annals of soccer, "An Outstanding Back and an Excellent Halfcentre if Called on" (106.35–6). As Joyce says, "The proteiform graph itself is a polyhedron of scripture" (107.8).

To some, such a polyhedron might look like a travesty of the novel form, not to say of holy scripture. There's no guarantee that it would ever make sense, that those scrambled phonemes and morphemes would ever yield anything coherent. For Joyce, scrambling is the point. Overrun by "Plurabilities," this no longer sacred Qur'an yields a weak faith and a superabundant micro archive, a repository for the jetsam and flotsam of the world, an Irish mamafesta not exclusively Irish.

EZRA POUND: FAITH UNDER DURESS

Ezra Pound was famously critical of *Finnegans Wake*, telling Joyce that "nothing so far as I can make out, nothing short of divine vision or a new cure for the clap, can possibly be worth all the circumambient peripherization."[57] Yet a weak Islam, fragmentary and gestural, would end up being a refuge for this poet, perhaps even more so than for Joyce. During 1945, probably the darkest year in Pound's life, a book-nurtured faith began to appear, scattered throughout *The Pisan Cantos*. He wrote the poems while he was detained, from May to November, by the US Army at the Disciplinary Training Center in Pisa on charges of treason for his pro-fascist Rome Radio broadcast.

Pound was initially kept outdoors in a six-by-six-foot steel cage, but he was moved indoors after three weeks and even given a writing table made from a packing box. Poetry writing seemed to have continued apace under these circumstances, with no break in its output and no diminishment in its encyclopedic range. Islam, a micro archive combined and recombined here as in *Finnegans Wake*, shows up in loosely connected throwaway lines with many references to Spain and North Africa and one specific reference to Joyce himself. In canto 74, while talking about his first visit to Gibraltar in 1898 with his aunt, during which he had also traveled north to Granada and south to Tangier, Pound juxtaposes all three locations, rounding out the trio with a nod to Joyce:

> And thence to Al Hambra, the lion court and el
> mirador de la reina Lindaraja
>
> orient reaching to Tangier, the cliffs the villa of Perdicaris
>
> Rais Uli, periplum
> Mr Joyce also preoccupied with Gibraltar[58]

The word that leaps out here is a word that ordinarily connotes secondariness but here concedes priority: *also*—"Mr Joyce also preoccupied with Gibraltar." When it comes to writing about Gibraltar, Joyce was there first. But as the laid-backness of *also* suggests, Joyce's priority is not much of a concern here, for there is in fact no competition between the two authors when it comes to that city.

NORTH TO GRANADA

Unlike Joyce's atmospheric Gibraltar, Pound's comes with well-defined coordinates, linked north and south to two specific compass points: on the one hand, the Alhambra in Granada, and on the other hand, the Villa of Perdicaris in Tangier. In 1492, Granada was the last Moorish stronghold to fall to Ferdinand and Isabella, shortly after which both Jews and Arabs were banished from the city. But Pound's reference is not to that fateful year. Rather, it's to an earlier time, before the Reconquista, when the great Islamic cities Granada and Cordoba were centers of learning for all Europe, of unsurpassed beauty and refinement. The Court of Lions and the Mirador de la Reina Lindaraja in particular are enduring testimonies to the magnificence of that period.

This medieval Islam was familiar to Pound in part through his life-long dedication to the work of Guido Cavalcanti, whose sonnets he translated in 1912 and who would be the subject of one of the three radio operas he wrote in 1931, commissioned by the BBC. In his essay on Cavalcanti, Pound specifically cites the inspiration the Italian poet received from two Islamic philosophers, Avicenna and Averroes, referred to by their Arabic names, Ibn Sina and Ibn Rashd: "From this poem and from passages elsewhere it would seem that Guido had derived certain notions from the Aristotelian commentators, the '*filosofica famiglia*,' Ibn Sina, for the *spiriti, spiriti* of the eyes, of the senses; Ibn Rashd, *che il gran comento feo*, for the demand for intelligence on the part of the recipients."[59]

This is what Islam means to Pound: intellectual labor and intellectual dedication, a symbol of enlightened reason that Cavalcanti embraced in the thirteenth century and that Pound hoped would once again be available to himself in the twentieth, especially now that he was locked up in a cage awaiting trial. To this incarcerated poet, the northward arc to Granada is largely a temporal arc, a journey necessarily abstract, making up for the bleakness of the present by reaching back to various idealized locales in the past. This is the "beyond" that he craves: Spain under Islam, China under Confucius, the seven-walled city of Dioce, the Aegean Sea of Homer—these are the receded and all the more necessary anchors that bring hope and solace.

SOUTH TO WAGADU

Complementing that temporal arc is another, heading south and traversed in space. Arriving in Tangier, it comes face to face with Mulai Ahmed er Raisuli, a Berber bandit who in 1904 kidnapped Ion Perdicaris and his nephew Cromwell Varley to collect eighty thousand dollars in ransom. For Pound, this is a quintessential twentieth-century story, and Tangier, as the setting for that story, is the epicenter of an Islam debased to the point where it becomes synonymous with greed and barbarism.

And yet a southward journey need not stop with Mulai Ahmed er Raisuli. Earlier in canto 74, Pound has already made a reference to the kidnapping of Perdicaris but against a differently imagined Tangier, not a haven of the depraved but the site for an unlikely miracle, a curious case of living fire coming from dead straw:

But in Tangier I saw dead straw ignition
> From a snake bite
Fire came to the straw
From the fakir blowing
Foul straw and an arm-long snake
That bit the tongue of the fakir making small holes
> And from the blood of the holes
> Came fire when he stuffed the straw into his mouth
Dirty straw that he took from the roadway
> First smoke and then the dull flame
That wd/ have been in the time of Rais Uli
> When I rode out to Elson's
> Near the villa of Perdicaris[60]

Perdicaris remains a live issue, but beyond the debased Islam encoded in that episode is something else, a feat of "dead straw ignition" that must have seemed both improbable and electrifying to a man condemned to political death. Nor is Tangier the only place where the dead could come back to life under such sordid circumstances. Earlier in canto 74, Pound has mentioned another city still further south, the pre-Islamic Wagadu, vanquished and resurrected again and again:

> 4 times was the city rebuilded, Hooo Fasa
> > Gassir, Hooo Fasa dell'Italia tradita
> Now in the mind indestructible, Gassir, Hooo Fasa
> With the four giants at the four corners
> And four gates mid-wall Hooo Fasa. . . .
> Hooo Fasa, and in a dance the renewal[61]

Hooo is the Soninke word for "hail"; *Fasa* is a tribe of heroes in North Africa. The phrase "Hooo! Fasa!" is a refrain in the Soninke epic *Gassire's Lute*, opening with these words about the endlessly resurrected Wagadu: "Four times Wagadu stood there in all her splendor. Four times Wagadu disappeared and was lost to human sight. . . . Four times Wagadu changed her name. First she was called Dierra, then Agada, then Ganna, then Silla. . . . [But] she endures no matter whether she be built of stone, wood and earth, or lives but as a shadow in the mind and longing of her children. . . . Hooo! Dierra, Agada, Ganna, Silla! Hooo! Fasa!"[62]

PRE-ISLAMIC AFRICA

It makes sense that a man held at the Disciplinary Training Center, a "man on whom the sun has gone down,"[63] would want to stake his faith on a four-time-resurrected city. Pound had come across *Gassire's Lute* in Leo Frobenius's *Atlantis: Volksmärchen und Volksdichtung Afrikas* (1921), which he had started reading around 1928. Frobenius's account of African civilizations left a deep impression on him. He mentions Frobenius frequently in *The Pisan Cantos*, as in these lines: "Frobenius der Gehemrat / der im Baluba das Gewitter gemacht hat."[64] Through the "benignity" of the Baluba mask, one of the objects Frobenius discusses, Pound links the German ethnographer to the equally benign African American guards at the DTC, especially Henry Hudson Edwards, the GI who made him the writing table:

> And Mr. Edwards superb green and brown
> in ward No 4 a jacent benignity,
> of the Baluba mask: "doan you tell no one
> I made you that table."[65]

This wasn't the first time Pound felt a special affinity for African Americans, backed by a faith in the primacy of African civilizations. Fourteen years earlier, on December 26, 1931, he had sent a letter to the president of the Tuskegee Institute, urging him to make Frobenius's African research a part of the curriculum. Pound declared that Frobenius had, with "an unflagging enthusiasm for the beauty of its different civilizations," "done more than any other living man to give the black race its charter of intellectual liberties." He had been trying to get some of this pioneering work translated into English, and it occurred to him that this "shd. be made a racial act, with whatever university or other backing you can give it." He added:

There is no reason why a black University shd. be merely a copy of a white one. I have written elsewhere that our American universities are full of redundance. A great deal left undone and a lot done uselessly three times over. There shd. be (if there is not already) a course in Africanology in every black special school, it wd. be more interesting than another professorship of greek or latin.[66]

Since Pound didn't know Tuskegee's president personally and had no idea "whether he is the sort of man who will have sense enough to ACT on the suggestion," he thought it wise to send a carbon copy to Langston Hughes, adding, "The job ought to be done. I don't know that I can make the suggestion any stronger or clearer, but I will cooperate with any scheme you suggest for getting on with it" (211).

On April 22, 1932, Hughes wrote back, apologizing for the lateness of the response (he had been on tour) but then saying, "I was very much interested in what you had to say about Frobenius. Certainly I agree with you about the desirability of his being translated into English, and I have written to both Howard and Fisk Universities concerning what you say." As for Tuskegee, Hughes was "afraid they have little inclinations toward anything so spiritually important as translations of Frobenius would be to the Negro race" (213–14). He was pleased, however, to be able to include affirmative responses from Howard and Fisk.[67]

Hughes continued, "I have known your work for more than ten years and many of your poems insist on remaining in my head." And since Pound had asked to see some of his work, he was only too happy to oblige: "Some weeks ago I sent you my books in care of INDICE. I hope you have received them" (214). Pound responded on May 8 to say that the "INDICE has gone bust." On June 17, Hughes replied, "My books, sent to you c/o INDICE, came back, so I re-sent them directly to you. Also a Scottsboro booklet of mine, the proceeds of which go to the defense of the boys" (218).

LANGSTON HUGHES: BRANDING CHRISTIANITY

The boys in question were the black youths accused of raping two white women on a freight train near Painted Rock, Alabama, on March 25, 1921. The rushed trials, held in nearby Scottsboro, quickly produced death sentences for eight of the nine defendants. The presence of a lynch mob before the trials, along with the framed charges, inadequate legal counsel, and all-white juries, made *Scottsboro* a byword for racial injustice. The case was taken to the US Supreme Court twice on appeal, the first resulting in the landmark decision *Powell v. Alabama* (1932), which ordered new trials, and the second resulting in *Patterson v. Alabama* (1935), with the ruling that African Americans must be included on juries.[68]

On December 1, 1931, the magazine *Contempo*, with Ezra Pound on
its masthead, printed Hughes's "Christ in Alabama" on its front page.[69]
Along with three other poems and a verse play, the poem was then published in a booklet, *Scottsboro Limited* (1932).[70] Hughes wrote:

> Christ is a Nigger,
> Beaten and black—
> *O, bare your back.*
> Mary is his mother
> *Mammy of the south,*
> *Silence your mouth.*
> God's His Father—
> *White Master above,*
> *Grant him your love.*
> Most holy bastard
> Of the bleeding mouth
> *Nigger Christ*
> *On the Cross of the South.*[71]

Christ, nigger, South—these words, born of the crucible of Scottsboro,
would be an animating triad for Hughes all through the 1920s and
1930s. To name the racial injustice routinely suffered by African Americans, the language of Christianity was crucial, though not as a faith to
be affirmed. While in his teens and living in Lawrence, Kansas, Hughes
had come under the influence of his aunt Mary Reed, spending considerable time in her church, the Methodist Episcopal St. Luke's, as well as
the more down-home Warren Street Baptist Church.[72] But his salvation,
announced at a revival meeting, quickly backfired—his lackluster faith
became apparent that very evening.[73] Christianity would henceforth be a
negative touchstone for him.[74] In such a guise, as a disparaging term with
maximum name recognition, it served a key function. Emptied of spiritual content, it became a brand name, a coded label that could be speed-
ily and reflexively processed, to be used wherever Hughes saw fit.

It's this branding of Christianity that enables Hughes, in his celebrated 1926 essay, "The Negro Artist and the Racial Mountain," to name
the following five fatal temptations for aspiring black writers: "Nordic
manners, Nordic faces, Nordic hair, Nordic art (if any), and an Episcopal
heaven." These five, magnets of a whiteness seen as "the symbol of all

virtues," make any "racial art" impossible.[75] An "Episcopal heaven"—
harking back to Aunt Mary's Methodist Episcopal St. Luke's—might not
belong obviously to this list. Its inclusion here makes it clear just how
far Christianity has been rhetoricized, a brand name no different from
the other "Nordic" ones and subject to the same reflexive judgment.
In time, this branding is to spread across the entire religious spectrum.
Other faiths, notably Islam, are now susceptible in the same way, becoming handy labels because strategically out of focus.

SOVIET UNION: OUT-OF-FOCUS ISLAM

On March 3, 1964, Hughes wrote a note to Cassius Clay, soon to join the
Nation of Islam and become Muhammad Ali: "I hear you are interested
in history. Well, history is no mystery. Why, out of the fact that some
are black, others try to make a twistery, is the only mystery."[76] The note
directed Clay's attention to page 333 of the new revised edition of *A Pictorial History of the Negro in America* (1963), which Hughes had written
with historian Milton Meltzer.[77] Featured there is "The Black Muslims."
   This cryptic, roundabout note, bracketing an Islam silently invoked
only as a "twistery," is in keeping with Hughes's off-key skirmishes with
this religion, granting its mass appeal but not its spiritual meaning. Earlier, writing about his 1931-32 trip across Soviet Central Asia in *I Wonder
as I Wander* (1956), he notes the suppression of Islam with the same strategic offhandedness—alluding vaguely to the decline of the faith while
giving top billing to a new development far more important, the elimination of beggars in Samarkand:

> Begging, however, that scourge of the Orient, had almost disappeared.
> With work for all, the building of homes for the aged and the infirm,
> and the creation in Samarkand of six communes for homeless chil-
> dren, the old familiar cry of the East, "Alms, alms, for the love of Al-
> lah," was seldom heard, except from a few holy beggars whose religion
> demanded that they live by charity.
>   The whirling dervishes—whose fanatic rites once greatly excited a
> portion of the populace, and who in wild frenzy would slash their flesh
> into strips in public—had been forbidden to dance. Some, however,
> were still said to hold secret rites. Calmer Mohammedan sects gath-
> ered at the few mosques still open, but among them not many young

men were seen. The young men of Samarkand were almost all going to
school rather than to mosques.[78]

Hughes was writing at a moment when Soviet anti-religious campaigns
were just moving into high gear. Launched in 1919 with the *Revolutsiia i
tserkov*, the first anti-religious monthly published by the People's Com-
missariat of Justice, the decades ahead would bring incendiary editori-
als ("Let the Five Year Plan Slam Religion on the Head") followed by
legislation outlawing religious activities.[79] While the Russian Orthodox
Church bore the brunt of the attacks,[80] mosques and Muslim clerics
were also increasingly targeted.[81] The 1929 law concerning religious associations resulted in the dissolution of all Islamic courts, putting an end
to Sharia law and customary law. Mosque landholdings were liquidated,
and Qur'anic schools were banned. Of the twenty thousand mosques in
Soviet Central Asia in 1917, fewer than four thousand remained in 1929.
By 1935, fewer than sixty still functioned in Uzbekistan, which held half
the Muslim population in Soviet Central Asia.[82]

Given Hughes's off-key approach to religion, his vague descriptions
of these events aren't surprising: whatever bad was happening to Islam
was offset by all the other spectacular progress in the Soviet Union. Even
though *I Wonder as I Wander* was published in 1956, long after the atrocities of Stalin had turned away many early sympathizers, Hughes's allegiance remained unchanged, along with his hope in a socialist state dedicated to eliminating poverty and illiteracy. This utopian experiment,
disappointing to so many, was to him still important to honor twenty
years later, more important than the fate of any religion.

"GENERAL FRANCO'S MOORS"

Hughes's loyalty to utopian experiments made for a similarly vague portrait of black Muslim soldiers during the Spanish Civil War. In "General
Franco's Moors," a 1937 piece for the *Baltimore Afro-American* later included in *I Wonder as I Wander*, he begins with the startling sight of a
black man in a Madrid prison hospital, his "blackness . . . accentuated by
a white hospital gown flopping about his bare legs, and a white bandage
around his head."[83] Here is an incarnation of Islam not to be shrugged
away. "Before I left home," Hughes says, "American papers had carried
photographs of turbaned Mohammedan troops marching in the streets

of Burgos, Seville and Malaga" (350–51). He is now greeted with this sight in Madrid as well, for the fascists, "in spite of their Christian cast," had "encamped thousands of pagan Moors at Casa del Campo" (351). Any right-thinking person would know what to make of this "union of the Cross and the Crescent." A wounded Muslim soldier inside a Madrid prison, however, is a different story, beset by "the irony of the colonial Moors—victims themselves of oppression in North Africa—fighting against a Republic that had been seeking to work out a liberal policy toward Morocco" (353).

Some thirty years before that cryptic note to Cassius Clay, Hughes had already tried to come to terms with a black Muslim, whose all too tangible wounds made it clear that faith is not just a matter of doctrine but often an embodied fact, bearing witness to the material forces of history. What to do with an Islam on the receiving end of those material forces, an Islam injured, disabled, and black? "General Franco's Moors" ends with a poem, written in the voice of an African American fighting in the International Brigades, urging common cause on this Muslim "as dark as me." It is a vain appeal: "But the wounded Moor was dying / So he didn't understand" (354). A flesh-and-blood Muslim dying inside a Madrid prison would perhaps always be a reproach to Hughes. Yet the physicality of the soldier is also its own solution. Victimized not by religious persecution but by colonial geopolitics, this wounded body occupies the narrative foreground only as an emblem of racial oppression. The tragedy here, as staged by Hughes, is failed solidarity, a tragedy of race failing to break down the dividing walls of colonialism, eclipsing the tragedy of an ostracized faith, banished from Spain in 1492 and viewed with suspicion ever since. Dissolving once again into an atmospheric blur, this out-of-focus religion, variously summoned and deployed by Matisse, Joyce, Pound, and now Hughes, shows why a weak Islam is often key to experimentation—and at what cost. If nothing else, the unhealed wounds of the black Muslim soldier call out for redress, a call that will be the subject of the next chapter.

6 · Remotely Japanese

WILLIAM FAULKNER INDIGENOUS
AND TRANS-PACIFIC

What does *reparation* mean in literature, if anything at all? How might one begin to make amends, and how to ensure that such efforts aren't fantasies? In this chapter, I look at the long-distance atonement of William Faulkner as he reaches out in apology to Japan after World War II, hoping in the same gesture to reach out in apology to displaced indigenous populations in Mississippi. This attempt at reparation, largely wishful, becomes less so when it is crowdsourced by chance, distributed to authors far from Faulkner's orbit, whose weak connectivity makes them resourceful mediators.

REPARATIVE VERSUS PARANOID

I begin not with Faulkner, though, but with Eve Kosofsky Sedgwick's now-classic plea on behalf of the reparative impulse. Sedgwick distinguishes between two ways of reading texts and two ways of reading the world, one strong and one weak: the former confident in its analytic totality and the latter hobbled by specters of what isn't redressed or resolved. The strong reading she has in mind is what Paul Ricoeur calls a "hermeneutics of suspicion" and what she herself calls "paranoid reading."[1] Seeing the world as a field of symptoms masking their systemic cause, such readings unmask with gusto. Anything that weakens this muscular exercise is not to be credited. Since this has been the case for some time, the critical reflex at play now in literary studies is winnowed down to a single, powerful, and powerfully negative one, discounting anything less.[2] For Sedgwick, it's tantamount to the loss of biodiversity, the overwhelming ability of one dominant gene to eliminate all others, leaving us with a "shallow gene pool" that seriously erodes our "ability to respond to environmental (i.e. political) change."[3]

Given such losses, reparative reading has no choice but to be "additive and accretive." It must do a different kind of evidentiary bookkeeping, making the discounted once again count. Taking the world not as a giant mask but as a torn web with gaping holes—the result of missed cues and failed connections—it makes repairs its most immediate task, prompted more by needs from the ground up than edicts from the top down. It sees weak mastery as a small price to pay for the job at hand. Rather than stripping away what mystifies, reparative reading wants to add layers of mediation to the world. It "wants to assemble and confer plenitude on an object that will then have resources to offer to an inchoate self."[4] And toward that end, it's willing to err on the side of the inconclusive, bringing more to the table than strictly necessary, canvassing more than would clinch the case, giving up the satisfaction of the knockout punch line for the uncertain benefit of crowdsourced agency, improvised networks, and less-than-guaranteed outcomes.

REPARATIVE JUSTICE, PUNITIVE JUSTICE

Focusing on the reparative-paranoid binary, Sedgwick doesn't consider another pair of terms equally pertinent to her analysis and perhaps with more direct impact on the world: reparative justice versus punitive justice. In this chapter, I'd like to open up that conversation as a methodological debate—between two investigative procedures and two attendant outcomes: mitigating circumstances versus punishable deed, ongoing contextualization versus terminal verdict. One cuts through the evidence and delivers a clean, final, targeted judgment, while the other thickens the plot and prolongs the commutation process thanks to a decentered and multilayered mediating network. Taking the former as a strongly institutionalized norm and the latter as a weakly experimental alternative, I'd like to make a case for reparative justice as an unorthodox but not implausible way of writing literary history, its scope and efficacy as yet to be tested but with consequences already palpable in adjacent disciplines.

In criminal law, an especially interesting example of reparative justice is a program called Alternatives to Incarceration (ATI). An ATI is any informal program of activity required of offenders, a substitute for penal action leading to reduced jail time. Given the well-documented abuses of US prisons, sentencing reform has long been a top priority among lawmakers as well as community activists, culminating in the passing of the 2018 bipartisan criminal justice reform bill.[5] Many cities have programs such as the ATI. New York City leads the way, boasting many reparative networks and a rehabilitation rate of 60 percent. According to a study commissioned by the city,

> [New York] has expanded the network of actors in the courtroom to encourage the use of alternative sentences. City officials have created an ATI system that includes not only programs for offenders, but also court representatives whose job is to persuade even reluctant judges, assistant DAs, and public defenders to use these programs routinely in appropriate cases. As a result, the ATI system plays a dual role in the criminal justice process, trying to shape plea bargains and sentencing decisions in court as well as administering the sentences themselves.[6]

Active both inside and outside the courtroom before, during, and after sentencing, the ATI as implemented in New York is a crowdsourced mechanism dedicated to turning jailed offenders into ordinary citizens. Community groups, working together on an ad hoc, case-by-case basis, spearhead this action, guided by the understanding that punitive sentences are counterproductive in criminal justice, that the more necessary, and necessarily incremental, work is in fact that of repairing lives, giving a second chance to those who perhaps have never had much of one to begin with.[7] Reparative justice of this sort has already borne fruit in criminal law. What might parallel efforts in literary studies look like, and how might they complement and extend these legal, legislative, and community alternatives to harsh sentences?

INCREMENTAL MEDIATION

The equivalent of sentencing reform in literary studies would seem to require, at the very least, a suspension of the punitive impulse, the impulse to deliver a quick, maximum-strength, terminal verdict. To resist that impulse, thinking further about mediation seems important, a task for which literary studies is especially suited, not being caught up in administrative hurtles and not duty-bound to wrap up within a fixed time frame. If it turns out that stipulated closure is indeed incompatible with mediation, reparative justice would seem to be particularly weak in relation to one criterion: the ticking clock. Continually improvised and slow moving, it's interminable, never done because never without some fresh input, a field perpetually amendable and incomplete.

The amending typically develops over time, the incremental and by no means unified effort of many. Its crowdsourced genesis suggests that any individual effort can be counted on to come up short—in the sense that it cannot be its own end point—precisely because it is singular, the work of one pair of hands, and arrested at one particular moment in time. Coming up short is less a failing than a spur to the work of others. The codependency that results binds any given author to a large, self-appointed, and impromptu repair team, a mediating network ancillary to but not without bearing on the original corpus. Untried options subsequently explored, roads not taken subsequently visited: these time-delayed amendments make up the incremental path of reparative justice. Through these prolonged and shakily executed weak reparations, happening as much by chance as by design, traces of the unactualized past can be carried into the future, and unredressed injuries can be given alternate outlines.

I'll be using weak reparation as a way to think about the incremental path set into motion by Faulkner, trying to reach out and atone for the past and, in not quite succeeding, leaving room for input from others. The crowdsourced mediation born of such fallible efforts is arguably a more reliable way to think about nonpunitive justice, not to say the capabilities and limits of literature. But first, a brief look at a strong theory on the other end of the spectrum, one doubling down on Faulkner as a case of mediation, hegemonic mediation, a top-down verdict absolute in its sentencing power.

TOP-DOWN VERDICTS

In *The World Republic of Letters* (1999), Pascale Casanova sees world literature as a series of unchallenged verdicts from a dominant hub. According to her, the handful of texts able to circulate beyond national borders do so only when they have satisfied one demand—"consecrat[ion] in Paris," the "Greenwich meridian" of literature—a rare but necessary occurrence that puts them at the very top and grants them connectivity at that elevation, the freedom to hobnob with other texts similarly elevated and adept at border crossing.[8]

Top-down consecration is the driving force in the global totality Casanova envisions, for "Paris is not only the capital of the literary world. It is also, as a result, the gateway to the 'world market of intellectual goods,' as Goethe put it; the chief place of consecration in the world of literature."[9] She points to the translations of Faulkner into French by Maurice-Edgar Coindreau, which, she claims, contributed significantly to his worldwide recognition, culminating in the 1949 Nobel Prize in literature. And that prize, in turn, connects Faulkner to the literary greats across space and time, the likes of Samuel Beckett, Octavio Paz, and Gabriel García Márquez, all Nobel Laureates and all given the nod in Paris before ascending to the very top in Stockholm.

Not only is there a strong presumption here in favor of literature as an institutional artifact, this strong presumption also carries with it a predictable outcome, giving us what we might expect from a strong theory: a fully rationalized and fully hegemonic regime in which a single, unvarying metropolitan center dominates a globalized field, dominates even those texts with no chance of ever being consecrated. Such a paradigm needs qualification on factual grounds—did those French translations alone catapult Faulkner to fame, and is Paris always the sentencing hub? And it needs qualification, most of all, as a conceptual template for theorizing mediation in literature. If only as a thought experiment, it's worth exploring peripheral networks below Casanova's radar: at some distance from seats of power, without institutional prestige, but also without the restrictiveness of prestige, decentralized formations too far down to be fully dominated, too far down to be coopted or even noticed by high authorities. Low-bar networks of this sort are input-accepting to a fault. Not overly efficient in gatekeeping, their flexible membership might be our best bet for a form of mediation unsupervised, unguaranteed, but nonetheless reliably incremental.

LOW-BAR NETWORKS

Here, I'd especially like to draw from the work of sociologist Mark Granovetter, whose memorable oxymoron—"the strength of weak ties"—captures just this paradox of low-bar networking, the aggregate effects of loose connectivity.[10] Granovetter's theory has been updated more recently by Lee Rainie and Barry Wellman, taking into account the loose connectivity afforded by the internet. In *Networked* (2012), Rainie and Wellman analyze the multiple weak ties developed online in terms of "partial membership": filiations existing in the plural, operating on multiple fronts and improvising as the need arises, rather than institutionally given and centrally dictated.[11] The resulting ties don't amount to much, but they're also difficult to stamp out, a downstream cascade likely to grow, interfering with any strong claim about closed-circuit domination and top-down verdicts.

I'll be using low-bar networks as an analytic tool to think about forms of mediation different from those described by Casanova, peripheral and incremental rather than absolute, and, in this case, extending across the Pacific rather than revolving around Paris. To the terms proposed by Granovetter and Rainie and Wellman, I'd like to add two more. The low-bar networks I'll be exploring are for the most part affective, based on inchoate sentiments, what Raymond Williams calls "structure of feeling": not quite a philosophy or worldview but simply a "practical consciousness of a present kind, in a living and interrelating continuity." Inarticulate feeling of this sort, Williams goes on to say, "cannot without loss be reduced to belief-systems, institutions, or explicit general relationships, though it may include all these as lived and experienced, with or without tension."[12]

And within this inarticulate continuum, the emotion associated with losing—finding oneself on the wrong side of history, the wrong side of any terminal event—is especially interesting, at once deeply traumatic and all too common. Losing is a low-bar experience known to many; it's the most ordinary of ordinary affects.[13] Could a network be built on it, a negative basis for kinship, creating a meaningful tie among those who otherwise might not have much in common? And could it be the basis for a weak form of reparation, perhaps more aspirational than actual, but nonetheless signaling an acknowledgment that something needs to be done?

TRANS-PACIFIC TRAUMA

Without further ado, I test these possibilities by turning directly to Faulkner and his reparative project, a trans-Pacific atonement, offering the defeat of the South after the American Civil War in solidarity with the defeat of Japan after World War II. Faulkner was in Nagano, Japan, as part of the US State Department's exchange of persons program, the same program that sent jazz musicians all over the world as goodwill ambassadors. By the time he went, in August 1955, he was at a low point himself, a confirmed alcoholic, so shaky in his general demeanor that the State Department apparently thought of cutting the tour short and sending him home. But Faulkner evidently rallied under the challenge of on-site adjustment to a foreign environment. For ten days, he was able to meet with members of the Nagano Seminar—fifty or so Japanese professors of American literature—every afternoon or evening, giving talks and interacting with them in Q&A sessions. Some of his remarks were quite odd, not what one would expect from someone in Japan under State Department sponsorship, such as the following, from a talk entitled "To the Youth of Japan":

> A hundred years ago, my country, the United States, was not one economy and culture, but two of them, so opposed to each other that ninety-five years ago they went to war against each other to test which one should prevail. My side, the South, lost that war, the battles of which were fought not on neutral ground in the waste of the ocean, but in our own homes, our gardens, our farms, as if Okinawa and Guadalcanal had been not islands in the distant Pacific but the precincts of Honshu and Hokkaido. Our land, our homes were invaded by a conqueror who remained after we were defeated; we were not only devastated by the battles which we lost, the conqueror spent the next ten years after our defeat and surrender despoiling us of what little war had left.[14]

As Civil War history, Faulkner's account is atrocious, one-sided, and reductive. He never mentioned slavery at all; his depiction of the Civil War was only as a war between two incompatible regions of the United States, eternally divided by their cultural and economic differences, with one side triumphing over the other and trampling the other underfoot.

What makes this peculiar account slightly more excusable is the presence here of *two* regional contexts. The first is obviously Oxford, Mississippi, and the conduct of the Union army in 1863: "That night the town was occupied by Federal troops; two nights later, it was on fire (the Square, the stores and shops and the professional offices), gutted (the courthouse too), the blackened jagged topless jumbles of brick wall enclosing like a ruined jaw the blackened shell of the courthouse . . . and so in effect it was a whole year in advance of Appomattox."[15] The other context, perhaps even more present to Faulkner at that moment, is what Japan went through at the end of World War II. The giveaway phrase, I think, is this: "The conqueror spent the next ten years after our defeat and surrender despoiling us of what little war had left."

Why ten years? Faulkner was probably thinking less about the year 1875, ten years after Appomattox, than about 1955, the year of the Nagano Seminar, ten years after Japan surrendered. And he seemed to know intuitively that though Allied occupation had ended formally in April 1952, the emotional ramifications of defeat would persist long after. For the Japanese in 1955, what struck a responsive chord in Faulkner's account of the American Civil War was no doubt this shared feeling: that in every war there was going to be a losing side, an existential condition known only to those who have been subjected to it. Reaching out to a war-traumatized audience on just that basis, Faulkner's regionalism was now both rooted and extended, based in Oxford, Mississippi, but offering Japanese professors a new prism to understand both their own recent history and the history of the American South. Familiar names such as Appomattox now gave way to four others: Okinawa, Guadalcanal, Honshu, Hokkaido. Significantly, these were not the best-known names, not the two atomic epicenters, Hiroshima and Nagasaki, but names far more ordinary, bringing to mind no spectacular destruction, only the steady-state, weakly but persistently gnawing sense of having been brought low.

It was a deliberate choice on Faulkner's part. Regional cities were in fact the reference points for him, not cosmopolitan cities like London and Paris. In his meeting with the citizens of Nagano, while trying to clarify his fictional world for this Japanese audience he came up with a comparative mapping of two pairs of cities: "My country lies between New Orleans and Memphis. New Orleans is the big, important city that in my country is like Tokyo here. That is, Nagano would be Memphis, Tokyo would be New Orleans, because Tokyo is the larger city. My country would be between Nagano and Tokyo. They were important in my work only because they were the big cities—the life in my land, the land I know, is country, it is farmland."[16]

This, in and of itself, seems to me a regional manifesto. New Orleans is the counterpart to Tokyo only on a very special map, one that leaves out New York, Chicago, and Los Angeles. And that seemed to be the point. Even though New York had been a shorthand for Faulkner elsewhere, say, in *The Sound and the Fury* (1929), and even though he knew Los Angeles well from his stint as a screenwriter in Hollywood, for this particular audience he wanted New Orleans to set the standard for a metropolitan center. And it was with New Orleans as the standard that he could then go down to the next level, to Memphis. But even this was too large a city for him. His country was nondescript farm country, he said, agrarian in what seemed to be the most traditional sense.

And yet, even as this was being put forward, two other cities, Tokyo and Nagano, were also very much in the picture. This cross-mapping, linking the cartography of an intimately known South to that of an unknown Asia, was something that Faulkner did fairly consistently throughout his stay in Japan. Rather than settling comfortably into some tried-and-tested binary—North versus South, city versus country—his world was now far more volatile, at once extended and ill-defined, a world in which unfamiliar names, perhaps seen together for the first time, produced fault lines as well as lines of filiation, giving us a sense of history far less predictable than the earlier North-as-conqueror-and-South-as-victim script.

VARIETIES OF LOSING

Such a world produced new contexts for old enmities and grievances, to the point where even *winning* and *losing* began to shed their customary character, taking on new meanings. There's no better example of this than Faulkner's musings on the conduct of war, specifically the conduct of the occupying forces, when this question came from his Nagano audience:

> The scene of soldiers drinking liquor which appears in the beginning of the book *Soldier's* [sic] *Pay* made me recall an occurrence which arose just after the end of the Pacific war. When I was standing on one of the platforms at Nagoya, some American soldiers came along and forcibly held my neck, making me drink whisky. They then passed the bottle among themselves, drinking from the same bottle that I had drunk from. Since considerable time has elapsed since the time that *Soldier's* [sic] *Pay* was written of, and since things are quite peaceful now, I don't

imagine that such things happen nowadays. Could you tell me whether such scenes can be seen? (141)

The remark is interesting for at least three reasons. First, it illustrates how broad the Faulkner canon in Japan was: not only on this occasion but throughout the entire ten days, references were made not just to the standard-bearers, *The Sound and the Fury* (1929), *Light in August* (1932), and *Absalom, Absalom!* (1936), but also to works such as *The Wild Palms* (1939), *Intruder in the Dust* (1948), and here, *Soldiers' Pay* (1926). Second, Faulkner was right about the basis for emotional connection between postbellum South and Japan in 1955: this shared sense of humiliation was exactly what his Japanese interlocutor picked up on and responded to. Finally, perhaps most interesting of all was the response from Faulkner himself, the explanation he offered for why these American soldiers would behave in that way:

> I wouldn't say that that is typical of American soldiers. If I said that was typical, I'd say that it is probably typical of all soldiers, that in this gentleman's case, these were young men who had never been this far from home before—they were in a strange country, they had been fighting in combat—suddenly combat was over, they were free of being afraid, and so they lost control temporarily. They wouldn't act like that always every time—it was the relief that anyone who has been a soldier and knows what it is to be fighting—when he gets over being in fighting, he's really not accountable for what he might do. (141-42)

This must be one of the most counterintuitive accounts of the effect of war, focusing not on the out-of-control behavior of soldiers while the fighting is in process but on their out-of-control behavior once the fighting is over. According to Faulkner, this relaxing of extreme fear could have an adverse effect still less calculable. Whether or not we agree with this theory, it seems clear that with Japan in the foreground, he was suddenly able to see military occupation in a different light, replacing the erstwhile conquerors with a vulnerable group of young men away from home for the first time, barely making it through and undone by the very burden of winning.

A skeptic might say that Faulkner is having his cake and eating it: claiming victimhood on the one hand and exonerating the atrocious behavior of his victorious compatriots on the other. Still, suddenly finding himself on the winning side did throw into relief a psychological truth: There are no victors in war. No one wins, since winning is never an option. We all lose one way or another: whether militarily, in a public surrender; or psychologically, in a mental unraveling. All of us end up being undone by war, thrown off-kilter by it. This ironic twist—that supposed winners do not in fact win—makes the imagined connection between Faulkner and his Japanese audience not just a fantasy on his part but a fantasy perhaps with some grounding in truth. Perhaps there is indeed a low common denominator to war in that it permits only varieties of losing. That irony points to the possibility of a further common ground, something like a nontragic sequel to World War II and perhaps all wars: a leveling out at the absolute low point, with a hint of an upturn.

NONTRAGIC SEQUELS

A hint is all we could hope for, Faulkner said, for there's no way to deny the catastrophe of war, no way to erase the two atomic bombs: "We can't go back to a condition in which there were no wars, in which there was no bomb. We got to accept that bomb and do something about it, eliminate that bomb, eliminate the war, not retrograde to a condition before it exists" (78). History is linear in the sense that it's made up of a series of irrevocable acts; but it's not the case that each of those acts marks a dead end, a point of no return. On the contrary, it's the in-progress and amendable nature of the narrative that gives Faulkner hope. In response to an observation from the Tokyo audience—that there were new literary movements in postwar Japan and new poetry being written—Faulkner had this to say: "I think what is primarily responsible for that sort of alternation in the sound, the style, the shape of work, is disaster. I think I said before that it's hard believing, but disaster seems to be good for people. But if they are too successful too long, something dies, it dries up, and then they have to collapse with their own weight, which has happened with so many empires" (37-38).

Defeat as a spur to experimentation: this is the low-bar starting point for a nontragic sequel to World War II. The example of Japan suggests that a similar narrative might be unfolding in the United States as well. Could it be that here, too, some glimmer of the nontragic could come out of the tragedy of slavery, the tragedy of the Civil War? Faulkner would like to think so. This is what he offers in *Absalom, Absalom!*—a low point where things bottom out, also marking the beginning of a tentative reparation. Here it takes the form of a bare-bones network of three women—two white and one black—trying their best to survive and succeeding because they have managed to eke out an aggregate life, not a real partnership but enough of one to keep them going:

> not as two white women and a negress, not as three negroes or three whites, not even as three women, but merely as three creatures who still possessed the need to eat but took no pleasure in it, the need to sleep but from no joy in weariness or regeneration. . . . We grew and tended and harvested with our own hands the food we ate, made and worked that garden just as we cooked and ate the food which came out of it: with no distinction among the three of us of age or color. . . . It was as though we were one being, interchangeable and indiscriminate.[17]

This is the regionalism that rises from the ashes of defeat to give us a glimpse of the world as it could be: a desolate world, it is true, but one where blacks and whites could commingle, interchangeable and indiscriminate. This is the reparative experiment Faulkner had imagined back in 1936. Japan seemed to offer an affirmation, an actualization.

A cautionary word from historians is helpful here. Cooperation between black and white women fueled by economic hardship was indeed a possible outcome from the Civil War; however, as Drew Gilpin Faust and Thavolia Glymph have noted, such partnership was relatively rare. Often, economic hardship gave rise less to shared need than to intensified fear, with many mistresses reverting to or perhaps even developing new tactics of managing their slaves.[18] The harsh treatment of blacks after Reconstruction was not an unheralded turn of events but a continuation of racial oppression before, during, and after the Civil War, practiced by white women no less than white men. However tempting it is to imagine an interracial utopia based on scarcity and flourishing on the axis of gender, the practice was limited. William Faulkner's utopian hope might have been just that.

MAKING UP INDIANS

Still, the example of Japan, defeated not so long ago but already on the mend, must have given Faulkner the idea to experiment with a parallel story, one speaking not only to slavery and the Civil War but equally to America's other catastrophe, the dispossession of indigenous peoples, especially the Choctaw and Chickasaw in Mississippi. When asked about the origin of the word *Yoknapatawpha*, he said, "Yes, it's a Chickasaw Indian word. They were the Indians that we dispossessed in my country. That word means 'water flowing slow through the flatland,' which to me was a pleasant image, though the word in Chickasaw might be pleasanter to a Chickasaw ear than to our ear, but that's the meaning of it."[19]

The dispossession of Indians need not have come up at all for a question on etymology. Faulkner seemed to have gone out of his way to bring it up, perhaps to show that *this* catastrophe could also now be looked in the eye. Perhaps his novels and stories, experimenting with *Yoknapatawpha* and giving it an extended life scarcely imaginable when it was only a Chickasaw word, could be a form of reparation? Grounding his fictional world, this Chickasaw word was as good a candidate as any for an interracial utopia, a nontragic sequel to New World genocide, as peaceful and steadfast as "water flowing slow through the flatland."

Oddly, even as Faulkner laid out this theory, some doubt seemed already to have crept up, giving him pause and making him add this qualification—that the sound of "Yoknapatawpha" might be pleasanter to a Chickasaw ear than to his own. Peace might not translate easily between winners and losers, whether black and white or Anglo and Indian. The alienness of the word *Yoknapatawpha* was only the most obvious sign of the often insurmountable barriers. And nowhere were those barriers harder to ignore than in Japan. Indeed, simply being there, and needing to explain both the word *Yoknapatawpha* and what happened to the Chickasaw, and who they were to begin with, seemed to have brought home to Faulkner the daunting gulf between cultures. Was he ever any closer to the Chickasaw than he was to the Japanese, and how steadfast was his dedication to them?

The penitent gesture in Japan in 1955, a tribute to a defeated but honored people, was in fact a relatively recent development in Faulkner, the tail end of a long experiment with indigeneity, whose earlier iterations he might not have been eager to recall. Native Americans in late Faulkner, say, in *Requiem for a Nun* (1951), were indeed much like those invoked and mourned in Japan. *Requiem* begins by observing that "the settlement had the records; even the simple dispossession of Indians begot in time a minuscule of archive."[20] The novel repeats a variant of the word *dispossession* in a long-drawn-out parenthetical aside as it recounts the bickering over whether the town should be called Jefferson or Habersham—the latter name coming from the old doctor, town founder and "friend of old Issetibbeha, the Chickasaw chief (the motherless Habersham boy, now a man of twenty-five, married one of Issetibbeha's grand-daughters and in the thirties emigrated to Oklahoma with his wife's dispossessed people)."[21] The sentence is lopsided, like the equally lopsided fight between the Chickasaw and the US government: Habersham loses out in more senses than one. What the name signifies—friendship with Native Americans and continued landholding by them—was the road not taken by a nation with an official policy of Indian removal, a nation whose Founding Fathers counted Thomas Jefferson but not any Indians.

Requiem for a Nun is in many ways the high-water mark for a Faulkner mindful of Native Americans as "dispossessed," robbed of what was rightfully theirs. And yet, even here, his sympathies can't be said to be solidly on their side. In act 3, "The Jail," he recounts the fateful day when Mohataha, the Chickasaw matriarch, came "to set her capital X on the paper which ratified the dispossession of her people forever," doing so while "seated in a rocking chair beneath a French parasol held by a Negro slave girl," a figure "grotesque and regal, bizarre and moribund, like obsolescence's self riding off the stage enthroned on its own obsolete catafalque."[22] This isn't the first time those two words, *dispossessed* and *obsolete*, are entwined to suggest a doomed people, slave owning, with inflated egos and effete bodies, destined to die out in their ignorance. This is the refrain throughout *Requiem for a Nun*: "the obsolete and the dispossessed, dispossessed by those who were dispossessed in turn because they were obsolete."[23]

These two are also the operative words in the short-fiction collection *Go Down, Moses* (1942), especially in "The Bear," although in that earlier work Faulkner is much less interested in dispossession as a historical fact than as a spiritual malaise, afflicting anyone who gets it into his head that he can own the land, buy or sell or bequeath it. The big woods, we are told as soon as the story opens, are "bigger and older than any recorded document:—of white man fatuous enough to believe he had bought any fragment of it, of Indian ruthless enough to pretend that any fragment of it had been his to convey."[24]

"Fatuous" whites and "ruthless" Indians are almost equal partners here. Ikkemotubbe, the Chickasaw chief, and L. Q. C. McCaslin, Ike's grandfather, are equally culpable and equally deluded: "because it was never old Ikkemotubbe's to sell to Grandfather for bequeathment and repudiation. Because it was never Ikkemotubbe's fathers' fathers' to bequeath Ikkemotubbe to sell to Grandfather or any man because on the instant when Ikkemotubbe discovered, realised, that he could sell it for money, on that instant it ceased ever to have been his forever."[25] Dispossession in "The Bear" is a providential judgment, a curse incurred by Indians and Anglos both. Rather than being the outcome of a federal policy, written in a legal document and signing away the right to vast tracts of Native lands, it operates here by an entirely different syntax—"Dispossessed of Eden. Dispossessed of Canaan"[26]—a syntax that judges those who sell even more harshly than those who buy. L. Q. C. McCaslin is merely "fatuous"; it is Ikkemotubbe who is "ruthless."

That startling adjective, *ruthless*, out of the blue here, seems to have been carried over from an early phase of Faulkner, especially from stories such as "Red Leaves" (1930) and "A Justice" (1931), where it would have been entirely fitting. In "A Justice," Ikkemotubbe—"not born to be the Man [the chief], because [his] mother's brother was the Man, and the Man had a son of his own, as well as a brother"—takes to calling himself Doom, from the expression *du homme* that he had picked up in New Orleans from his French companion.[27] Armed with a little "gold box of New Orleans salt" upon his return, he does indeed spell doom: beginning with a puppy brought along for demonstration, then making quick work of the Man and his son, sparing the brother only because the latter, upon seeing what's happening, has covered his head with a blanket and taken himself out of the line of succession.[28]

That succession is just about to take place in "Red Leaves." Like "A Justice," this story also features ruthlessness of a sort, though manifest here not in Moketubbe, Issetibbeha's son and heir, who is obese and lethargic, "diseased with flesh," and not much of a schemer.[29] Ruthlessness inheres, rather, in the tribe as a whole, in its low-energy but unrelenting pursuit and capture of a black slave who has run away to escape being buried alive with Issetibbeha, his old master.

How credible is this portrait of Native Americans? "Red Leaves" has been challenged on multiple fronts, not least for its depiction of the burial

practices of Native Americans in Mississippi.[30] Faulkner, when asked by
a contemporary local historian "where he got his Indians," famously
replied, "I made them up."[31] In a letter to *Scribner's* accompanying
the submission of "Red Leaves," he also said, "So here is another story.
Few people know that Miss. Indians owned slaves; that's why I suggest you all buy it. Not because it is a good story; you can find lots of
good stories. It's because I need the money."[32] Faulkner's financial
needs might indeed have been dire, since he'd just bought a wreck of a
house (later named Rowan Oak). And the muckraking impulse to show
that whites weren't the only slave owners might indeed have been irre-
sistible.[33] Whatever the reason, historical accuracy couldn't be said to
be his top priority, which is why the names and identities of individuals and even of whole tribes could be switched from story to story. Indians, identified as Chickasaw in *Requiem for a Nun*, had started out in
the early stories as Choctaw. As Robert Dale Parker and Robert Woods
Sayre point out, Native Americans in early Faulkner were figments of
his imagination, grotesque "projections and introjections" of the slave-
owning South: archaic, degenerate, and doomed.[34]

With the effete Moketubbe setting the tone, the other two Indians
in "Red Leaves" are also "burgher-like" and "paunchy," one wearing
an "enameled snuff box" in his ear, and both receding into "a certain
blurred serenity like carved heads on a ruined wall in Siam or Sumatra,
looming out of a mist."[35] These made-up Indians have nothing to do with
the Native populations who had stayed on in Mississippi after the Treaty
of the Dancing Rabbit Creek in 1830, after even the Second Choctaw Removal of 1903, struggling to safeguard their communal holdings against
land frauds and the influx of white settlers, protecting the livelihood of
small subsistence farmers while debating citizenship rights.[36]

GERALD VIZENOR, JIM BARNES, AND LUCIEN STRYK: ROAD TO REPAIR

What to do with this distortion in Faulkner, this substitution of actual
Native Americans with ones of his own making? As it turns out, a mediating network—extending by chance but with some persistence across
the Pacific—does offer some reparation of sorts. For historical reasons
that warrant a full-length study in itself, many Native authors have felt
specially drawn to Japan, much like Faulkner. Their attachments stand

as both supplement and counterpoint to his. Gerald Vizenor, who posted there in 1953 with the occupation forces, was so taken with the haiku form that he wrote haiku for the rest of his life.[37] The overlapping catastrophes of the atomic bomb and New World genocide also resulted in a novel, *Hiroshima Bugi* (2003). Featuring a character named Ronin, a composite ghost from the Native American and Japanese pasts, it shows mass extermination as an unreceded legacy, at once dead and undead, born again and again in the present: "I am dead, the one who shatters nuclear peace. Some of my deaths have been reported in obituaries around the world. Dead Amerika Indian, hafu peace boy out to sea, was the report of my second death at the orphanage. I am forever an orphan, a tatari of the ruins."[38]

Is peace ever possible for such a ghost, peace that's not a travesty, not an insult to the continual presence of the dead? Vizenor writes that "peace is untrue by nature, a common counterfeit of nations."[39] And there's "no more treacherous a peace than the nuclear commerce / of the Peace Memorial Museum in Hiroshima," with feel-good messages emblazoned on every souvenir T-shirt: "No More Hiroshima, August 6, 1945," and "Hiroshima Loves Peace."[40] Against such phoniness, the only truth is the *tatari*, "spirits of retribution and vengeance, a curse of kami." This is what haunts the Japanese: "the tatari of the dead, that is, the vengeance of people who had been killed, or killed themselves, after being falsely accused or unfairly treated." The *tatari* will "persecute its enemies, strike at the innocent in passing," and stop at nothing.[41]

Here is a rejoinder of sorts, not specifically aimed at Faulkner but devastating all the same. And yet, such is the nature of mediation that it's not the last word, not the absolute verdict. I'd like to temper its finality with an in-progress sequel, adding to Vizenor's unappeasable voice a different voice, from two poems by the Choctaw-Welsh poet Jim Barnes: one, a direct response to Faulkner, carefully staged; and the other, not intended as a response at all but, in its trans-Pacific arc and its many accidental echoes, as good a response as any.

In "The Only Photograph of Quentin at Harvard" (1982), Barnes begins and ends with two pairs of hands and a book:

> On the far left, at the edge,
> a pair of hands holds
> an open book.

At the right-hand bottom corner
a pair of shoes hangs
pegged to the wall,

the soles outward and soiled.
At the end of a word Shreve laces
his hands in his lap.
Central, across the checkered table,
Quentin counts the silence in his throat
below a half-
curtained bookcase. A mirror
reflects pictures pyramided
up a wall.
The one window is draped in white
gauze. Time is stilled
forever
in a hushed tone of sand.
The hands are about
to turn a page.[42]

The photo is of course apocryphal, as there can be no photo of a fictional character. The scene here, though, could easily have come from either *The Sound and the Fury* or *Absalom, Absalom!*—more likely the latter, given the tenor of the composition. Everything is in pairs here: the shoes, the pictures (thanks to the mirror), and the two friends, one lapsing into silence and the other about to speak, their hands cross-stitched in their gesture of expectancy. This is a Quentin not alone, not in despair, a Quentin literally and metaphorically with an open book, about to turn a page.

Without being asked, Barnes has come up with a nontragic sequel to Faulkner. It can't undo the tragedy already in the script; but while the open book remains open and while the companionship lasts, that ending can be momentarily put off, a weakly reparative action that turns the indefinite back-and-forth into a shared lifeline. This indefinite back-and-forth is also what Barnes highlights in a poem featuring not a photograph but a postcard—"After a Postcard from Stryk in Japan" (2001)—its very structure of sending and receiving already affirming a long-standing bond between the two friends:

Lucien, all
the green river,
falling
green beneath
the green bridge,
all
the green houses,
their windows
opening light
onto the river
falling
now beyond
the green bridge
into the green sky,
and now
    all
        quiet
the green night blossoms.[43]

The "Lucien" in question is Lucien Stryk, poet and translator of Zen poetry, born in Poland, professor for more than thirty years at Northern
Illinois University, with a lifelong attachment to the haiku of Issa and
Bashō, and visiting Japan often to teach at Niigata University and Yama-
guchi University.[44] In this postcard, there's no hint of the atomic bombs
and no hint of catastrophe anywhere in the world, though elsewhere,
notably in the poem "Choctaw Cemetery," Barnes is pointed about the
infant mortality and decimated populations among Native peoples:

Familiar glyphs:
ushi holitopa
The dates:
short years[45]

Instead, the postcard, like the apocryphal photo of Quentin, celebrates
the life-giving force of continuity across different experiential registers:
the green bridge mirroring the green river, the houses and the sky mirroring both, making even the night green.

This is what Faulkner was hoping to find in the word *Yoknapatawpha*—"water flowing slow through the flatland"—a peace impossible to achieve as an absolute outcome. It can take shape slowly and collaboratively, however, as an oblique and incremental arc, a nonlinear process beginning with Jim Barnes and Lucien Stryk and to be continued by others. These two names are almost never seen in the company of Faulkner. Unbeknownst to him, however, they have done what they can to ground his hoped-for atonement. This trans-Pacific network, low-key and steadfast, links the catastrophe of New World genocide to the catastrophe of the atomic bombs without stopping with either. Speaking on Faulkner's behalf and perhaps in his despite, Jim Barnes and Lucien Stryk show that weak reparation could indeed open into nontragic sequels.

Afterword

NOT PARALYZED

Many things came to me during my four weeks at Spaulding Rehab: consolatory emails, cards, some flowers, and a care package from *PMLA* that kept me going for the entirety of my stay. What I never expected was a translation of a story by the Japanese writer Shiga Naoya, sent by the translator, Scott Miller, Dean of Humanities at Brigham Young University.

I had visited BYU—for a symposium entitled, with singular prescience, "On Being Vulnerable"—just three weeks before being struck by a car. Scott was in attendance almost the entire time. We talked briefly, and I learned that his missionary work in Japan had affected him deeply, leaving him with an abiding love for Japanese cinema and early sound recordings as well as literature of all genres, all periods.

"Impressions from Kinosaki," the story by Shiga, features a protagonist recuperating at the Kinosaki hot springs to avoid contracting a spine disease after being struck by a train. There is no plot, just a sequence of musings as he encounters a dead wasp, a rat pierced through the throat by a skewer but still struggling to stay alive, and a newt that he accidentally kills.[1] Hermetic in its eerie details, the story nonetheless spoke to me, to my matter-of-fact surroundings at Spaulding, with great immediacy. I read it at one sitting and felt unaccountably renewed at the end.

Was it the last line: "At least I managed to avoid contracting the spine disease"? Was it the luminous prose of the translator, an unobtrusive conduit for Shiga's equally unobtrusive art? Or was it the teasing coincidence between that story and my life, an offbeat forecast of my chances for survival, as gratefully received as it was unsought? Scott Miller had no idea of me, or of my accident, when he translated the story. Yet here I was, an ideal recipient for his work—ideal, both because it arrived at a moment of need and because it was only by the merest chance that I read it at all. Why was it that someone like me could nonetheless get a boost that seemingly came from nowhere, released from paralysis as a left-field beneficiary?

Collateral resilience is the term I propose to highlight such left-field developments, nonlinear agency multiplying through the off-course cascading of events. Emerging on the other side of the spectrum from *collateral damage*, it adds an odd twist to our fatalistic sense that side effects can only take the form of harm. Reversing that fatalism, the asymmetry here between deed and consequence works in the opposite direction. Just as harm radiates outward to a larger circle of recipients than the intended target, so, too, the chance to rebound ripples unpredictably, bearing fruit in circumstances far removed from its primary sphere of operation.

In a recent *PMLA* column,[2] I point to the resurgence of indigenous languages as an example of such nonlinear agency, a networked effect emerging peripherally and against all odds, allowing the historically handicapped to be tenacious survivors. I'd like to wrap up here by returning briefly to that argument. I begin with Luther Standing Bear's *My People the Sioux* (1928), an indigenous autobiography showing us just what collateral resilience might do when its weak input into the future is recognized—as not more but also not less than what it sets out to be.

A writer, orator, and eventual leader of the Oglala Lakota Nation, Standing Bear worked for the Wanamaker Department Store while a student at the Carlisle Indian Industrial School in Pennsylvania. He had a chance to see Sitting Bull in a Philadelphia theater when, for four months in 1885, the legendary Lakota chief toured with Buffalo Bill's Wild West Show:

> On the stage sat four Indian men, one of whom was Sitting Bull. There were two women and two children with them. A white man came on stage and introduced Sitting Bull as the man who had killed General Custer (which, of course, was absolutely false). Sitting Bull arose and addressed the audience in the Sioux tongue, as he did not speak nor understand English. He said, "My friends, white people, we Indians are on our way to Washington to see the Grandfather, or President of the

United States. I see so many white people and what they are doing, that it makes me glad to know that some day my children will be educated also. There is no use fighting any longer. The buffalo are all gone, as well as the rest of the game. Now I am going to shake the hand of the Great Father at Washington, and I am going to tell him all these things." Then Sitting Bull sat down. He never even mentioned Custer's name.[3]

Sitting Bull, celebrated for his war prowess since he was fourteen, was less military minded in his last decades. Though popularly credited with the destruction of Lieutenant Colonel George A. Custer's Seventh Cavalry at the 1876 Battle of the Little Bighorn, he was in fact not present, the fighting being done by his nephew White Bull and the Oglala Lakota warrior Crazy Horse. When the US Army retaliated with intensified attacks and systematic destruction of the buffalo, Sitting Bull went into exile in Canada for four years. He surrendered to the US government in July 1881, and was held prisoner for two years before being assigned to the Standing Rock Reservation in North Dakota. In 1890, he was killed during a scuffle with the reservation police.

The year 1885 marked a special point of vulnerability for Sitting Bull. As part of Buffalo Bill's Wild West Show, he was an exhibit in a vast entertainment industry. And he had a further disadvantage. Unable to speak English, he was at the mercy of the fabrications of the white stage manager, able to get his story across to non-Lakota-speakers only if someone fluent in both languages happened to be present.

That linguistic disability gives Sitting Bull a far more vital future than if he had been able to speak English. There's no better example of non-paralysis than this aging warrior, hemmed in by circumstances, his exploits told secondhand, but able to survive with the help of others, those who obliquely reach back to his linguistic disability and turn it into the beginning of a path forward. Standing Bear's *My People the Sioux*, keeping Sitting Bull's memory alive when it was first published by Houghton Mifflin in 1928, was reissued by the University of Nebraska Press in 1975, and reissued again in 2006 as a Bison Books edition, with a new introduction by Virginia Driving Hawk Sneve. Two new books on Sitting Bull himself—focusing specifically on Buffalo Bill's Wild West Show—came out in 2016 and 2017.[4] Above all, the Lakota language, apparently doomed in the late nineteenth century, is showing signs of revival, and on the very Standing Rock Reservation where Sitting Bull was killed.

The Standing Rock Sioux Tribe made history when, for almost three years, it held up the construction of the Dakota Access pipeline, a feat reported all around the world. Even though the Trump administration eventually prevailed, the tribe continues to monitor oil leaks, most recently filing a motion against the pipeline's expansion while persisting in its opposition to the Keystone XL, and gearing up for a new fight, against the innocuously named Line 3.[5] Hundreds of reporters have gone to the Standing Rock Reservation, but one of them, Patrick Cox, was recently there for a different reason: to write a story about the language classes at the Lakota Summer Institute and the making of a new Lakota grammar with the help of a Czech linguist.

The first Lakota grammar was created in 1902 by Father Eugene Buechel, a Jesuit missionary untrained in phonetics. Tribal elders have long been unhappy with it, finding that many of the sounds unique to Lakota are lost in the written form. Recently, an ally showed up in the form of Jan Ullrich, who, growing up in Czechoslovakia under the Soviet Union, "sympathized with other people who had a history of being colonized."[6] Ullrich began learning Lakota from a dictionary found in a Prague library. He is now in a position to advise the tribes on all aspects of grammar, including pronunciation, spelling, and neologisms. Meanwhile, Sitting Bull College, a public college serving the Standing Rock Sioux community, has received a one-hundred-thousand-dollar NEH grant for a "Lakota-Dakota Language Project," making video as well as audio recordings of Native speakers to pass on to a new generation.[7]

The money will run out in three years. And, all these efforts notwithstanding, the number of Lakota speakers will no doubt continue to decline for many years to come. Still, the grammar and the recordings and the language classes aren't trivial. Testaments to nonparalysis, they turn Sitting Bull's late-life frailty into an incremental lifeline. The Standing Rock Sioux Tribe's climate activism he couldn't have foreseen, but its collateral effects he most certainly would have applauded. Weak but not without help from others, defeated again and again but so far uneliminated from the field, these subjunctive experiments might turn out to be coextensive with the planet itself, their hoped-for future marginally but meaningfully within the realm of possibility.

Acknowledgments

I thank the many people who made the writing of this book as slow as it has been—by asking questions, raising doubts, pointing out alternatives, and suggesting more readings than I could do in several lifetimes: Nancy Armstrong, Lauren Berlant, Daphne Brooks, Mary Campbell, Margaret Cohen, Heather Dubrow, Susan Stanford Friedman, Brandon Menke, Paul Saint-Amour, Susan Staves, Jesse Oak Taylor, Karen Thornber, Hap Veeser, and Kyle Powys Whyte. Edgar Garcia, Kyle Hutzler, Jordan Brower, and Nick Rinehart, coeditors for the *American Literature in the World* anthology, taught me what collaboration means. Bob Wallace, Harriet McGurk, and the Frank Stella Studio helped with high-resolution image files that anchor the book technically, philosophically, and emotionally. Tilda St. Pierre, Lakota artist, turns the book cover into a visual argument beyond my wildest dreams.

Weak Planet is about assisted life; the writing process exemplified it. Randy Petilos and Alan Thomas at the University of Chicago Press shamed me into finishing by putting more into the project than any editor would. Sandy Hazel's copyediting saved the day in countless ways. June Sawyers's index is a work of art. Tim Lyu and Zoe Siegelnickel, the next generation, launched the book with their superb proofreading. Zoe and Rae Ganci Hammers also put their magical touch on the cover design. Sara Pastel, Angela Gibson, Isabel Guan, Joe Wallace, Barney Latimer, and Annabel Schneider, the extraordinary team at *PMLA*, fortified me with their sane and steadfast rhythms. All of this would have come to nothing, of course, if Amy Allen and Lindsay Dodge, physical therapists at Spaulding Rehab, hadn't been there at a critical moment. Liz Liberge, Steve Shennan and Tori Hricko, Sarah Dunlap and Mike Itz, David Kopp and Andy Bergman, Allen Davis and Barbara Sweet took care of me, walked my dog, and carried me up and down three flights of stairs for doctors' appointments. I can't say how lucky I am to be sustained by such networks.

* * *

Earlier, much revised versions of three chapters appeared as follows: chapter 1 in *Early American Literature* 50, no. 1 (2015); chapter 4 in *Critical Inquiry* 39, no. 4 (Summer 2013); and chapter 6 in *Modernism/Modernity* 25, no. 3 (September 2018). I thank the editors of these journals for allowing me to think through some of the ideas first in their pages.

Notes

INTRODUCTION

1. On October 11, 2018, I was admitted to Mt. Auburn Hospital in Cambridge, Massachusetts, and then transferred to Spaulding Rehabilitation Hospital in Allston, with fractures to my right shoulder and left knee. Four months in a wheelchair gave me a unique perspective on the importance of assisted survival. Reinjuring my shoulder in January 2019 made it clear that experiments in nonparalysis are best undertaken collectively.

2. Wai Chee Dimock, "Weak Theory," *Critical Inquiry* 39 (Summer 2013): 732–53. See also Paul K. Saint-Amour, ed., "Weak Theory, Weak Modernism," special issue, *Modernism/Modernity* 3 (2018).

3. For the effect of genocide on the climate, see Jonathan Amos, "America Colonisation 'Cooled Earth's Climate,'" BBC, January 31, 2019, https://www.bbc.com/news/science-environment-47063973; and Lauren Kent, "European Colonizers Killed So Many Native Americans That It Changed the World's Climate," CNN, February 2, 2019, https://www.cnn.com/2019/02/01/world/european-colonization-climate-change-trnd/index.html.

4. Here, I follow David Treuer, Gerald Vizenor, Kyle Powys Whyte, and Dan Wildcat, who see Native history as resourceful survival in the face of devastations. See Treuer, *The Heartbeat of Wounded Knee: Native America from 1890 to the Present* (New York: Penguin Random House, 2019); Vizenor, *Survivance: Narratives of Native Presence* (Lincoln: University of Nebraska Press, 2008); Whyte, "Our Ancestors' Dystopia Now: Indigenous Conservation and the Anthropocene," in *The Routledge Companion to the Environmental Humanities*, ed. Ursula Heise, Jon Christensen, and Michelle Niemann (New York: Routledge, 2016), 206–15; Whyte, "Indigenous Climate Change Studies: Indigenizing Futures, Decolonizing the Anthropocene," *English Language Notes* 55 (Fall 2017): 153–62; Whyte, "Critical Investigations of Resilience: A Brief Introduction to Indigenous Environmental Studies and Sciences," *Daedalus* 147 (2018): 136–47; and Wildcat, *Red*

Alert: Saving the Planet with Indigenous Knowledge (Golden, CO: Fulcrum Press, 2009). See also Vine Deloria's discussion of resilient tribalism in *We Talk, You Listen: New Tribes, New Turfs* (New York: Dell, 1970); and Pekka Hamalainen, *Lakota America: A New History of Indigenous Power* (New Haven, CT: Yale University Press, 2019); and Jonathan Lear, *Radical Hope: Ethics in Face of Cultural Devastation* (Cambridge, MA: Harvard University Press, 2006), on the nondespair of Plenty Coups, Chief of the Crow Nation.

5. The crucial presence of indigenous tribes against deforestation in the Amazon both before and during the devastating fires is the clearest example of such non-paralysis. See Naomi Klein, "The Amazon Is On Fire—Indigenous Rights Can Help Put It Out," *Boston Globe*, August 25, 2019, https://www.bostonglobe.com /opinion/2019/08/26/the-amazon-fire-indigenous-rights-can-help-put-out/Qylc SQzyPPh52cYzwEvVSO/story.html.

6. Interestingly, *vulnerability* is emerging as a key term in social psychology. See Brené Brown's June 2010 TED Talk, "The Power of Vulnerability," https://www .ted.com/talks/brene_brown_on_vulnerability?language=en; and a related inter-view with *Forbes*, "Brené Brown: How Vulnerability Can Make Our Lives Better," *Forbes*, April 21, 2013, https://www.forbes.com/sites/danschawbel/2013/04/21 /brene-brown-how-vulnerability-can-make-our-lives-better/#838611136c72.

7. See especially Lennard J. Davis, *The Disability Studies Reader* (New York, Rout-ledge, 1997); Elizabeth Ellcessor, Mack Hagood, and Bill Kirkpatrick, eds., *Disability Media Studies* (New York: New York University Press, 2017); Rosemarie Garland-Thomson, *Extraordinary Bodies: Figuring Physical Disability in American Literature* (New York: Columbia University Press, 1997); Alison Kafer, *Feminist, Queer, Crip* (Bloomington: Indiana University Press, 2013); Simi Linton, *Claiming Disability* (New York: New York University Press, 1998); and Tobin Siebers, *Disability Theory* (Ann Arbor: University of Michigan Press, 2009).

8. Robert McRuer, *Crip Theory: Cultural Signs of Queerness and Disability* (New York: New York University Press, 2006); McRuer, *Crip Times: Disability, Globalization, Resistance* (New York: New York University Press, 2018). See also Eunjung Kim, *Curative Violence: Rehabilitating Disability, Gender, and Sexuality in North Korea* (Durham, NC: Duke University Press, 2017).

9. Aimi Hamraie, *Building Access: Universal Design and the Politics of Disability* (Minneapolis: University of Minnesota Press, 2017); Bess Williamson, *Accessible America: A History of Disability and Design* (New York; New York University Press, 2019). For recent scientific work exploring disability as an alter-nate form of ability, see Scott Barry Kaufman, "Autism: More Than Meets the Eye; How Ability Grows out of Seeming Disability," *Scientific American*, June 19, 2019, https://blogs.scientificamerican.com/beautiful-minds/autism -more-than-meets-the-eye/.

10. Donna Haraway, *Staying with the Trouble: Making Kin in the Chthulucene* (Durham, NC: Duke University Press, 2016).

11. Anthony Hallam and P. B. Wignall, *Mass Extinctions and Their Aftermaths* (Oxford: Oxford University Press, 1997), 1. For an update, see Elizabeth Kolbert, *The Sixth Extinction: An Unnatural History* (New York: Henry Holt, 2014). For projected economic disruptions, see the Fourth U.S. National Climate Assessment, released on November 22, 2018. Summarizing its findings, the assessment states that "climate change creates new risks and exacerbates existing vulnerabilities in communities across the United States, presenting growing challenges to human health and safety, quality of life, and the rate of economic growth," and that "without substantial and sustained global mitigation and regional adaptation efforts, climate change is expected to cause growing losses to American infrastructure and property and impede the rate of economic growth over this century." https://nca2018.globalchange.gov/.

12. Stephen Leahy, "One Million Species at Risk of Extinction," *National Geographic*, May 6, 2019, https://www.nationalgeographic.com/environment/2019/05/ipbes-un-biodiversity-report-warns-one-million-species-at-risk/.

13. Dipesh Chakrabarty, "The Climate of History: Four Theses," *Critical Inquiry* 35 (2009): 197–222; quotation is from p. 213. Timothy Morton's argument about individual humans as "subscending" from the human species offers an interesting variation on Chakrabarty's argument. See Morton, *Humankind: Solidarity with Nonhuman People* (New York: Verso, 2017), especially 101–20.

14. Elizabeth A. Povinelli, "The Ends of Humans: Anthropocene, Autonomism, Antagonism, and the Illusions of Our Epoch," *South Atlantic Quarterly* 116 (2017): 293–310; quotation is from p. 293. Sylvia Wynter calls attention to the coloniality embedded in the concept of the human. See "Unsettling the Coloniality of Being/Power/Truth/Freedom: Towards the Human, after Man, Its Overrepresentation—an Argument," *CR: The New Centennial Review* 3 (2003): 257–337. For a critique of humanism focusing on geology, see Kathryn Yusoff, *A Million Black Anthropocenes or None* (Minneapolis: University of Minnesota Press, 2018).

15. In the 1844 *Political and Economic Manuscripts*, Marx describes humans as "species-beings" constituted by free productive labor. Rob Nixon highlights the unequal distribution of harm as well as unequal distribution of labor. See *Slow Violence and the Environmentalism of the Poor* (Cambridge, MA: Harvard University Press, 2011). For Jedidiah Purdy's damage-responsive politics, see *After Nature: A Politics for the Anthropocene* (Cambridge, MA: Harvard University Press, 2015).

16. While Judith Butler focuses on the troubling link between vulnerability and aggression in the context of 9/11, I'd like to call attention to vulnerability as a condition for resilience in climate crisis. See Butler, *Precarious Life: The Powers of Mourning and Violence* (New York: Verso, 2004). For queer, African-American, and Asian-American accounts of vulnerability as energizing, see Viet Thanh Nguyen's short story collection, *The Refugees* (New York: Grove Atlantic, 2017); Stephen Best, *The Fugitive Properties: Law and the Poetics of Possession* (Chicago:

University of Chicago Press, 2004); Dorinne Kondo, *Worldmaking: Race, Performance, and the Role of Creativity* (Durham, NC: Duke University Press, 2018); Fred Moten and Stefano Harney, *The Undercommons: Fugitive Planning and Black Study* (Wivenhoe, UK: Minor Compositions, 2013); José Esteban Muñoz, *Cruising Utopia: The Then and There of Queer Futurity* (New York: New York University Press, 2009); and Christina Sharpe, *In the Wake: On Blackness and Being* (Durham, NC: Duke University Press, 2016). See also Rebecca Solnit, *A Paradise Built in Hell: The Extraordinary Communities That Arise in Disasters* (New York: Penguin, 2009).

17.   Friedrich Kittler, "There Is No Software," in *The Truth of the Technological World: Essays on the Genealogy of Presence* (Stanford, CA: Stanford University Press, 2014), 220.

18.   The work of Jane Bennett, Donna Haraway, and Anna Lowenhaupt Tsing is especially important here. See Bennett, *Vibrant Matter* (Durham, NC: Duke University Press, 2010); Haraway, *Staying with the Trouble*; Haraway, *When Species Meet* (Minneapolis: U of Minnesota P, 2006); Haraway, *Simians, Cyborgs, and Women* (New York: Routledge, 1991); Tsing et al., *Arts of Living on a Damaged Planet* (Minneapolis: University of Minnesota Press, 2017); and Tsing, *The Mushroom at the End of the World: On the Possibility of Life in Capitalist Ruins* (Princeton, NJ: Princeton University Press, 2015).

19.   Benjamin Bratton, *The Stack: On Software and Sovereignty* (Cambridge, MA: MIT Press, 2016).

20.   The rhizome's multiple and lateral connectivity is the central argument in Gilles Deleuze and Feliz Guattari, *A Thousand Plateaus*, trans. Brian Massumi (Minneapolis: University of Minnesota Press, 1987). Lauren Berlant discusses "lateral agency" versus "sovereign agency" in *Cruel Optimism* (Durham, NC: Duke University Press, 2011).

21.   Bruno Latour, *Reassembling the Social: An Introduction to Actor-Network Theory* (Oxford: Oxford University Press, 2005), 55.

22.   Latour, 37-42.

23.   The #MeToo movement is a good example of such a nonparalyzed weak network. While media attention has typically focused on the glamorous and visible, *Time* magazine, by naming #MeToo as the 2017 Person of the Year, has performed an invaluable service in highlighting the agency of ordinary women: dishwashers, housekeepers, and hospitality workers. "The Silence Breakers," *Time*, December 18, 2017, http://time.com/time-person-of-the-year-2017-silence-breakers/.

24.   Manuel Castells, *The Rise of the Network Society*, 2nd ed. (Oxford: Blackwell, 2000), 384, 388.

25.   Lee Rainie and Barry Wellman, *Networked: The New Social Operating System* (Cambridge, MA: MIT Press, 2012).

26.   Mark S. Granovetter, "The Strength of Weak Ties," *American Journal of Sociology* 78, no. 6 (May 1973): 1360-80; Granovetter, *Getting a Job: A Study of Contacts and Careers* (Cambridge, MA: Harvard University Press, 1974), 4.

27.   Granovetter, "The Strength of Weak Ties," 1360.

28. For an important discussion of genre as empirical rather than logical, see Ralph Cohen, "History and Theory," *New Literary History* 17 (1986): 203–21. See also Wai Chee Dimock, "Genres as Fields of Knowledge," *PMLA* 122 (October 2007): 1377–88.

29. Gianni Vattimo and Pier Aldo Rovatti, eds., *Weak Thought*, trans. Peter Carravetta (Albany: SUNY Press, 2012).

30. Howard Rheingold's discussion of virtual reality and virtual community is especially helpful here. Rheingold, *Virtual Reality* (New York: Summit Book, 1991); Rheingold, *The Virtual Community: Homesteading on the Electronic Frontier* (New York, Addison-Wesley, 1993). See also Katherine N. Hayles, "Embodied Virtuality: Or How to Put Bodies Back into the Picture," in *Immersed in Technology: Art and Virtual Environments*, ed. M. A. Moser and D. MacLeod (Cambridge, MA: MIT Press, 1996), 1–28.

31. Arjun Appadurai, *Modernity at Large: Cultural Dimensions of Globalization* (Minneapolis: University of Minnesota Press, 1996).

32. Lisa Parks and Nicole Starosielski, eds., *Signal Traffic: Critical Studies of Media Infrastructures* (Urbana: University of Illinois Press, 2015). Patrick Jagoda distinguishes between the linear media forms of novel, film, and television and the distributed media forms of digital and alternate reality games in *Network Aesthetic* (Chicago: University of Chicago Press, 2016). See also Tung-Hui Hu, *A Prehistory of the Cloud* (Cambridge, MA: MIT Press, 2015); and John Durham Peters, *The Marvelous Clouds: Toward a Philosophy of Elemental Media* (Chicago: University of Chicago Press, 2015).

33. Benedict Anderson, *Imagined Communities: Reflections on the Origin and Spread of Nationalism* (London: Verso, 1983).

34. Marshall McLuhan, *The Gutenberg Galaxy: The Making of Typographic Man* (Toronto: University of Toronto Press, 1962). He was thinking especially of radio and television, two media that challenge print. See also McLuhan, *Understanding Media: The Extensions of Man* (New York: McGraw Hill, 1964). For other accounts of the auditory and the visual, see Jacques Rancière, *The Politics of Aesthetics: The Distribution of the Sensible*, trans. Gabriel Rockhill (New York: Continuum, 2005). For the importance of visual forms to contemporary fiction, see Debjani Ganguly, *This Thing Called the World: Contemporary Novel as Global Form* (Durham, NC: Duke University Press, 2016). For the ascendancy of audiobooks, see "New Chapter? UK Print Book Sales Fall while Audiobooks Surge by 43%," *Guardian* (US edition), June 25, 2019, https://www.theguard ian.com/books/2019/jun/26/new-chapter-uk-print-book-sales-fall-while-au diobooks-surge-43; and Ellen Duffer, "Audiobooks Revenue Soared in 2018," *Forbes*, June 25, 2019, https://www.forbes.com/sites/ellenduffer/2019/06/25 /audiobook-revenues-soared-in-2018/#354e6845219f.

35. Henry Jenkins, *Textual Poachers: Television Fans and Participatory Culture* (New York: Routledge, 1992); Jenkins, *Participatory Culture in a Networked Era*

(Cambridge: Polity Press, 2015); and Jenkins, *By Any Media Necessary: The Partic-ipatory Culture of American Youth* (New York: New York University Press, 2016). See also Anne Jamison, *Fic: Why Fanfiction Is Taking Over the World* (Dallas: BenBella Books, 2013). For public recognition of the fan fiction site An Archive of Our Own, see "An Archive of Our Own Is Now a Hugo Nominee," *Vox*, April 11, 2019, https://www.vox.com/2019/4/11/18292419/archive-of-our-own-hugo-award-nomination-related-work. For fans as accomplished information organiz-ers, see Gretchen McCullogh, "Fans Are Better Than Tech in Organizing Infor-mation Online," *Wired*, June 11, 2019, https://www.wired.com/story/archive-of-our-own-fans-better-than-tech-organizing-information/.

36. For a sustained engagement with Eve Sedgwick's indispensable work on "repar-ative reading," see chapter 6. Here, my sense of literary history as imperfect and incessant draws from her account of error as generative in the systems theory of Silvan Tomkins. See Eve Kosofsky Sedgwick and Adam Frank, "Shame in the Cybernetic Fold: Reading Silvan Tomkins," *Critical Inquiry* 21 (1995): 496–522.

37. Without specifically using the language of crowdsourcing, T. S. Eliot, in his es-say "Tradition and the Individual Talent" (1919), also sees literature as input-accepting and continually updated.

38. John Dewey, "Escape from Peril," in *The Later Works, 1925–1953*, ed. Jo Ann Boydston, vol. 4, *1929* (Carbondale: Southern Illinois University Press, 1988), 4, 17, 5, 6.

39. William James, "The Present Dilemma in Philosophy," in *Pragmatism and Other Essays* (New York: Washington Square Books, 1963), 21.

40. James, 21. See also James's discussion of "the 'possible' as something less than the actual and more than the wholly unreal": "Pragmatism and Common Sense," in ibid., 73–86; quotation is from p. 80.

41. Henri Matisse, answer to Alfred Barr's questionnaire, 1945; archive of the Mu-seum of Modern Art, New York. Quoted in Jack Cowart, National Gallery of Art, et al., *Matisse in Morocco: The Paintings and Drawings, 1912–1913*, exhibition cata-log (Washington, DC: National Gallery of Art, 1990), 110.

CHAPTER ONE

1. Emma Coleman recorded the names of more than 750 New England captives taken to Canada during the French and Indian War alone; she estimates that thousands more, whose names have been lost, might have died along the way or been adopted by the Indians. Another survey compiled by Alden Vaughan and Daniel Richter documents 1,641 New Englanders being captured by Indians be-tween 1675 and 1763. For the nineteenth century, Wilcomb E. Washburn of the Smithsonian Institution estimated that "900 to 1,000 Mexican captives, and a much smaller though not insignificant number of Anglo captives were among the Comanches in 1850." Kathryn Zabelle Derounian-Stodola and James Ar-

thur Levernier speculate that cumulatively, "the incidence of captivity among this single Western tribe must have been well into the thousands. As statistical research continues, other Western tribes such as the Apache and Sioux will no doubt be shown to have trafficked in similarly large number of captives." See Emma Coleman, *New England Captives Carried to Canada* (Portland, ME: Southworth Press, 1925); Alden T. Vaughan and Daniel K. Richter, "Crossing the Cultural Divide: Indians and New Englanders, 1605–1763," *Proceedings of the American Antiquarian Society* 90 (1980): 91; Wilcomb E. Washburn, introduction to *Narratives of North American Captivity: A Selective Bibliography*, ed. Alden T. Vaughan (New York: Garland, 1983), xviii; and Kathryn Zabelle Derounian-Stodola and James Arthur Levernier, *The Indian Captivity Narrative, 1550–1900* (New York: Twayne, 1993), 2.

2. Michelle Burnham, *Captivity and Sentiment: Cultural Exchange in American Literature, 1682–1861* (Hanover, NH: University Press of New England, 1997), 26.

3. Alden T. Vaughan and Edward W. Clark, eds., *Puritans among the Indians: Accounts of Captivity and Redemption* (Cambridge, MA: Harvard University Press, 1981), 2.

4. Linda Colley, "Perceiving Low Literature: The Captivity Narrative," *Essays in Criticism* 53 (2003): 199–218; quotation is from p. 200. Subsequent references are given in the text.

5. Linda Colley is best known, of course, for *Captives* (New York: Pantheon Books, 2002), chronicling British captives held in India and North Africa as well as America. For related works, see Lisa Voigt, *Writing Captivity in the Early Modern Atlantic: Circulations of Knowledge and Authority in the Iberian and English Imperial Worlds* (Chapel Hill: University of North Carolina Press, 2009); and Gordon Sayre, "Renegades in Barbary," *Early American Literature* 45 (2010): 325–38.

6. Mary Rowlandson, *The Sovereignty and Goodness of God, together with the Faithfulness of His Promises Displayed, Being a Narrative of the Captivity and Restoration of Mrs. Mary Rowlandson and Related Documents*. Ed. Neal Salisbury (Boston: Bedford-St. Martin's, 1997), 95.

7. "A Narrative of Hannah Swarton, containing Wonderful Passages, related to her Captivity and her Deliverance," from Cotton Mather, *Magnalia Christi Americana*, bk. 4; included in Vaughan and Clark, *Puritans among the Indians*, 148–57; quotation is from p. 149.

8. "A Narrative of Hannah Swarton," 148–49.

9. "A Narrative of Hannah Swarton," 150.

10. Rowlandson, *The Sovereignty and Goodness of God*, 96.

11. Richard Slotkin, Amanda Porterfield, Mitchell Breitwieser, and Jordan Alexander Stein have likewise been struck by this passage. While Slotkin and Porterfield see this as an instance of cultural hypocrisy, Breitwieser reads it as a double-edged moment: a "protesting too much that betrays the vitality of what it seeks to deny," and a "surprisingly candid . . . desire to *live* rather than to *live for*." Stein

emphasizes the extent to which hunger in Rowlandson is "deinstrumentalized, a matter of taste and not just need." See Richard Slotkin, *Regeneration through Violence: Mythology of the American Frontier, 1600–1800* (Middletown, CT: Wesleyan University Press, 1969), 110; Amanda Porterfield, *Female Piety in Puritan America* (New York: Oxford University Press, 1991), 139; Mitchell Breitwieser, *American Puritanism and the Defense of Mourning: Religion, Grief, and Ethnology in Mary White Rowlandson's Captivity Narrative* (Madison: University of Wisconsin Press, 1990), 141; and Jordan Alexander Stein, "Mary Rowlandson's Hunger and the Historiography of Sexuality," *American Literature* 81 (2009): 469–95; quotation is from p. 474.

12.   Rowlandson, *The Sovereignty and Goodness of God*, 93.

13.   Rowlandson, 111.

14.   Giorgio Agamben, *Homo Sacer: Sovereign Power and Bare Life*, trans. Daniel Heller-Roazen (1995; Stanford, CA: Stanford University Press, 1998), 104.

15.   Agamben, 9.

16.   Louise Erdrich, introduction to *The Falcon: A Narrative of the Captivity and Adventures of John Tanner during Thirty Years Residence among the Indians in the Interior of North America* (New York: Penguin, 1994), xi–xv; quotation is from p. xi. Subsequent references are given in the text.

17.   Gordon M. Sayre, "Abridging between Two Worlds: John Tanner as American Indian Autobiographer," *American Literary History* 11 (Autumn 2001): 481–99; quotations are from pp. 485, 484. Gordon Brotherston, perhaps the foremost authority on Native American writing systems, cites Edwin James's pictographs and translations of Ojibwa "Metai" songs in his *Book of the Fourth World: Reading the Native Americas through Their Literature* (Cambridge: Cambridge University Press, 1992), 283–84. For a detailed discussion of the coauthorship of John Tanner and Edwin James as a precedent-setting cross-cultural collaboration, see Kyhl D. Lyndgaard, *Captivity Literature and the Environment: Nineteenth-Century American Cross-Cultural Collaborations* (Oxon: Routledge, 2017), 64–98.

18.   In a somewhat different language, T. S. Eliot describes the same phenomenon in his 1919 essay "Tradition and the Individual Talent."

19.   W. V. Quine, "Speaking of Objects," in *Ontological Relativity and Other Essays* (New York: Columbia University Press, 1969), 1–25; quotation is from p. 23.

20.   Michel-Rolph Trouillot, *Silencing the Past: Power and the Production of History* (Boston: Beacon Press, 2015), 3.

21.   Mark Ward, "Tuning in to the Background Hum of the Net," BBC, November 10, 2010, http://www.bbc.com/news/technology-11863294.

22.   For a technical discussion, see Alain Barrat, Marc Barthelemy, and Alessandro Vespignani, *Dynamical Processes in Complex Networks* (Cambridge: Cambridge University Press, 2012).

23.   Matt Cohen, *The Networked Wilderness: Communicating in Early New England* (Minneapolis: University of Minnesota Press, 2010).

NOTES TO PAGES 29-31

185

24. Birgit Brander Rasmussen's *Queequeg's Coffin: Indigenous Literacies and Early American Literature* (Durham, NC: Duke University Press, 2012); Jeffrey Glover's *Paper Sovereigns: Anglo-Native Treaties and the Law of Nations, 1604-1664* (Philadelphia: University of Pennsylvania Press, 2014); and Sarah Rivett's *Unscripted America: Indigenous Languages and the Origins of a Literary Nation* (New York: Oxford University Press, 2017).

25. For networked indigeneity in the twenty-first century, see Marisa Elena Duarte, *Network Sovereignty: Building the Internet across Indian Country* (Seattle: University of Washington Press, 2017).

26. Arnold Krupat argues that Native American autobiography as a genre attests to interracial collaborations. These autobiographies, he says, "are not actually self-written, but are, rather, texts marked by the principle of original, bicultural composite composition. That is to say, these texts are the end-products of a rather complex process involving a three-part collaboration between a white editor-amanuensis who edits, polishes, revises, or otherwise fixes the 'form' of the text in writing, a Native 'subject' whose orally presented life story serves as the 'content' of the autobiographical narrative, and, in almost all cases, a mixed-blood interpreter/translator whose exact contribution to the autobiographical project remains one of the least understood aspects of Indian autobiography." See Arnold Krupat, ed., *Native American Autobiography: An Anthology* (Madison: University of Wisconsin Press, 1994), 3-4.

27. Thomas Greene, *The Vulnerable Text: Essays on Renaissance Literature* (New York: Columbia University Press, 1986).

28. Greene, xiv.

29. Greene, 103.

30. Wai Chee Dimock, "A Theory of Resonance," *PMLA* 112 (October 1997): 1060-71.

31. Roy Harvey Pearce, "The Significances of the Captivity Narrative," *American Literature* 19 (1947): 1-20; Richard VanDerBeets, ed., *Held Captive by Indians: Selected Narratives, 1642-1836* (Knoxville: University of Tennessee Press, 1973).

32. Excerpt from Louise Erdrich, "Captivity," in *Jacklight: Poems* (New York: Holt, 1984), 27.

33. Rowlandson, *The Sovereignty and Goodness of God*, 111.

34. Susan Howe, *My Emily Dickinson* (Berkeley, CA: North Atlantic Books, 1985), 21.

35. Howe, 43.

36. Mitchell Breitwieser, *American Puritanism and the Defense of Mourning: Religion, Grief, and Ethnology in Mary White Rowlandson's Captivity Narrative* (Madison: University of Wisconsin Press, 1990); Michelle Burnham, "The Journey Between: Liminality and Dialogism in Mary White Rowlandson's Captivity Narrative," *Early American Literature* 28 (1993): 60-75; Christopher Castiglia, *Bound and Determined: Captivity, Culture-Crossing, and White Womanhood from Mary Rowlandson to Patty Hearst* (Chicago: University of Chicago Press, 1996);

Kathryn Zabelle Derounian-Stodola, "Captivity, Liberty, and Early American Consciousness," *Early American Literature* 43 (2008): 715-24; Kathryn Zabelle Derounian-Stodola, "Puritan Orthodoxy and the 'Survivor Syndrome' in Mary Rowlandson's Indian Captivity Narrative," *Early American Literature* 22 (1987): 82-93; and Teresa Toulouse, *The Captive's Position: Female Narrative, Male Identity, and Royal Authority in Colonial New England* (Philadelphia: University of Pennsylvania Press, 2007).

37.   Howe, *My Emily Dickinson*, 43.

38.   Rowlandson, *The Sovereignty and Goodness of God*, 87.

39.   Lee Rainie and Barry Wellman, *Networked: The New Social Operating System* (Cambridge, MA: MIT Press, 2012).

40.   Increase Mather, preface to Rowlandson, *The Sovereignty and Goodness of God*, 67.

41.   Mather, 67.

42.   Rowlandson, *The Sovereignty and Goodness of God*, 82.

43.   Sherman Alexie, *The Absolutely True Diary of a Part-Time Indian* (New York: Little, Brown, 2007), 7-8.

44.   On new frameworks for Native language learning as well as a historical perspective on language policies in reservation public schools, see Phyllis Bo-Yuen Ngai, "An Emerging Native Language Education Framework on Reservation Public Schools with Mixed Populations," *Journal of American Indian Education* 47 (2008): 22-50.

45.   Richard Henry Pratt, *Battlefield and Classroom: Four Decades with the American Indian, 1867-1904* (New Haven, CT: Yale University Press, 1964), 247, 335.

46.   Pratt, 286.

47.   Sherman Alexie, "Captivity," in *The First Indian on the Moon* (Brooklyn: Hanging Loose Press, 1993), 98.

48.   Even though I will not be discussing Samson Occom (1723-1792), Presbyterian minister and first Native American to publish his writings in English, his language acquisition is very much on my mind.

49.   William Apess, "A Eulogy on King Philip" (1836), in *On Our Own Ground: The Complete Writings of William Apess, A Pequot*, ed. and with an introduction by Barry O'Connell (Amherst: University of Massachusetts Press, 1992), 277.

50.   Philip Gura, *The Life of William Apess, Pequot* (Chapel Hill: University of North Carolina Press, 2015), 105.

51.   Gura, 106.

52.   Apess, "A Eulogy on King Philip," 296.

53.   Barry O'Connell, introduction to *On Our Own Ground*, xx.

54.   Rowlandson, *The Sovereignty and Goodness of God*, 111.

55.   For the relation between settler colonialism, slavery, and indentured labor, see Lisa Lowe, *The Intimacies of Four Continents* (Durham, NC: Duke University Press, 2015). For enslavement of Native Americans, see Jill Lepore, *The Name*

of War: King Philip's War and the Origins of American Identity (New York: Knopf, 1998).

56. Alexie, "Captivity," 98.

57. Erdrich, "Captivity," 26.

58. Yael Ben-Zvi, "Up and Down with Mary Rowlandson: Erdrich's and Alexie's Versions of Captivity," *Studies in American Indian Literatures* 24 (2012): 21-46.

59. John Gyles, *Memoirs of Odd Adventures, Strange Deliverances, etc. in the Captivity of John Gyles, Esq., Commander of the Garrison on St. George River, in the District of Maine, Written by Himself*, in *Held Captive by Indians: Selected Narratives, 1642-1836*, ed. Richard VanDerBeets (Knoxville: University of Tennessee Press, 1973), 98.

60. Jared Hickman, "Globalization and the Gods," *Early American Literature* 45 (2010): 145-82.

61. Benedict Anderson, "Exodus," *Critical Inquiry* 20, no. 2 (1994): 314-27; Ralph Bauer, "Creole Identities in Colonial Space: The Narrative of Mary White Rowlandson and Francisco Nunez de Pineda y Bascunan," *American Literature* 69 (1997): 665-95.

62. Bridget Bennett, "The Crisis of Restoration: Mary Rowlandson's Lost Home," *Early American Literature* 49 (2014): 327-56.

63. Paul Baepler, "The Barbary Captivity Narrative in American Culture," *Early American Literature* 39 (2004): 217-46; Paul Baepler, ed., *White Slaves, African Masters: An Anthology of American Barbary Narratives* (Chicago: University of Chicago Press, 1999); Robert C. Davis, ed., *Christian Slaves, Muslim Masters: White Slavery in the Mediterranean, the Barbary Coast, and Italy, 1500-1800* (Basingstoke, UK: Palgrave Macmillan, 2004); Nabil Matar, "Introduction: England and Mediterranean Captivity, 1577-1704," in *Piracy, Slavery, and Redemption: Barbary Captivity Narratives from Early Modern England*, ed. Daniel J. Vitkus (New York: Columbia University Press, 2001), 1-52; Nabil Matar, *Turks, Moors and Englishmen in the Age of Discovery* (New York: Columbia University Press, 1999); Gordon M. Sayre, ed., *American Captivity Narratives* (Boston: Houghton Mifflin, 2000); Gordon M. Sayre, "Renegades from Barbary: The Transnational Turn in Captivity Studies," *Early American Literature* 45, no. 2 (2010): 325-38; Daniel J. Vitkus, ed., *Piracy, Slavery, and Redemption: Barbary Captivity Narratives from Early Modern England* (New York: Columbia University Press, 2001); and Lisa Voigt, *Writing Captivity in the Early Modern Atlantic: Circulations of Knowledge and Authority in the Iberian and English Imperial Worlds* (Chapel Hill: University of North Carolina Press, 2009).

64. John Williams, *The Redeemed Captive*, ed. Edward W. Clark (Amherst: University of Massachusetts Press, 1976), 74.

65. Edward W. Clark, introduction to Williams, 1-25.

66. James Axtell, *Natives and Newcomers: The Cultural Origins of North America* (New York: Oxford University Press, 2001); James Axtell, "The White Indians of

Colonial America," *William and Mary Quarterly* 32 (1975): 55-88; June Namias, *White Captives: Gender and Ethnicity on the American Frontier* (Chapel Hill: University of North Carolina Press, 1993); Alden T Vaughan, *New England Frontier: Puritans and Indians 1620-1675* (Boston: Little, Brown, 1965).

67. Colin G. Calloway, "An Uncertain Destiny: Indian Captivities on the Upper Connecticut Rivers," *Journal of American Studies* 17 (1983): 189-210; quotation is from p. 194.

68. Wilcomb E. Washburn, introduction to *Narratives of North American Indian Captivity: A Selective Bibliography*, ed. Alden T. Vaughan (New York: Garland, 1983), xi-liii; quotation is from p. xiiv.

69. Kathryn Zabelle Derounian-Stodola and James Arthur Levernier, eds., *The Indian Captivity Narrative, 1550-1900* (New York: Twayne, 1993), 5.

70. Axtell, "The White Indians of Colonial America," 61.

71. J. Hector St. John de Crevecoeur, *Letters from an American Farmer* (New York: Dutton, 1971), 219.

72. Zabelle Derounian-Stodola and Levernier, *The Indian Captivity Narrative*, 6.

73. John Demos, *The Unredeemed Captive* (New York: Knopf, 1994), 3-9. For a full-throated subjunctive story recounting the friendship between the fictional Bethia Mayfield, a young Puritan woman, and the historical Caleb Cheeshahteaumack, a member of the Wampanoag tribe and the first Native American to graduate from Harvard College, see Geraldine Brooks, *Caleb's Crossing* (New York: Viking Penguin, 2011). I thank Michael Warner for alerting me to this novel.

CHAPTER TWO

1. The elimination of humanities departments seems to be a world trend. For a broad overview, see Ella Delany, "Humanities Studies under Strain around the Globe," *New York Times*, December 1, 2013, https://www.nytimes.com/2013/12/02/us /humanities-studies-under-strain-around-the-globe.html. For across-the-board cuts in Japan, see Nash Jenkins, "Alarm over Huge Cuts to Humanities and Social Sciences," *Time*, September 16, 2015, http://time.com/4035819/japan-university-liberal-arts-humanities-social-sciences-cuts/. For recent developments in the United States, see Ben Felder, "How Colleges Are Adapting to Declines in Liberal Arts Majors," *PBS News Hour*, November 30, 2018, https://www.pbs.org /newshour/education/how-colleges-are-adapting-to-the-decline-in-liberal arts-majors; Reshmi Dutt-Ballerstadt, "Academic Prioritization or Killing the Liberal Arts?" *Inside Higher Education*, March 1, 2019, https://www.insidehighered.com /advice/2019/03/01/shrinking-liberal-arts-programs-raise-alarm-bells-among -faculty; and Liam Knox, "U of Tulsa Faculty to Ask Oklahoma's Attorney General to Halt Controversial Restructuring Plan," *Chronicle of Higher Education*, August 22, 2019, https://www.chronicle.com/article/U-of-Tulsa-Faculty-to-Ask/246997.

2. On the importance of putting extinction on the table, see Ursula K. Heise, *Imagining Extinction: The Cultural Meanings of Endangered Species* (Chicago: University of Chicago Press, 2016).

3. Bernie Krause, *The Great Animal Orchestra: Finding the Origins of Music in the World's Wild Places* (Boston: Little, Brown, 2012).

4. Online at http://www.wildsanctuary.com/, accessed January 3, 2020.

5. Krause, *The Great Animal Orchestra*, 178.

6. Krause, 180–81.

7. Anne L. Klinck, *The Old English Elegies: A Critical Edition and Genre Study* (Montreal: McGill-Queen's University Press, 1992), 124.

8. Stuart Curran, "Romantic Elegiac Hybridity," in *The Oxford Handbook of the Elegy*, ed. Karen Weisman (Oxford: Oxford University Press, 2010), 238, 240.

9. Timothy Morton, "The Dark Ecology of Elegy," in Weisman, *The Oxford Handbook of the Elegy*, 251, 254. Also important here is Jesse Oak Taylor's sense of elegy as a backward look from the future, proleptically mourning the demise of the human species itself. See Taylor, "Mourning Species: *In Memoriam* in an Age of Extinction," in *Ecological Form*, ed. Nathan Hensley and Philip Steer (New York: Fordham University Press, 2019), 42–62.

10. Milton's *Lycidas*, of course, has concluded with this invitation: "Tomorrow to fresh woods, and pastures new," suggesting that the "new pastoral" has perhaps always been implicit in its earlier forms.

11. William Empson, *Some Versions of Pastoral* (New York: New Directions, 1974), 3. Jeffrey S. Theis points out that when early modern pastoral writing is set in forests, where the poor migrated during times of population increases and land scarcity, the genre becomes a site where social conflict is highlighted. See Theis, *Writing the Forest in Early Modern England: A Sylvan Pastoral Nation* (State College: Pennsylvania State University Press, 2005).

12. Empson, *Some Versions of Pastoral*, 19, 22.

13. Raymond Williams, "Pastoral and Counter-Pastoral," in *The Country and the City* (New York: Oxford University Press, 1973), 18, 20.

14. Williams, 32. Heather Dubrow notes that pastoral has "a predilection for binary oppositions so fundamental that if the genre did not exist the structuralists would have invented it." See Dubrow, *Genre* (New York: Methuen, 1982), 117.

15. Paul Alpers, *What Is Pastoral?* (Chicago: University of Chicago Press, 1993), 93, 92.

16. Leo Marx, "Does Pastoral Have a Future?," in *The Pastoral Landscape*, ed. John Dixon Hunt (Washington, DC: National Gallery of Art, 1992), 208–25; quotation is from p. 210.

17. Lawrence Buell, *The Environmental Imagination: Thoreau, Nature Writing, and the Formation of American Culture* (Cambridge, MA: Belknap Press of Harvard University Press, 1995), 32.

18.   Kenneth Hiltner, *What Else Is Pastoral?* (Ithaca, NY: Cornell University Press, 2011), 7.

19.   Seamus Heaney, "Eclogues 'In Extremis': On the Staying Power of Pastoral," *Proceedings of the Royal Irish Academy* 103C, no. 1 (2003), pp. 1–12; quotations are from pp. 3, 11, 9.

20.   Terry Gifford, "Post-Pastoral as a Tool for Ecocriticism," in *Pastoral and the Humanities*, ed. Mathilde Skoie and Sonia Bjornstad Velazquez (Exeter, UK: Bristol Phoenix Press, 2006), 14–24; quotation is from p. 15.

21.   Henry David Thoreau, *Walden*, ed. Lyndon Shanley (Princeton, NJ: Princeton University Press, 1971), 126.

22.   Anthony Hallam and P. B. Wignall, *Mass Extinctions and Their Aftermaths* (Oxford: Oxford University Press, 1997), 1.

23.   Edmund O. Wilson, *The Future of Life* (New York: Knopf, 2001), xxiii.

24.   Elizabeth Kolbert, *The Sixth Extinction: An Unnatural History* (New York: Henry Holt, 2014), 17–18.

25.   Stephen Leahy, "One Million Species at Risk of Extinction," *National Geographic*, May 6, 2019, https://www.nationalgeographic.com/environment/2019/05/ipbes -un-biodiversity-report-warns-one-million-species-at-risk/.

26.   D. B. Wake and V. T. Vredenburg, "Colloquium Paper: Are We in the Midst of the Sixth Mass Extinction? A View from the World of Amphibians," *Proceedings of the National Academy of Sciences* 105 (2008): 11466–73.

27.   "Frogs: A Thin Green Line," PBS, April 5, 2009, http://www.pbs.org/wnet/nature /episodes/frogs-the-thin-green-line/introduction/4763/.

28.   "Amphibians Face Terrifying Rate of Extinction," *Guardian* (US edition), November 16, 2011, https://www.theguardian.com/environment/2011/nov/16/am phibians-terrifying-extinction-threat.

29.   John Upton, "Despite Deadly Fungus, Frog Imports Continue," *New York Times*, April 7, 2012, http://www.nytimes.com/2012/04/08/us/chytrid-fungus-in-frogs -threatens-amphibian-extinction.html.

30.   Laura Gibbs, introduction to *Aesop's Fables: A New Translation by Laura Gibbs* (Oxford: Oxford University Press, 2002), xix.

31.   These commonplace book entries from 1837 to 1847 are in the *Journal of Henry David Thoreau*, ed. Bradford Torrey and Francis Allen, 14 vols. (Boston: Houghton Mifflin, 1906), 1:470.

32.   For recent research on animal intelligence, see Frans De Waal, *Are We Smart Enough to Know How Smart Animals Are?* (New York: Norton, 2017); and Carl Safina, *Beyond Words: What Animals Think and Feel* (New York: Henry Holt, 2015). For a memorable account of the intelligence of parrots, see Allora & Calzadilla and Ted Chiang, "The Great Silence," *Planetary Computing*, May 8, 2015, http://supercommunity.e-flux.com/texts/the-great-silence/. My thanks to Kyle Hutzler for calling my attention to this piece.

33. Thoreau, *Journal*, 1:470.

34. Christopher Benfey, "The Lost Wolves of New England," *New York Review of Books*, January 22, 2013, http://www.nybooks.com/blogs/nyrblog/2013/jan/22/lost-wolves-new-england/.

35. Massachusetts Office of Energy and Environmental Affairs, "State Mammal List," http://www.mass.gov/eea/agencies/dfg/dfw/fish-wildlife-plants/state-mammal-list.html, accessed January 3, 2020.

36. Thoreau, *Walden*, 236.

37. Massachusetts Office of Energy and Environmental Affairs, "Loons, Lead Sinkers and Jigs," http://www.mass.gov/eea/agencies/dfg/dfw/hunting-fishing-wildlife-watching/fishing/loons-lead-sinkers-and-jigs.html, accessed January 3, 2020.

38. Diane Toomey, "Maya Lin's Memorial to Vanishing Nature," June 25, 2012, https://e360.yale.edu/features/maya_lin_a_memorial_to_a_vanishing_natural_world.

39. Honoring the Future, "Maya Lin's Project, 'What Is Missing,'" https://www.honoringthefuture.org/climate-smarts/artist-to-know/maya-lins-project-whats-missing/, accessed January 3, 2020.

40. Honoring the Future.

41. All About Birds, Cornell Lab of Ornithology, "What Is Missing? Q & A with Maya Lin," All About Birds, June 15, 2012, https://www.allaboutbirds.org/what-is-missing-qa-with-maya-lin/.

42. Toomey, "Maya Lin's Memorial to Vanishing Nature."

43. Cornell Lab of Ornithology, "New Maya Lin Work Highlights Extinction," September 17, 2009, http://www.birds.cornell.edu/page.aspx?pid=1422.

44. Climate Central, "Maya Lin's 'Last Memorial' Honors 'What Is Missing,'" August 6, 2012, http://www.climatecentral.org/blogs/maya-lins-last-memorial-honors-what-is-missing.

45. Pat Leonard, "Earth Day 2016: Get Inspired by Maya Lin's What Is Missing Website," April 22, 2016, https://www.allaboutbirds.org/earth-day-2016-get-inspired-by-maya-lins-what-is-missing-website-2/.

46. All About Birds, Cornell Lab of Ornithology, "Cornell Lab Helps Artist Maya Lin Ask 'What Is Missing' on Earth Day 2012," April 24, 2012, https://www.allaboutbirds.org/cornell-lab-helps-artist-maya-lin-ask-what-is-missing-on-earth-day-2012/.

47. Leonard, "Earth Day 2016."

48. Stanley Cavell, *The Senses of Walden: An Expanded Edition* (Chicago: University of Chicago Press, 1992), 19–20.

49. For the importance of this rhetorical tradition, see Sacvan Bercovitch, *The American Jeremiad* (Madison: University of Wisconsin Press, 1978).

50. Jer. 9:10.

51. Charles Darwin, *The Origin of Species by Means of Natural Selection; or, The Preservations of Favoured Races in the Struggle for Life* (1859; New York: New American Library, 1958), 108–9.

52. Thoreau, *Journal*, 8:221.

53. Henry David Thoreau, *The Maine Woods* (1864; New York: Penguin, 1988), 6. *The Maine Woods*, published posthumously, comprises three essays, "Ktaadn," "Chesuncook," and "The Allegash and East Branch." As Robert F. Sayre points out, the ideology of Western progress and Indian demise is especially pronounced in the first essay, "Ktaadn." See Sayre, *Thoreau and the American Indian* (Princeton, NJ: Princeton University Press, 1977).

54. According to the *Oxford English Dictionary*, the adjective *extinct*, referring to "that has died out or come to an end," first appeared in 1581. The word *extinction* appeared shortly thereafter, in 1602.

55. Washington Irving, "Traits of Indian Character," in *The Sketch Book* (1820; New York: Signet, 1961), 273.

56. Irving, 280–81.

57. Irving, 282.

58. Irving, 282.

59. Herman Melville, *Moby-Dick*, ed. Harrison Hayford and Hershel Parker (New York: Norton, 1967), 67.

60. Melville, 78.

61. Melville, 265.

62. Melville, 520.

63. The epilogue was added to *Moby-Dick* only after English reviewers raised the reasonable objection that if everyone had perished, as was the case in the English edition, no one should have been left to tell the story.

64. For a diluted sequel to that all-destroying vortex, see the work of C. L. R. James, Frank Stella, and Amitav Ghosh, discussed in chapter 3.

65. *The Indians of Thoreau: Selections from the Indian Notebooks*, ed. Richard Fleck (Albuquerque: Hummingbird Press, 1974), 174.

66. Robert Sattelmeyer, *Thoreau's Reading: A Study in Intellectual History with Bibliographical Catalogue* (Princeton, NJ: Princeton University Press, 1988), 107.

67. See especially John J. Kucich, "Lost in the Maine Woods: Henry David Thoreau, John Nicolar, and the Penobscot World," *Concord Saunterer* 19/20 (2011–12): 22–52. See also Laura Dassow Walls, *Henry David Thoreau: A Life* (Chicago: University of Chicago Press, 2018), 333–421.

68. Thoreau, *The Maine Woods*, 185.

69. Joe Leydon, "Rumble: The Indians Who Rocked the World," Sundance film review, *Variety*, January 23, 2017, https://variety.com/2017/film/reviews/rumble-the-indians-who-rocked-the-world-review-1201966605/.

70. Videos of NMAI performances, https://www.si.edu/spotlight/native-american-music/videos-of-nmai-performances, accessed January 3, 2020.

71. John Nichols, "No Native American Woman Had Ever Been Elected to Congress—Until Last Year," *Nation*, August 6, 2019, https://www.thenation.com/podcast

/deb-haaland-next-left. Both Deb Haaland, a member of the Pueblo of Laguna, and Sharice Davids, a member of the Ho-Chunk Nation, were elected in 2018 to the House of Representatives. For the growing importance of the Native American vote, see Delilah Fiedler, "The Rise of the Native American Electorate," *Mother Jones*, August 27, 2019, https://www.motherjones.com/politics /2019/08/the-rise-of-the-native-american-electorate/. For Elizabeth Warren's extensive policy agenda for Native Americans (including revoking the permits for the Keystone XL and Dakota Access pipelines), see Thomas Kaplan, "Elizabeth Warren Offers a Policy Agenda for Native Americans," *New York Times*, August 16, 2019, https://www.nytimes.com/2019/08/16/us/politics/elizabeth -warren-native-american.html.

72. MIT Indigenous Languages Initiative, http://linguistics.mit.edu/mitili/, accessed January 3, 2020.

73. Yale Group for the Study of Native America, "Native American Language Program Offers Eight Indigenous Languages," https://ygsna.sites.yale.edu/news/native -american-language-program-offers-8-indigenous-languages-spring-2016-0, accessed January 3, 2020. This program offers classes conducted via Skype with Cherokee, Choctaw, and Mohawk speakers in Oklahoma and Canada.

74. American Indian Studies Research Institute, https://www.indiana.edu/~aisri /projects/educational.html, accessed January 3, 2020. In this context, see also the work of the National Breath of Life Archival Institute for Indigenous Languages at http://nationalbreathoflife.org, accessed January 3, 2020. For indigenous language programs at Brigham Young University and the University of Washington, see Wai Chee Dimock, "Collateral Resilience," *PMLA* 134 (2019): 441–49.

75. Standing Rock Lakota/ Dakota Language Project, accessed January 3, 2020, https:// humanitiesforall.org/projects/standing-rock-lakota-dakota-language-project.

76. See, for instance, by Kyle Powys Whyte: "Justice Forward: Tribes, Climate Adaptation and Responsibility," Climate Change, March 2013, https://nwclimate science.org/sites/default/files/2013bootcamp/readings/Whyte_2013b.pdf; "Indigenous Climate Change Studies: Indigenizing Futures, Decolonizing the Anthropocene," *English Language Notes* 55 (Fall 2017): 153–62; and "Indigenous Science (Fiction) for the Anthropocene: Ancestral Dystopias and Fantasies of Climate Change Crises," *Environment and Planning*, March 30, 2018, http://jour nals.sagepub.com/doi/10.1177/2514848618777621.

77. Tracey Osborne, "Native American Fighting Fossil Fuels," *Scientific American*, April 9, 2018, https://blogs.scientificamerican.com/voices/native-americans-fight ing-fossil-fuels/.

78. National Caucus of Native American State Legislators, accessed January 3, 2020, http://www.ncsl.org/research/state-tribal-institute/national-caucus-native -american-state-legislators.aspx.

79. Hari M. Osofsky, "Climate Change and Dispute Resolution Processes," in *International Law in the Era of Climate Change*, ed. Rosemary Gail Rayfuse and Shirley V. Scott (Cheltenham, UK: Edward Elgar, 2012), 353.

80. Naomi Klein, "The Amazon Is On Fire—Indigenous Rights Can Help Put It Out," *Boston Globe*, August 25, 2019, https://www.bostonglobe.com/opinion/2019/08/26/the-amazon-fire-indigenous-rights-can-help-put-out/QylcSQzyPPh52cYzwEvVSO/story.html.

81. "Dakota Access Pipeline: What to Know about the Controversy," *Time*, October 26, 2017, http://time.com/4548566/dakota-access-pipeline-standing-rock-sioux/.

82. James MacPherson, "Standing Rock Sioux Tribe Seeks to Intervene in Dakota Access Pipeline Expansion," *Time*, August 28, 2019. https://time.com/5663860/standing-rock-sioux-tribe-dapl-expansion/.

83. "Rosebud Sioux Tribe Promises Continued Vigilance on the Keystone XL Pipeline," *Business Wire*, November 21, 2017, https://www.businesswire.com/news/home/20171121005310/en/Rosebud-Sioux-Tribe-Promises-Continued-Vigilance-Keystone. On November 8, 2018, judge Brian Morris of the District Court of Montana blocked construction of the Keystone XL pipeline by ordering the US State Department to conduct a supplement environmental impact review. Reuters, "U.S. to Conduct Additional Keystone XL Pipeline Review," November 30, 2018, https://www.reuters.com/article/us-usa-keystone-pipeline/u-s-to-conduct-additional-keystone-xl-pipeline-review-idUSKCN1NZ2TH.

84. Bill McKibben, "Anti-Pipeline Activists Are Fighting to Stop Line 3. Will They Succeed?," *Guardian* (US edition), June 27, 2018, https://www.theguardian.com/environment/commentisfree/2018/jun/27/anti-pipeline-activists-fighting-to-stop-line-3.

CHAPTER THREE

1. George Steiner, *The Death of Tragedy* (1961; reprint, New Haven, CT: Yale University Press, 1996), xi–xii. Subsequent references are given in the text.

2. Aristotle, *Poetics*, trans. Gerald F. Else (Ann Arbor: University of Michigan Press, 1970), 27–31.

3. Aristotle, 31–32.

4. Aristotle, 65.

5. Steiner, *The Death of Tragedy*, 292. See also Steiner, "Tragedy, Reconsidered," in *Rethinking Tragedy*, ed. Rita Felski (Baltimore: Johns Hopkins University Press, 2008), 29–44; quotation is from p. 32.

6. Raymond Williams, *Modern Tragedy*, ed. Pamela McCallum (1966; reprint, Peterborough, ON: Broadview Press, 2006), 33–34. Williams is, of course, not primarily concerned with Greek tragedy. Terry Eagleton, also not primarily concerned with Greek tragedy, has similarly argued for an important link between tragedy

and modernity. See his *Sweet Violence: The Idea of the Tragic* (London: Blackwell, 2003).

7. Glenn Most, "Generating Genres: The Idea of the Tragic," in *Matrices of Genre: Authors, Canons, and Society,* ed. Mary Depew and Dirk Obbink (Cambridge, MA: Harvard University Press, 2000), 15–36; Adrian Poole, *Tragedy: A Very Short Introduction* (Oxford: Oxford University Press, 2005).

8. Eagleton, *Sweet Violence*, 2.

9. Especially pertinent here is Lauren Berlant and Sianne Ngai's discussion of comedy as a "vernacular form" in which "the funny is always tripping over the not funny, sometimes appearing identical to it." Berlant and Ngai, "Comedy Has Issues," *Critical Inquiry* (Winter 2017): 233–49; quotation is from p. 234. Relatedly, see also Joshua Clover's discussion of tragedy and comedy as dialectically intertwined. Clover, "Genres of the Dialectic," *Critical Inquiry* 43 (Winter 2017): 431–50.

10. David T. Hirst, *Tragicomedy* (London: Methuen, 1984), 15–36.

11. In fact, even in the *Poetics*, Aristotle already senses that tragedy is a less unified genre than he has taken it to be, and that unity of purpose and outcome is to not to be found in all of them. Conceding that there are four kinds of tragedy (complex, fatal, moral, and episodic), and that all of them exhibit the features that he credits them with, he rather drolly says that "one must try if possible to have all these features, or if not, the biggest ones and as many of them as one can manage" (50).

12. John Kekes, *Facing Evil* (Princeton, NJ: Princeton University Press, 1990).

13. Zygmunt Bauman, *Collateral Damage: Social Inequalities in a Global Age* (Cambridge: Polity Press, 2011), 5.

14. Stanley Corngold, "Sebald's Tragedy," in *Rethinking Tragedy*, ed. Rita Felski (Baltimore: Johns Hopkins University Press, 2008), 218–40; quotation is from p. 234. The Sebald work that chronicles the mass destruction of herrings and silkworms, as well as trees, is *The Rings of Saturn*, trans. Michale Hulse (New York: New Directions, 1998).

15. C. L. R. James, *Mariners, Renegades and Castaways: The Story of Herman Melville and the World We Live In*, ed. Donald E. Pease (Lebanon, NH: University Press of New England, 2001), 3.

16. James, 3.

17. Frank Rosengarten, *Urbane Revolutionary: C. L. R. James and the Struggle for a New Society* (Jackson: University of Mississippi Press, 2008), 193. The "Leyda" in the "Leyda letter" was Jay Leyda, author of the *Melville Log*, with whom James was corresponding.

18. Herman Melville, *Moby-Dick*, ed. Hershel Parker and Harrison Hayford (New York: Norton, 1967), 104.

19. James, *Mariners, Renegades and Castaways*, 45.

20. James, 45.

21. James, 22.

22. James, 21.

23. Melville, *Moby-Dick*, 240.

24. James, *Mariners, Renegades and Castaways*, 25.

25. James, 20.

26. Peter Linebaugh and Marcus Rediker, *The Many-Headed Hydra: Sailors, Slaves, Commoners, and the Hidden History of the Revolutionary Atlantic* (Boston: Beacon Press, 2000), 1.

27. C. L. R. James, *The Black Jacobins: Troussaint L'Overture and the San Domingo Revolution* (1938; reprint, Harmondsworth, UK: Penguin, 2001), xviii. For a helpful historical overview, see Robin Blackburn, "*The Black Jacobins* and New World Slavery," in *C. L. R. James: His Intellectual Legacies*, ed. Selwyn Cudjoe and William Cain (Amherst: University of Massachusetts Press, 1995), 81-97.

28. James, *The Black Jacobins*, 98.

29. James, xvi-xvii.

30. James, xv.

31. Kent Worcester, *C. L. R. James: A Political Biography* (Albany: State University of New York Press, 1996), 48.

32. These arguments were developed in detail in two books James coauthored with Grace Lee and Raya Dunayeskaya: *Notes on Dialectics*, privately circulated in 1948, published in 1980; and *State Capitalism and World Revolution*, prepared for the World Congress of the Fourth International in 1951.

33. Raymond Williams, *The Country and the City* (London: Chatto and Windus, 1973), 132.

34. C. L. R. James, *Beyond a Boundary* (London: Hutchinson, 1963), 50.

35. James, 71. For the centrality of cricket to James's thinking, see Sylvia Wynter, "Beyond the Categories of the Master Conception: The Counterdoctrine of the Jamesian Poiesis," and Neil Lazarus, "Cricket and National Culture in the Writings of C. L. R. James," both in *C. L. James's Caribbean*, ed. Paget Henry and Paul Buhle (Durham, NC: Duke University Press, 1992), 63-91, 92-110; Sylvia Wynter, "In Search of Matthew Bondman: Some Cultural Notes on the Jamesian Journey," in *C. L. R. James: His Life and Work*, ed. Paul Buhle (London: Allison and Busby, 1986), 131-45; Grant Farred, "The Maple Man: How Cricket Made a Postcolonial Intellectual," in *Rethinking C. L. R. James*, ed. Grant Farred (Cambridge: Blackwell, 1996), 165-86; and Christopher Gair, "Beyond Boundaries: Cricket, Herman Melville, and C. L. R. James's Cold War," in *Beyond Boundaries: C. L. R. James and Postnational Studies*, ed. Christopher Gair (Ann Arbor, MI: Pluto Press, 2006), 89-107.

36. C. L. R. James, "Every Cook Can Govern: A Study of Democracy in Ancient Greece," in *The Future in the Present* (London: Allison and Busby, 1977), 160-74; quotation is from p. 163.

37. James, *Mariners, Renegades and Castaways*, 154.

38. For three critical accounts of *Mariners, Renegades and Castaways* from three different perspectives—focusing on Ahab, Ishmael, and the crew, respectively—see Cedric Robinson, "C. L. R. James and the World-System," and William Cain, "The Triumph of the Will and the Failure of Resistance: C. L. R. James's Reading of *Moby-Dick* and *Othello*," both in Cudjoe and Cain, *C. L. R. James: His Intellectual Legacies*, 244–59, 260–76; and Donald Pease, "Doing Justice to C. L. R. James's *Mariners, Renegades and Castaways*," *boundary 2* (2000): 1–19.

39. Frank Stella, *The Marriage of Reason and Squalor II*, https://www.moma.org/learn/moma_learning/frank-stella-the-marriage-of-reason-and-squalor-ii-1959/.

40. William S. Rubin, *Frank Stella* (New York: Museum of Modern Art, 1970), 15, 151.

41. Paul Goldberger, *Frank Stella: Painting into Architecture*, exhibition catalog (New York and New Haven, CT: Metropolitan Museum of Art and Yale University Press, 2007).

42. Robert Hughes, *Frank Stella: The Swan Engravings* (Fort Worth, TX: Fort Worth Museum of Art, 1984), 5.

43. Richard Axsom, *The Prints of Frank Stella: 1967–1982* (Ann Arbor and New York: University of Michigan Museum of Art and Hudson Hills Press, 1983), 14.

44. Franz-Joachim Verspohl, ed., with Ulrich Müller and Reinhard Wagner, *The Writings of Frank Stella / Die Schriften Frank Stellas*, trans. into German by Bernhard Jendricke in collaboration with Kollektiv Druck-Reif (Jena, Germany: König, 2001), 209, 211.

45. Elizabeth A. Schultz, *Unpainted to the Last: "Moby-Dick" and Twentieth-Century American Art* (Lawrence: University of Kansas Press, 1995), 148.

46. Barry Schwabsky, "Frank Stella at the Gagosian Gallery," *Artforum*, September 1995, 88.

47. Philip Leider, "Shakespearean Fish," *Art in America*, October 1, 1990, https://www.artnews.com/art-in-america/features/shakespearean-fish-63119/.

48. Leider.

49. Frank Stella, *Working Space: The Charles Eliot Norton Lectures, 1983–84* (Cambridge, MA: Harvard University Press, 1986), 97.

50. Frank Stella, "1989 Previews for 36 Creative Artists," *New York Times*, January 1, 1989.

51. Siri Engberg, *Frank Stella at Tyler Graphics* (Minneapolis: Walker Art Center, 1997), 13.

52. Leider, "Shakespearean Fish."

53. Leider.

54. Robert K. Wallace, *Frank Stella's "Moby-Dick": Words and Shapes* (New York: Blue Heron Press, 2006), 9.

55. Wallace, 9.

56. Daniel Sheets Dye, *Chinese Lattice Design*, 2nd ed. (New York, Dover, 1974).

57. Melville, *Moby-Dick*, 388–89.

58. Melville, 385–86.

59. Melville, 433.
60. Amitav Ghosh, interview by Christopher Lydon, *Open Source*, WBUR, Boston, November 19, 2008, http://radioopensource.org/amitav-ghosh-and-his-sea-of -poppies/.
61. Amitav Ghosh, "Of Fanas and Forecastles: The Indian Ocean and Some Lost Languages of the Age of Sail," *Economic and Political Weekly* (Mumbai), June 21–27, 2008, 56–62; quotation is from p. 57. https://www.amitavghosh.com/docs /Of%20Fanas%20and%20Forecastles.pdf.
62. Ghosh, 60.
63. Amitav Ghosh, *Sea of Poppies* (New York: Farrar, Straus and Giroux, 2008), 186–87.
64. Amitav Ghosh, *River of Smoke* (New York: Farrar, Straus and Giroux, 2011), 67–68.
65. Amitav Ghosh, *Flood of Fire* (London: John Murray, 2015), 173, 174.
66. Ghosh, 607.
67. Melville, *Moby-Dick*, 469.
68. Ghosh, *Flood of Fire*, 586.
69. Ghosh, *Sea of Poppies*, 14.

CHAPTER FOUR

1. Jacques Derrida, *Of Hospitality: Anne Dufourmantelle Invites Derrida to Respond*, trans. Rachel Bowlby (Stanford, CA: Stanford University Press, 2000).
2. Henry James to Mr. and Mrs. William James, February 2, 1895, in *Henry James: Letters*, ed. Leon Edel, vol. 3, *1883–1895* (Cambridge, MA: Belknap Press of Harvard University Press, 1980), 514.
3. Colm Tóibín, *The Master* (New York: Scribner, 2004), 15.
4. Henry James to Mr. and Mrs. William James, February 2, 1895.
5. On viral social media, see Ryan Milner, *The World Made Meme* (Cambridge, MA: MIT Press, 2018); Karine Nahon and Jeff Hemsley, *Going Viral* (Cambridge: Polity Press, 2013); and Limor Shifman, *Memes in Digital Culture* (Cambridge, MA: MIT Press, 2013). On viral pandemics, see Laurie Garrett, *The Coming Plague: Newly Emerging Diseases in a World Out of Balance* (New York: Farrar Straus and Giroux, 1994); David Quammen, *Ebola: The Natural and Human History of a Deadly Virus* (New York: Norton, 2014); Sonia Shah, *Pandemic: Tracking Contagions from Cholera to Ebola and Beyond* (New York: MacMillan, 2016); and Nathan Wolfe, *The Viral Storm: The Dawn of a New Pandemic Age* (New York: Penguin, 2011).
6. Colm Tóibín, "A More Elaborate Web," in *All a Novelist Needs: Colm Tóibín on Henry James*, ed. Susan Griffin (Baltimore: Johns Hopkins University Press, 2010), 24–37; quotations are from pp. 31, 30.

7. J. Hillis Miller, "The Critic as Host," in *Deconstruction and Criticism* (New York: Continuum, 1979), 217–54, especially 219–22.

8. The World Health Organization has identified climate change as a major cause of emerging infectious diseases. See its "Climate Change and Human Health," accessed January 3, 2020, https://www.who.int/globalchange/climate/summary /en/index5.html. For the most recent findings, see Olivia Willis, "The Health Impacts of Climate Change and Why Calls to Action Are Growing Louder," *ABC News*, July 5, 2019, https://www.abc.net.au/news/health/2019-07-06/health -impacts-of-climate-change/11282926.

9. Leon Edel writes, "The James family was founded in America by an Irish immigrant who arrived in the United States immediately after the Revolution. He was a Protestant from County Cavan and bore the name William James. His father had been a William also, and among the thirteen children the immigrant fathered in the New World there was still another William and also a Henry who in turn became the father of still another William and of a Henry, a philosopher and a novelist. The names had become dynastic symbols, as if the family were a royal line and there was a throne to be filled." See Leon Edel, *Henry James: The Untried Years, 1943–1870* (1953; reprint, New York: Avon, 1978), 19.

10. Tóibín, *The Master*, 34–35.

11. Henry James, *The Golden Bowl* (New York: Scribner's, 1905), 4–5.

12. Eve Kosofsky Sedgwick, "The Beast in the Closet: James and the Writing of Homosexual Panic," in *Epistemology of the Closet* (Berkeley: University of California Press, 1990), 182–212; Michael Moon, *A Small Boy and Others: Imitation and Initiation from Henry James to Andy Warhol* (Durham, NC: Duke University Press, 1998); Eric Haralson, *Henry James and Queer Modernity* (New York: Cambridge University Press, 2003); Kevin Ohi, *Henry James and the Queerness of Style* (Philadelphia: University of Pennsylvania Press, 2011).

13. Tóibín, *The Master*, 29.

14. "Symptomatic reading" was a phrase coined by Louis Althusser and Étienne Balibar to anchor a hermeneutic that allows for transcoding across different structural levels. See Althusser and Balibar, *Reading Capital*, trans. Ben Brewster (London: Verso, 1979). Fredric Jameson's *The Political Unconscious* is sometimes seen as an unduly dogmatic instance of this hermeneutic. Here, though, I want to highlight the extent to which Jameson cautions against such flattening in the transcoding process. See *The Political Unconscious: Narrative as a Socially Symbolic Act* (Ithaca, NY: Cornell University Press, 1981); quotations are from pp. 41, 43. In this context, Jameson might even be said to have anticipated Stephen Best and Sharon Marcus's critique. See Best and Marcus, "Surface Reading: An Introduction," *Representations* 108 (Fall 2009): 1–21. See also Rita Felski, *The Limits of Critique* (Chicago: University of Chicago Press, 2015); and Heather Love, "Close but Not Deep," *New Literary History* 41 (2010): 371–91.

15. Henry James to Edmund Gosse, April 8, 1895, in *Henry James: Letters*, vol. 4, *1895–1916*, ed. Leon Edel (Cambridge, MA: Belknap Press of Harvard University Press, 1984), 9–10.

16. Caroline Levine's concept of "affordances" is especially helpful here. See Levine, *Forms: Whole, Rhythm, Hierarchy, Network* (Princeton, NJ: Princeton University Press, 2015), 1–23.

17. Carl Zimmer, "Ancient Viruses Are Buried in Your DNA," *New York Times*, October 4, 2017, https://www.nytimes.com/2017/10/04/science/ancient-viruses-dna-genome.html.

18. Donna Haraway, *When Species Meet* (Minneapolis: University of Minnesota Press, 2006), 3–4.

19. Dorothy H. Crawford, *Viruses: A Very Short Introduction* (New York: Oxford University Press, 2011), 1.

20. Wolfe, *The Viral Storm*, 12–13.

21. Judy Diamond and Charles Wood, foreword to *A Planet of Viruses*, by Carl Zimmer (Chicago: University of Chicago Press, 2011), ix.

22. As Priscilla Wald reminds us, the standard vocabulary of virology more often than not emphasizes the danger of hybridity. "The most dangerous viruses are themselves frequently hybrids: the mutant strains produced when animal and human viruses recombine in animal hosts," she explains. "In their new incarnations, hybrid viruses can jump the species barrier (be 'recognized') and produce outbreaks of especially virulent and untreatable diseases." See Wald, *Contagious: Cultures, Carriers, and the Outbreak Narrative* (Durham, NC: Duke University Press, 2008), 260.

23. Michael G. Cordingley, *Viruses: Agents of Evolutionary Invention* (Cambridge, MA: Harvard University Press, 2017), 1.

24. M. J. Roossinck and E. R. Bazan, "Symbiosis: Viruses as Intimate Partners," *Annual Review of Virology* 4 (2017), https://www.ncbi.nlm.nih.gov/pubmed/28787582.

25. Colm Tóibín, *The Blackwater Lightship* (London: Picador, 1999), 273.

26. Colm Tóibín, *Love in a Dark Time: Gay Lives from Wilde to Almodovar* (London: Picardor, 2002); Tóibín, *On Elizabeth Bishop* (Princeton, NJ: Princeton University Press, 2015); Tóibín, *House of Names* (New York: Scribner, 2017).

27. "O's Top 20 Books to Read this Summer," Oprah.com, June 8, 2017, http://www.oprah.com/book/os-top-20-books-to-read-this-summer-house-of-names?editors_pick_id=69248.

28. Carole Burns, "Off the Page: Colm Tóibín," *Washington Post*, July 22, 2004.

29. Burns. For more on this online discussion, see Anders Olsson, "'The Broken Place': Memory, Language, Tradition, and Storytelling in Colm Tóibín's Texts," in *Recovering Memory: Irish Representations of Past and Present*, ed. Hedda Friberg et al. (Cambridge: Cambridge Scholars, 2007), 128–48.

30. Colm Tóibín, *Beauty in a Broken Place* (Dublin: Lilliput Press, 2004), 46–47.

31. Tóibín, 52–53.

32. Tóibín seems intensely aware of cross-genre authorship as a genetic legacy from Yeats. In "Writers and Their Families," a February 17, 2012, article in the US edition of the *Guardian*, he speaks of Yeats as an inspiration and an Oedipal shadow cast over his entire novelistic career: http://www.guardian.co.uk/books/2012/feb/17/colm-toibin-how-i-killed-my-mother?newsfeed=true. My thanks to Lauren Berlant for alerting me to this essay.

33. Lady Gregory, *Our Irish Theatre: A Chapter of Autobiography* (London: G. P. Putnam's Sons, 1913), 19: "Mr. Martyn had written two, *The Heather Field* and *Maeve*. They had been offered to London managers, and now he thought of trying to have them produced in Germany, where there seemed to be more room for new drama than in England. I said it was a pity we had no Irish theatre where such plays could be given. Mr. Yeats said that had always been a dream of his, but he had of late thought it an impossible one, for it could not at first pay its way, and there was no money to be found for such a thing in Ireland."

34. W. B. Yeats, "The Irish Dramatic Movement," in *Plays and Controversies* (London: Macmillan, 1923), 1–218; quotation is from p. 5.

35. Gregory, *Our Irish Theatre*, 20: "We are confident of the support of all Irish people, who are weary of misrepresentation, in carrying out a work that is outside all the political questions that divide us."

36. The riots caused by Sean O'Casey's play *The Plough and the Stars* were neither the first nor the worst. Some twenty years earlier, in 1907, a bigger uproar, and an even more spectacular show of force, had erupted over J. M. Synge's *The Playboy of the Western World*.

37. Gregory, *Our Irish Theatre*, 68.

38. Colm Tóibín, *Lady Gregory's Toothbrush* (Dublin: Lilliput Press, 2002), 61. Tóibín's account of the riots surrounding *The Plough and the Stars* is very close to O'Casey's own account: "We think it necessary that the police should be sent for immediately, so that the mob may be kept from preventing us carrying on the work we have set our hands to do, said Yeats. We want your consent, O'Casey, to send for the police, as you happen to be the author of the play. The police! Sean to agree to send for the police—never! His Irish soul revolted from the idea; though Yeats and others reminded him that the police were no longer in a foreign service, but were now in Ireland's own. . . . Even so, Sean couldn't see his way to ask them to come. No, no; never! But a wild roar heard in the theater, seeming to shake the room where they all stood, told him to make up his mind quick; and swearing he could ne'er consent, consented." Sean O'Casey, *Mirror in My House: The Autobiographies of Sean O'Casey*, 2 vols. (New York: Macmillan, 1956), 2:237–38.

39. "Easter 1916," in W. B. Yeats, *The Poems*, ed. Richard Finneran (New York: Macmillan, 1983), 180–82; the excerpt is from p. 181.

40. For an extended discussion, see Lauren Arrington, *W. B. Yeats, the Abbey Theatre, Censorship, and the Irish State* (Oxford: Oxford University Press, 2010).

41. Ezra Pound, "Henry James," special issue, *Little Review*, August 1918; collected in *Literary Essays of Ezra Pound* (New York: New Directions, 1968), 296–302.

42. Leon Edel, *Henry James: The Master, 1901–1916* (New York: Avon Books, 1972), 518–27.

43. Lady Gregory, *Seventy Years: Being the Autobiography of Lady Gregory*, ed. Colin Smythe (Gerrards Cross, UK: Colin Smythe, 1974), 184.

44. W. B. Yeats to Henry James, August 20, 1915, in *The Letters of W. B. Yeats*, ed. Allan Wade (London: Rupert Hart-Davis, 1954), 599–600. "A Reason for Keeping Silent" was published on March 16, 1916, in *The Book of the Homeless*. It was reprinted in Yeats's poetry collection *The Wild Swans at Coole* under the title "On Being Asked for a War Poem."

45. W. B. Yeats, "An Irish Airman Foresees His Death," in *The Poems*, 135.

46. Edel, *Henry James*, 527.

47. "Henry James's First Interview: Noted Critic and Novelist Breaks His Rule of Years to Tell of the Good Works of the American Ambulance Corps," *New York Times*, March 21, 1915, https://www.nytimes.com/1915/03/21/archives/henry -jamess-first-interview-noted-critic-and-novelist-breaks-his.html.

48. Ernest Hemingway, *A Farewell to Arms* (1929; reprint, New York: Scribners, 2003), 165.

49. Henry James to Edith Wharton, March 5, 1915, in *The Letters of Henry James*, ed. Percy Lubbock, 2 vols. (New York: Octagon Books, 1970), 2:452. For more on James, Wharton, and World War I, see Hazel Hutchinson, *The War That Used Up Words: American Writers and the First World War* (New Haven, CT: Yale University Press, 2015).

50. Henry James to Edith Wharton, March 24, 1915, in *Henry James: Letters*, ed. Leon Edel, vol. 4, *1895–1916* (Cambridge, MA: Belknap Press of Harvard University Press, 1984), 741.

51. "Henry James's First Interview."

52. Of course, James and Yeats aren't the only ones. As Cecilia Watson points out, numerous other authors are attached to the semicolon; there are four-thousand-odd of them in *Moby-Dick*. See Watson, *Semi-Colon: The Past, Present, and Future of a Misunderstood Mark* (New York: HarperCollins, 2019).

53. Henry James to Edmund Gosse, June 25, 1915, in *Henry James: Letters*, ed. Leon Edel, vol. 4, *1895–1916* (Cambridge, MA: Belknap Press of Harvard University Press, 1984), 763.

54. On July 27, 1915, the day after he became a British citizen, James sent his "Reasons for Naturalization" to James Brand Pinker, his agent. Pinker published the statement the following day in the London *Times*. See *Henry James: A Life in Letters*, ed. Philip Horne (New York: Penguin, 2001), 556–57.

55. Rudyard Kipling to Henry James, July 28, 1915, in *The Letters of Rudyard Kipling*, ed. Thomas Pinney, vol. 4, *1911–19* (Iowa City: University of Iowa Press, 1990), 309.

56. Leon Edel, *Henry James: The Master, 1901–1916* (New York: Avon Books, 1972), 526.

57. Colm Tóibín, "Their Vilest Hour," *New York Times*, March 23, 2008.

58. Nicholson Baker, *Human Smoke: The Beginnings of World War II, the End of Civilization* (New York: Simon and Schuster, 2008), 4.

59. Tóibín, "Their Vilest Hour."

60. Richard Overy, *The Bomber and the Bombed: Allied Air War over Europe, 1940–1945* (New York: Viking, 2014). Civilian casualties in World War II totaled 50 to 55 million, with 19 to 28 million dying from war-related disease and starvation. German civilian casualties totaled 4.3 million, according to the records of the German government.

61. Tóibín, "Their Vilest Hour."

62. Mrs. Hanna Sheehy-Skeffington to the *Irish Independent*, February 10, 1926, in *The Letters of Sean O'Casey*, ed. David Krause, vol. 1, *1910–41* (New York: Macmillan, 1975), 167–68.

63. Tóibín, *Beauty in a Broken Place*, 73.

64. Gish Jen, "Who's Irish?," in *Who's Irish?: Stories* (New York: Vintage, 2000), 15–16.

65. An interesting biographical detail: Gish Jen is married to David O'Connor, of Irish descent.

CHAPTER FIVE

1. Robert Irwin, "The Emergence of the Islamic World System, 1000–1500," in *The Cambridge Illustrated History of the Islamic World*, ed. Francis Robinson (Cambridge: Cambridge University Press, 1996), 32–61.

2. William McNeill, *The Rise of the West: A History of the Human Community* (1963; reprint, Chicago: University of Chicago Press, 1991), 488.

3. Fazlur Rahman, *Islam*, 2nd ed. (Chicago: University of Chicago Press, 1979), 153, 132, 154. Rahman's observation is echoed by John L. Esposito, who writes, "Throughout the ninth and tenth centuries, Sufism grew in Arabia, Egypt, Syria, and Iraq. Though its origins and sources . . . were clearly Islamic, outside influences were absorbed from the Christian hermits of Egypt and Lebanon, Buddhist monasticism in Afghanistan, Hindu devotionalism, and Neoplatonism." See Esposito, *Islam: The Straight Path* (New York: Oxford University Press, 1991), 102.

4. Marshall Hodgson, *The Venture of Islam*, vol. 1, *The Classical Age of Islam* (Chicago: University of Chicago Press, 1974), 57.

5. For a compelling study of vagueness with special attention to the pragmatism of William James and Charles S. Peirce and the "blasphemy and nonsense of James Joyce," see Megan Quigley, *Modernist Fiction and Vagueness: Philosophy, Form, and Language* (New York: Cambridge University Press, 2015), 1–34, 103–46.

6. Ian Finlayson, *Tangier: City of the Dream* (New York: HarperCollins, 1992), 73.

7. Allen Hibbard, *Paul Bowles: Magic and Morocco* (San Francisco: Cadmus, 2004).

8. Virginia Spencer Carr, *Paul Bowles: A Life* (New York: Scribner, 2004), 291.

9. Mel Gussow, "Writer Paul Bowles Dies at 88," *New York Times*, November 19, 1999, http://movies2.nytimes.com/library/books/111999obit-p-bowles.html.

10. David Pryce-Jones, "A Nihilist's Wasted Talent," *Wall Street Journal*, November 23, 1999.

11. Richard Brown, "Molly's Gibraltar: The Other Location in Joyce's *Ulysses*," in *A Companion to James Joyce*, ed. Richard Brown (Oxford: Blackwell, 2008), 157–73; quotation is from p. 158.

12. Robert Martin Adams, *Surface and Symbol: The Consistency of James Joyce's "Ulysses"* (New York: Oxford University Press, 1962), 231–33.

13. Henry M. Field, *Gibraltar* (New York: Scribner's, 1888), quoted in Brown, "Molly's Gibraltar," 166.

14. James Joyce, *Ulysses*, ed. Hans Walter Gabler, Wolfhard Steppe, and Claus Melchior (New York: Vintage, 1986): 18.859–60.

15. Don Gifford and Robert J. Seidman, *Notes for Joyce: An Annotation of James Joyce's "Ulysses"* (New York: Dutton, 1974), 509.

16. Andrew Gibson, *Joyce's Revenge: History, Politics, and Aesthetics in Joyce's "Ulysses"* (Oxford: Oxford University Press, 2002).

17. Joyce, *Ulysses*, 18.1586–89.

18. Mark Twain, *Innocents Abroad* (New York: Signet, 1966), 50.

19. Twain, 50.

20. Twain, 52.

21. Edith Wharton, *In Morocco* (New York: Scribner's, 1920), 148.

22. Paul Bowles, *Their Heads Are Green and Their Hands Are Blue* (1957), in *Collected Stories and Later Writings* (New York: Library of America, 2002), 730.

23. Bowles, 730–31.

24. Fredric Jameson, "*Ulysses* in History," in *James Joyce and Modern Literature*, ed. W. J. McCormack and Alistair Stead (London: Routledge and Kegan Paul, 1982), 126–41; Enda Duffy, *The Subaltern "Ulysses"* (Minneapolis: University of Minnesota Press, 1994).

25. Joyce, *Ulysses*, 18.855–68.

26. Phillip Herring, *Joyce's Uncertainty Principle* (Princeton, NJ: Princeton University Press, 1987), 117–40; Marilyn Reizbaum, *James Joyce's Judaic Others* (Stanford, CA: Stanford University Press, 1999), 130–32.

27. As several critics have pointed out, in 1921 Joyce had made a point of asking Frank Budgen to get him a book on the military history of Gibraltar, especially the sieges. James Joyce to Frank Budgen, August 16, 1921, in *Letters of James Joyce*, ed. Stuart Gilbert and Richard Ellmann, 3 vols. (London: Faber and Faber, 1957–66), 1:169.

28. Joyce, *Ulysses*, 12.1470–72.

29. Don Gifford, with Richard Seidman, *Ulysses Annotated* (Berkeley: University of California Press, 1998), 364.

30. Edwin R. Steinberg, "Persecuted . . . Sold . . . in Morocco Like Slaves," *James Joyce Quarterly* 29 (1992): 615-22.

31. Meaning "one who is garrisoned" in Arabic and "saint" in the Berber language, *marabout* (or *murābiṭ*) originally referred to a holy man—a Qur'anic scholar, an itinerant spiritual guide (primarily in the Sufi tradition), or a teacher in a religious school (*zaouïa*)—who served both clerical and military functions in Maghrebi society. The marabout typically resided within a castellated monastery called a *ribat* (or *ribāṭ*) that could be located at remote outposts along the frontier and offered respite to patrolling soldiers. The *ribat* also could be incorporated into the superstructure of the casbah (citadel) of cities such as Tangier. Gradually, the word also came to denote—as Matisse employs it in the title of his painting from 1912/13—the tomb of such a venerated figure, which often became a site of pilgrimage.

32. Roger Benjamin, *Orientalist Aesthetics: Art, Colonialism, and French North Africa, 1880-1930* (Berkeley: University of California Press, 2003), 178. Since the creation of the French protectorate in 1912, the Riffians' political autonomy gradually diminished, culminating in the loss of independence following their clash with Spanish forces in the Rif War of 1926, adding fuel to their legendary ferocity.

33. Jack Cowart, National Gallery of Art, et al., *Matisse in Morocco: The Paintings and Drawings, 1912-1913*, exhibition catalog (Washington, DC: National Gallery of Art, 1990), 94.

34. Pierre Schneider, "The Moroccan Hinge," in Cowart et al., *Matisse in Morocco*, 17-57.

35. Pierre Schneider, *Matisse*, trans. Michael Taylor and Bridget Stevens Romer (New York: Rizzoli, 1984), 458.

36. These geometric shapes seem especially significant given Islam's aniconic mandates against figurative representation.

37. Henri Matisse, response to Alfred Barr's Questionnaire, 1945. Archive of the Museum of Modern Art, New York. Quoted in Cowart et al., *Matisse in Morocco*, 110.

38. Schneider, *Matisse*, 488.

39. Alfred Barr, *Matisse: His Art and His Public* (New York: Museum of Modern Art, 1951), 173; quotation from Jack D. Flam, *Matisse: The Man and His Art* (Ithaca, NY: Cornell University Press, 1986), 414.

40. Barry Schwabsky, "Black Is Also a Color," *The Nation*, June 21, 2010, https://www.thenation.com/article/black-also-color/.

41. I am thinking especially of the *Blue Nudes* and of the *gouaches découpées* like *Souvenir d'Océanie* and *L'Escargot*, whose radiating and spiraling rhythms reside in the action and interaction of colors, centered on emerald green.

42. John Rawls, *A Theory of Justice* (Cambridge, MA: Harvard University Press, 1971).

43. The six episodes are "Cyclops," "Calypso," "Aeolus," "Nausicaa," "Circe," and "Ithaca."

44. Joyce, *Ulysses*, 4.92–98.

45. Joyce, 4.99–100.

46. James Atherton, *The Books at the Wake* (Mamaroneck, NY: Paul P. Appel, 1974), 201–17.

47. Atherton, 201–17.

48. The Notebooks are now at the State University of New York at Buffalo and have been published in facsimile as part of *The James Joyce Archive*, ed. Michael Groden, with Danis Rose, John O'Hanlan, and David Hayman (New York: Garland, 1978).

49. Danis Rose, *The Textual Diaries of James Joyce* (Dublin: Lilliput Press, 1995).

50. Aida Yared, "'In the Name of Annah': Islam and *Salam* in Joyce's *Finnegans Wake*," *James Joyce Quarterly* 35 (1998): 401–38.

51. James Joyce, *A Facsimile of Buffalo Notebooks* (New York: Garland, 1978), VI.B.24.209–16.

52. Joyce, VI.B.31.45–69.

53. Joyce, VI.B.31.45–69.

54. James Joyce, *Finnegans Wake* (1939; reprint, New York: Penguin, 1976), 5.14–18.

55. Roland McHugh, *The "Finnegans Wake" Experience* (Berkeley: University of California Press, 1981), 4.

56. Joyce, *Finnegans Wake*, 51.26. Subsequent references are given in the text.

57. Ezra Pound to James Joyce, November 25, 1926, quoted in Richard Ellmann, *James Joyce* (Oxford: Oxford University Press, 1983), 584.

58. Ezra Pound, *The Pisan Cantos*, ed. Richard Sieburth (1948; reprint, New York: New Directions, 2003), 74.785–89.

59. Ezra Pound, "Cavalcanti," in *Literary Essays of Ezra Pound*, ed. T. S. Eliot (New York: New Directions), 149–200; quotation is from p. 158.

60. Pound, *The Pisan Cantos*, 74.247–59.

61. Pound, 74.197–201, 205.

62. Carroll F. Terrell, *A Companion to the Cantos of Ezra Pound* (Berkeley: University of California Press, 1993), 370.

63. Pound, *The Pisan Cantos*, 74.178.

64. Pound, 74.384–85.

65. Pound, 74.317–20.

66. David Roessel, "'A Racial Act': The Letters of Langston Hughes and Ezra Pound," in *Ezra Pound and African American Modernism*, ed. Michael Coyle (Orono, ME: National Poetry Foundation, 2001), 207–44; quotation is from p. 212. Subsequent references are given in the text.

67. Howard wrote Hughes that "the University feels deeply indebted to you for bringing this interesting project to our attention and we shall take immediate steps toward interesting some members of our faculty in it"; president Thomas E.

Jones of Fisk wrote that although "Fisk has no money with which to get Frobenius translated into English," he would forward "the request to Professor Louis S.
Shores, our Librarian, for his information" (quoted in Roessel, 215).

68. Charges were eventually dropped for four of the defendants. Haywood Patterson, found guilty of rape, was sentenced to seventy-five years. Clarence Norris,
the oldest defendant and the only one sentenced to death, jumped parole in
1946 and went into hiding up north. In 1976 he was pardoned by Alabama governor George Wallace, who judged him not guilty, since by then all the convictions
had been studied from every angle and thoroughly discredited.

69. Arnold Rampersad, *Life of Langston Hughes, 1902–1941: I, Too, Sing America* (New
York: Oxford University Press, 1986), 224.

70. Langston Hughes, *Scottsboro Limited: Four Poems and a Play in Verse, with Illustra-
tions by Prentiss Taylor* (New York: Golden Stair Press, 1932).

71. Langston Hughes, "Christ in Alabama," accessed January 3, 2020, http://www
.english.illinois.edu/Maps/poets/g_l/hughes/christ.htm.

72. Rampersad, *Life of Langston Hughes*, 16.

73. Langston Hughes, *The Big Sea* (New York: Hill and Wang, 1963), 18–21.

74. In "Goodbye Christ," a 1932 poem written while in the Soviet Union, Hughes is
emphatic about his rejection of Christianity:

> Goodbye,
> Christ Jesus Lord God Jehova,
> Beat it on away from here now.
> Make way for a new guy with no religion at all—
> A real guy named
> Marx Communist Lenin Peasant Stalin Worker ME—
>
> I said, ME!
> Go ahead now,
> You're getting in the way of things, Lord.
> And please take Saint Ghandi with you when you go,
> And Saint Pope Pius,
> And Saint Aimee McPherson,
> And big black Saint Becton
> Of the Consecrated Dime.
> And step on the gas, Christ!
> Move!

See Wallace Best, "Concerning 'Goodbye Christ': Langston Hughes, Political
Poetry, and African American Religion," *Religion and Politics*, November 26, 2013,
https://religionandpolitics.org/2013/11/26/concerning-goodbye-christ-langston
-hughes-political-poetry-and-african-american-religion/.

75. Langston Hughes, "The Negro Artist and the Racial Mountain," accessed January 3, 2020, http://www.english.illinois.edu/Maps/poets/g_l/hughes/mountain.htm.

76. *Selected Letters of Langston Hughes*, ed. Arnold Rampersad and David Roessel (New York: Knopf, 2015), 395.

77. Langston Hughes and Milton Meltzer, *A Pictorial History of the Negro in America*, new rev. ed. (New York: Crown, 1963).

78. Langston Hughes, "South to Samarkand," in *I Wonder as I Wander* (New York: Hill and Wang, 1956), 186.

79. Dimitry Pospietovsky, *Soviet Antireligious Campaigns and Persecutions* (New York: St. Martin's Press, 1988), 19-90.

80. Between 1927 and 1940, the number of Orthodox churches in the USSR fell from 29,584 to less than 500. Theological seminaries were closed, and church publications were prohibited. More than 85,000 Orthodox priests were shot in 1937 alone. Only one-twelfth of the priests were left functioning in their parishes by 1941. See Dimitry Pospietovsky, *The Russian Church under the Soviet Regime, 1917-1982*, 2 vols. (Crestwood, NY: St. Vladimir Seminary Press, 1984), 1:175.

81. The late 1920s and the 1930s marked a clear shift away from the policy of tolerance toward Muslims begun by the Soviet government's 1917 statement, "To All Toiling Moslems of Russia and the East," promising them full religious rights in the new socialist state. See Bernhard Wilhelm, "Moslems in the Soviet Union," in *Aspects of Religion in the Soviet Union, 1917-1967*, ed. Richard H. Marshall Jr., with Thomas E. Byrd and Andrew Blane (Chicago: University of Chicago Press, 1971), 257-59.

82. Walter Kolarz, *Religion in the Soviet Union* (New York: St. Martin's Press, 1961), 400-447.

83. Langston Hughes, "General Franco's Moors," in *I Wonder as I Wander*, 349-354; quotation is from p. 349. Subsequent references are given in the text.

CHAPTER SIX

1. Paul Ricoeur, *Freud and Philosophy: An Essay on Interpretation*, trans. Denis Savage (New Haven, CT: Yale University Press, 1970), 32; Eve Kosofsky Sedgwick, "Paranoid Reading and Reparative Reading, or, You're So Paranoid, You Probably Think This Essay Is about You," in *Touching Feeling: Affect, Pedagogy, Performativity* (Durham, NC: Duke University Press, 2003), 123-52.

2. Rita Felski sees this negative reflex as a case of "affective inhibition." See *The Limits of Critique* (Chicago: University of Chicago Press, 2015), 188.

3. Sedgwick, "Paranoid Reading and Reparative Reading," 144.

4. Sedgwick, 149.

5. Jeremy Eagle, "Learning with: Senate Passes Bipartisan Criminal Justice Reform Bill," *New York Times*, December 20, 2018, https://www.nytimes.com/2018/12/20/learning/learning-with-senate-passes-bipartisan-criminal-justice-bill.html.

6. Rachel Porter, Sophia Lee, and Mary Lutz, *Balancing Punishment and Treatment: To Incarceration in New York City* (Vera Institute of Justice, May 2002), https://www.prisonpolicy.org/scans/vera/balancingpunishmentandtreatment.pdf.

7. For an account of the Brooklyn-based Common Justice, see Danielle Sered, *Until We Reckon: Violence, Mass Incarceration, and the Road to Repair* (New York: New Press, 2019).

8. Pascale Casanova, *The World Republic of Letters*, trans. M. B. DeBevoise (Cambridge, MA: Harvard University Press, 2007), 127.

9. Casanova, 127.

10. Mark S. Granovetter, "The Strength of Weak Ties," *American Journal of Sociology* 78, no. 6 (1973): 1360–80; Granovetter, *Getting a Job: A Study of Contacts and Careers* (Cambridge, MA: Harvard University Press, 1974), 4. For a more detailed discussion of Granovetter, see the introduction.

11. Lee Rainie and Barry Wellman, *Networked: The New Social Operating System* (Cambridge, MA: MIT Press, 2012), 12.

12. Raymond Williams, *Marxism and Literature* (Oxford: Oxford University Press, 1977), 132.

13. I am drawing inspiration here from Kathleen Stewart, *Ordinary Affects* (Durham, NC: Duke University Press, 2007).

14. Robert A. Jelliffe, ed., *Faulkner at Nagano* (Tokyo: Kenkyusha, 1956), 185.

15. William Faulkner, *Requiem for a Nun* (New York: Random House, 1951), 232–33.

16. Jelliffe, *Faulkner at Nagano*, 139–40. Subsequent references are given in the text.

17. William Faulkner, *Absalom, Absalom!* (1936; reprint, New York: Vintage, 1972), 155.

18. Drew Gilpin Faust, *Mothers of Invention: Women of the Slaveholding South in the American Civil War* (Chapel Hill: University of North Carolina Press, 1996); Thavolia Glymph, *Out of the House of Bondage: The Transformation of the Plantation Household* (Cambridge: Cambridge University Press, 2008).

19. Jelliffe, *Faulkner at Nagano*, 82.

20. William Faulkner, *Requiem for a Nun* (New York: Random House, 1951), 3.

21. Faulkner, 8.

22. Faulkner, 216–17.

23. Faulkner, 101. Here, Faulkner invokes not only the Chickasaw but also the "nameless though recorded predecessors" they had in turn displaced: "the wild Algonquian, Chickasaw and Choctaw and Natchez and Pascagoula" (101).

24. William Faulkner, *Go Down, Moses* (New York: Random House, 1942), 191.

25. Faulkner, 256–57.

26. Faulkner, 258.

27. William Faulkner, "A Justice," in *Collected Stories of William Faulkner* (1950; reprint, New York: Vintage, 1995), 343–60; quotation is from p. 346.

28. Faulkner, 345.

29. William Faulkner, "Red Leaves," in *Collected Stories of William Faulkner*, 313–42; quotation is from p. 321.

30. For a good summary of the controversies, see Gene M. Moore, "Faulkner's Incorrect 'Indians'?," *Faulkner Journal* 18, no. 1/2 (2002/2003): 3–8. For a detailed critique, see Howard Horsford, "Faulkner's (Mostly) Unreal Indians in Early Mississippi History," *American Literature* 64, no. 2 (1992): 311–30.

31. Lewis M. Dabney, *The Indians of Yoknapatawpha: A Study in Literature and History* (Baton Rouge: Louisiana State University Press, 1974), 11n15.

32. Joseph Blotner, ed., *Selected Letters of William Faulkner* (New York: Random House, 1977), 46–47.

33. Faulkner was on solid historical ground here: slaveholding was a common practice among Native Americans: "The Cherokee had the most slaves, with 1,600 before removal and about 2,500 in 1860. The Choctaw planters had the next highest number of slaves, with about 500 before removal and 2,350 in 1860. The Creek held 902 slaves in 1832 and 1,532 in 1860, while the Chickasaw had the fewest slaves—several hundred near removal and about 1,000 in 1860. The free Chickasaw population, however, was less than one-fourth the size of the Cherokee population, so the per capita slaveholding among the Chickasaw was relatively higher." See Duane Champagne, *Social Order and Political Change: Constitutional Governments among the Cherokee, the Choctaw, the Chickasaw, and the Creek* (Stanford, CA: Stanford University Press, 1992), 176–77.

34. Robert Dale Parker, "Red Slippers and Cottonmouth Moccasins: White Anxieties in Faulkner's Indian Stories," *Faulkner Journal* 18 (2002/2003): 81–99; Robert Woods Sayre, "Faulkner's Indians and the Romantic Vision," *Faulkner Journal* 18, nos. 2/3 (2002/2003): 33–49.

35. Faulkner, "Red Leaves," 313.

36. Daniel H. Usner Jr., "American Indians on the Cotton Frontier: Changing Economic Relations with Citizens and Slaves in the Mississippi Territory," *Journal of American History* 72, no. 2 (1985): 297–317; and Samuel J. Wells and Roseanna Tubby, eds., *After Removal: The Choctaw in Mississippi* (Jackson: University of Mississippi Press, 1986).

37. Gerald Vizenor's haiku are collected in *Raising the Moon Vines* (1964); *Empty Swings* (1967); *Matsushima: Pine Islands Collected Haiku* (1984); and *Favor of Crows: New and Collected Haiku* (2014).

38. Gerald Vizenor, "Ronin of the Imperial Moat," in *Hiroshima Bugi: Atomu 57* (Lincoln: University of Nebraska Press, 2003), 16–17.

39. Vizenor, 16.

40. Vizenor, 16–17.

41. Vizenor, 25.

42. Jim Barnes, "The Only Photograph of Quinten at Harvard," in *On a Wing of the Sun: Three Volumes of Poetry* (Urbana: University of Illinois Press, 2001), 45.

43. Jim Barnes, "After a Postcard from Stryk in Japan," in *On a Wing of the Sun*, 56.

44. As editor and translator, Lucien Stryk published *World of the Buddha: An Introduction to Buddhist Literature* (1968), *Zen Poems of China and Japan: The Crane's Bill* (1973), and, with Takashi Ikemoto, *The Penguin Book of Zen Poetry* (1977). *The Penguin Book of Zen Poetry* won the Islands and Continents Translation Award and the Society of Midland Authors Poetry Award. Stryk's other translations include *Bird of Time: Haiku of Basho* (1983), *Triumph of the Sparrow: Zen Poems of Shinkichi Takahashi* (1986), and, with Noboru Fujiwara, *The Dumpling Field: Haiku of Issa* (1991).

45. Jim Barnes, "Choctaw Cemetery," in *On a Wing of the Sun: Three Volumes of Poetry* (Urbana: University of Illinois Press, 2001), 123.

AFTERWORD

1. Scott Miller's translation is now online at https://www.academia.edu/38576900 /_Impressions_from_Kinosaki.

2. Wai Chee Dimock, "Collateral Resilience," *PMLA* 134 (May 2019): 1–13.

3. Luther Standing Bear, *My People the Sioux*, ed. E. A. Brininstool (1928; reprint, Lincoln: University of Nebraska Press, 1975), 185.

4. See Deanne Stillman, *Blood Brothers: The Story of the Strange Friendship between Sitting Bull and Buffalo Bill* (New York: Simon and Schuster, 2017); and Eric Vuillard, *Sorrow of the Earth: Buffalo Bill, Sitting Bull, and the Tragedy of Show Business* (London: Pushkin Press, 2016).

5. James MacPherson, "Standing Rock Sioux Tribe Seeks to Intervene in Dakota Access Pipeline Expansion," *Time*, August 28, 2019, https://time.com/5663860 /standing-rock-sioux-tribe-dapl-expansion/. On November 8, 2018, judge Brian Morris of the District Court of Montana blocked construction of the Keystone XL pipeline by ordering the US State Department to conduct a supplemental environmental impact review. See Reuters, "U.S. to Conduct Additional Keystone XL Pipeline Review," November 30, 2018, https://www.reuters.com/article/us -usa-keystone-pipeline/u-s-to-conduct-additional-keystone-xl-pipeline-re view-idUSKCN1NZ2TH. For a more detailed discussion of the Standing Rock Sioux Tribe, see chapter 2.

6. Patrick Cox, "The Standing Rock Sioux Are Also Fighting for Their Language," PRI, November 18, 2016, https://www.pri.org/stories/2016-11-17/standing-rock -sioux-are-also-fighting-their-language.

7. National Endowment for the Humanities, Standing Rock Lakota/Dakota Language Project, https://www.neh.gov/sites/default/files/inline-files/sitting_bull _college_lakota-dakota_language_revitalization.pdf.

Index

humans, 3, 51, 53, 66, 102, 104, 132, 179n13; and nonhumans, 8–9, 43, 52, 54–55; resilience of, 7; as species-beings, 179n15

Human Smoke (Baker), 115

hunger, 9, 17–22, 24–25, 27, 31, 35, 183–84n11

Husiash, J., 79–80

Hutzler, Kyle, 190n32

hybridity, 116; cross-genre, 108; danger of, 200n22; hybridized Islam, 119–20. *See also* portmanteau religion

hybridization, 10, 119

Ibis trilogy (Ghosh): *Flood of Fire*, 89, 91; pidgin English, 90–91; *River of Smoke*, 89–91; *Sea of Poppies*, 89–90; as weak tragedy, 92

immunity breakdown, 96–98, 104, 111. *See also* infectious diseases

"Impressions from Kinosaki" (Shiga), 171

indentured servants, 38–39

India, 119–20

Indian Ocean, 10, 88–90. *See also* Laskari language; pidgin tongues

Indian removal, 164

indigeneity, 163. *See also* Abenaki language; Algonquian; Apache; Cherokee; Chickasaw; Choctaw; Creek; Delaware (tribe); Haudenosaunee (Iroquois); Mashpee; Mohawk (tribe); Narragansett; Nipmuc; Oglala Lakota Nation; Ojibwa; Penobscot; Pequot; Potawatomi; Seneca Nation; Shawnee; Standing Rock Sioux Tribe; Wampanoag

indigenous agency, 9. *See also* climate activism; editing, Native American

indigenous languages, 63, 174; as "multimedial," 28; and nonlinear agency, 172. *See also* Abenaki language; Algonquian; Lakota/Dakota Language Project; Ojibwa

indigenous pastoral, 62–63

indigenous populations, 12, 61, 178n5; adaptation, as key to, 1–2, 63; dispossession of, 162–64; survival of, 1–2, 63–64

indigenous revitalization, 62–64, 173–74

induced Irishness, 117

induced vulnerability, 99

Industrial Revolution, 3, 48

infection, 11, 96–98; and coloniality, 99; and ethnicity, 99; and sexuality, 99

infectious diseases: and adaptation, 102–3; and HIV, 103–5; and measles, 103; and pandemics, 10, 63, 97; and viruses, 102–4

infrastructure, 6–7

Innocents Abroad (Twain), 121, 124–25

Inter-American Commission, 64

International Brigades, 150

International Congress of Women, 116

internet, 5

internet background noise (IBN), 27–29

In the Track of the Sun (Thompson), 137

Intruder in the Dust (Faulkner), 160

Inuit Circumpolar Council, 64

involuntary relocation, 63

Iraq, 119–20, 203n3

Ireland, 98, 100, 110, 112, 123, 201n38; pacifism, 116; theatre in, 201n33

"Irish Airman Foresees His Death, An" (Yeats), 110, 112

Irish Republican Brotherhood, 107

Irish Women's Franchise League, 116

Iroquois (Haudenosaunee), 28, 41

Irregular Shapes (Stella), 82

Irving, Washington, 59, 61; "Philip of Pokanoket," 36

Irwin, Robert, 119

Islam, 123–24, 133, 139–40, 142–44, 149; divergent forms of, 119; expansion of, 119; as hybridized, 120; jihad, 119; as low-resolution spectrum, 11, 137; suppression of, 148; vaguely Islamic, 120; weak, 11–12, 134, 141, 150. *See also* portmanteau religion

Issa, 169

Istiqlal Party, 122

Italy, 121

I Wonder as I Wander (L. Hughes), 148; "General Franco's Moors," 149–50

INDEX   227

Thompson, Frederick Diodati, *In the Track of the Sun*, 137

Thoreau, Henry David, 9, 43, 56; Darwin, admirer of, 57; extinction vs. extermination, 58–59; and a fox, 51–53; and frogs, 47–48, 50; involuntary nonbelonging, 62; and a loon, 52–54; *The Maine Woods*, 58, 192n53; on Native Americans, 61–62; *Walden*, 45–48, 50, 52–54, 56; wolves, 53

Thury, Louis Pierre, 40

Tóibín, Colm, 114, 118, 201n38; antiwar gene pool, corpus of, 116; *Beauty in a Broken Place*, 105, 116–17; *The Blackwater Lightship*, 11, 96, 104; contagious site, 115; globalized contagion of, 99–101; *House of Names*, 105; and Henry James, 10–11, 95–100, 115, 117; *Lady Gregory's Toothbrush*, 107; *The Master*, 10–11, 95–98, 105, 117; queerness, 99; risky symbiosis, 104–5; Yeats, as inspiration, 201n32

Toklas, Alice B., 121

Tokyo (Japan), 158–59, 161

Tomkins, Silvan, 182n36

Toulouse, Teresa, 31

tragedy, 74; collateral damage, 68–69; and comedy, 67–70, 88, 90–92, 195n9; fatalism of, 65–66; and fate, 69; harm, democratizing of, 69–70; as irreparable, 66; kinds of, 195n11; and modernity, 67, 194–95n6; and novel, 67–70, 88, 90–92; selective affinity, 69; undeserved harm, 68; user-amended sequels, 70; as user-friendly and user-amended, 10; zero distraction, 66

tragicomedy, 68

Transatlantic Review (magazine), 138

transition (magazine), 138

translation, 12, 25, 29; of Faulkner, 155; of Frobenius, 146; need for, 91; of Qur'an, 138

trans-Pacific networks, 12, 158–61, 166–70

Treaty of Fez, 121, 128, 132

Treaty of the Dancing Rabbit Creek, 166

Treaty of Utrecht, 128

Trenchard, Lord, 115

Treuer, David, 177–78n4

Trinidad, 77

Trouillot, Michel-Rolph, 27

Trump, Donald, 64, 174

Tsing, Anna Lowenhaupt, 180n18

Turtle Mountain Reservation, 24

Tuskegee Institute, 145–46

Twain, Mark, 11, 123; *Innocents Abroad*, 121, 124–25

Tyler, Ken, 81

Tyler Graphics, 81. *See also* Gemini G. E. L.

Ulama, 119

Ullrich, Jan, 174

Ulysses (Joyce), 11, 125–26, 138; "Aeolus" episode, 206n43; "Calypso" episode, 136–37, 206n43; "Circe" episode, 206n43; "Cyclops" episode, 128, 206n43; as factually incorrect, 123–24; and Islam, 137; "Ithaca" episode, 206n43; and Matisse, 136; and Morocco, 127–28; "Nausicaa" episode, 206n43; "Penelope" episode, 137

United Nations (UN), 3; Intergovernmental Panel on Climate Change, 49

United States, 42, 98, 116–17, 121, 157, 161–63, 179n11, 183n5; Indian reservations, 63; Old Testament prophets, 56–57

Unredeemed Captive, The (Demos), 42

user-amended sequels, 30–31, 35–36, 39, 70–71. *See also* counterfactual agency; need-based history

Uzbekistan, 149

Vandenburg, Vance T., 49

Vattimo, Gianni, 6

Vaudreuil, Pierre de Rigaud de, 41

Vaughan, Alden, 182–83n1

Virgil, 46

Virginia, 39

virtual history, 27. *See also* counterfactual agency; need-based history

viruses, 91, 102–4; as catalysts, 103; hybridity, danger of, 200n22; as

Made in the USA
Monee, IL
04 November 2022

17132004R00131